EXPØNENTIAL
PRØGRESS

*MIND-BENDING breakthrough technologies
to evolve over the next decade
and DOMINATE the century*

*Restrospective analysis of the advancement of emerging
technologies that are radically driving business model
innovation and reflecting the necessity of
collateral damage control*

FARABI SHAYOR *BSc, MSc, MIScT*

EXPONENTIAL PROGRESS: Mind-Bending Breakthrough Technologies
to Evolve Over the Next Decade and Dominate the Century

First Edition

Copyright © 2019-2020, research and design by IntelXSys Research, a
trading name of Research Intelligence Systems Ltd.
14, East Bay Lane, Press Centre, Here East,
London, E20 3BS, UK.

Correspondence Email: farabi@intelxsys.com

Publisher: Independent Publishing Network
Location: London, United Kingdom

A CIP catalogue record of this book
is available from the British Library.

ISBN: 9-781-8385-3333-5.

ep.intelxsys.com

Foreword

Exponential Progress takes readers on a journey through over seven decades of progress, as technology has shaped and controlled everything from banking and business to education, medicine, and the very basis of the human genome. It is a must read for anyone looking to learn about fascinating emerging technologies that will disrupt our lives over the next ten years.

Humanity is progressing towards a world that will be dominated by the end-results of scientific inventions evolving over the next decade. Technological progress has accelerated over the past decade – it was slow and buggy at the beginning, but the rate of improvement is now exponential. These technologies are not commercially available to consumers. However, scientists and researchers have made several breakthroughs and are continuously in pursuit of improving their startling inventions.

From a business perspective, these ground-breaking technologies are expected to deliver the highest return on investment. That is why investors, analysts and entrepreneurs are tenacious about investing in these technologies. Where did it all start? How far have we come in the past 70 years since the curious minds developed the first digital computer? If utilised properly, these technologies could substantially improve our lives, help stop viral outbreaks, and future pandemics. They could also affect us in a way that would be incomprehensible.

Thousands of innovators are in the process of developing the building blocks of these technologies, that will radically grow over the next decade and potentially dominate the century. Although technologists are focused on creating the next best product or service, we, as humans, are stepping into the unknown.

This book looks back at the history of these technologies, analyse current progress and what the researchers have achieved until now. The author attempts to comprehend the need for advancement and in parallel, the potential, reflecting the necessity of control, and the balance of ethical value and our rights.

Acknowledgement

A book like this involves a lot effort into research and extracting the most useful data. This book took almost 1 year and 2 months to complete. To be very honest, this book has allowed me to get through a difficult time in 2019. I am personally very grateful to all the people working with IntelXSys Research who were involved in completing this book, including Shama, Sharod, and my friends from Innovi. Very grateful to Santé Beasant et al. for their voiceover contributions.

I would also like to acknowledge the contributions of Dr. Sohag Saleh MEd PhD, Head of Year 2 (Biomedical Science) at *Imperial School of Medicine* for the research opportunity and collaboration; Alistair Drew-Yeates FRSA, ecosystem manager, *Barclays Eagle Lab at Plexal*, Chris Rossi, Hana Gilbert and the Plexal Squad for supporting my team from Imperial to conduct research in their premises.

This book is dedicated to my little nieces and nephews – Tiana, Dante and Konen. I hope this inspires them to become successful.

Competing Interest

The author works with Imperial College School of Medicine, Imperial College London as a Research Experience Lead for Clinical Research and Innovation (CRI) module. The author also conducts further research in partnership with Barclays Eagle Lab at Plexal. The author declares that he has no other competing interest and no financial association with any other companies for the purpose of product placement.

License

Author Contribution & Notes

The author confirms that he is the sole contributor to this work, except for chapter 6. Mr Shyeem Rahman, EEE grad student, has made contributions to that chapter.

As with any human endeavour, errors are inevitable and part of any process. **If you spot any mistake, or any incorrect information, please feel free to contact the author at farabi@intelxsys.com.** All the new information will be updated in the future editions.

FOR USE OF EDUCATIONAL, TRAINING AND RESEARCH PURPOSES ONLY.

Table of Contents

This page is left blank intentionally.

Introduction.

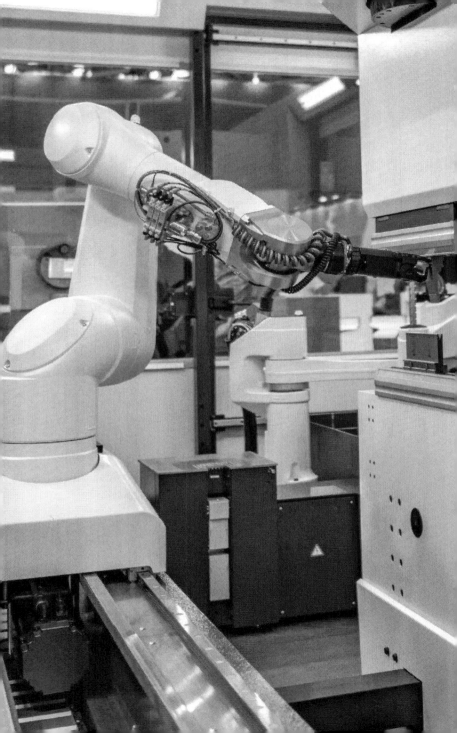

Achieve the Impossible

Collectively, at the end of the twenty-first century, humanity is struck with a perplexing reality – a society, fundamentally metamorphosed around the abstractions of artificial intelligence, is not the only civilisation residing on a circular astronomical object, floating through the multitudinous dimensions of space and time at a speed of 66,000 mph. The technologies that evolved over this century aided in discovering the reality - something that many scientists anticipated throughout their life. How did we get this far? How did we manage to overhaul from 'no electricity' to 'outer-terrestrial colonies' in just under 300 years? The credit goes to a handful of ideas invented in a span of a few decades. Since the dawn of civilisation, we have been assembling this planet from scratch, bootstrapping our supplies, working collectively as a cohesive team, irrespective of the race and gender, with the fundamental notion for ascertaining breakthrough visions that would transform the society for its greater good. We have fostered a world-wide coalition of disruptive intellectuals, and constructed a substantial network of progressive thinkers, researchers, investors, entrepreneurs, and scientists. To the future generation, the very few aspirant luminaries, thank you for bringing this book to your attention and taking some time out to read a book in the world of augmented digital content. This is where it all begins.

Let's transport back in time to 2020. Our consciousness, imprisoned in the present, continually looks out for drastic ways to predict the future – lower uncertainty, prognosticate barriers, and discover ways to take the next step. Every single day, we are exploiting the intricate knowledge that we retained from our past. The approach to solving these problems is driven from the desire to achieve the impossible; a thriving want at the bottom of our heart to achieve exponential progress.

1.1 – The Pale Blue Dot (centre-right)
© 2016 NASA Goddard Space Flight Center.

On July 19, 2013, NASA's Jet Propulsion Lab released a brain-melting image - recognised as the "Pale Blue Dot". The photo was taken from the Cassini spacecraft near the Saturn. Now take a moment to step back, breathe, and think - you and I, along with the billions of residents, live in that tiny dot. Everything we learned, and we know – all our existential knowledge is stuffed into the pale blue dot. In a grand scheme of things, we are a microorganism in the vast space of emptiness, yet the desire to achieve the impossible does not fade away. On a broader scale compared to the galaxy's existence, human life-span is absolutely nothing. Yet, we move on, grasping that mortality is inevitable, and unearthing ways to enhance lives, with a hope that it will be favourable to the future generations. Welcome to the philosophical and pragmatic analysis of the technologies that will help us take that quantum leap. From here, the future could go in any direction. It depends on how we utilise the resources we possess.

Beginning of A New Era

Over the past decade, we have witnessed the formation of some captivating inventions that are definitively going to set the course for humanity. Industries are currently going through a rapid transformation and being disrupted by these technological innovations. The outcome of the foundations built by these innovators in the next decade will reverberate for hundreds of years.

The internet has connected billions of people and completely changed our lives. Mobile phones have resulted in creating digital copies of ourselves – a fascinating extension of human beings which learns, recognises and stores every step. Internet fuelled the growth of e-commerce, and now blockchain is allowing users to exchange money globally in seconds. The question is, are these ideas driving humanity into an unknown territory? Are humans acting as the bootloader for what it seems to be the most cutting-edge invention in the history of modern discoveries? What happens if all these technologies are merged, resulting in the creation of a new species that would become more intelligent than humans? A looming catastrophic event won't be an asteroid hitting the surface of the earth and wiping out millions, because that is theoretically hundreds of years away. An imminent threat is the misuse or weaponisation of technologies. The ideas that are reshaping lives could at the same time, translate into a threat for the civilisation.

Experts believe that the entire world is now a *cybernetic collective*.[1] Every single user connected to the internet is contributing to the development of a unified network that we cannot live without. The growth of emerging technologies has resulted in developing eccentric ideas, such as machines that synchronise with the brain.[2] People who require prosthetics can have smart arms directly connected to the brain that would not have been possible even decades ago.

The discussion on the progress of technology is everywhere. Scientific progress has advanced more in the past seventy years than it did over the past thousand. Pyramids were built around 2500BC, a structure that would have required thousands of working hours to plan and execute efficiently.[3] The rate of progress stabilised over the past couple of centuries. Space technology, on the other hand, was developed long before the "internet-era". When astronauts successfully landed on the moon in 1969, millions of people witnessed the historical moment on their television. Neil Armstrong and his team inspired an entire generation to build upon the skills that were left by their ancestors. But the trend went downwards due to budget restraints – until recently, when technologists decided to rapidly advance towards the colonisation of Mars.[4]

History suggests that every type of technology hits the ceiling. Civil engineering has come a long way. Building construction processes haven't changed much over the past few decades but improved in terms of design and safety. In 50 years, aerospace engineering has grown significantly – we went from creating fuel-draining DCs to energy-efficient Boeing 787s.[5] But the growth of the invention slowed down because the aerospace industry demands affordability and safety over innovative design. The recent grounding of Boeing 737 Max is a great example in this scenario.[6]

The internet has created and fuelled many delightful concepts and helped different types of technologies to excel. After the dotcom boom in early 2000, Amazon has led the way for millions of e-commerce businesses, completely shifting global buyer behaviour pattern. Now, researchers can collaborate almost instantaneously to share crucial data. During the last decade, the world wide web has powered the development of internet banking. In the coming years, blockchain is going to become the next phase of this financial facelift. Blockchain-based ideas are going to have an enormous impact on various other market verticals, including supply-chain management. We could see ideas such as the *real-life tracking* of an object within a supply chain come into life.[7] In the forthcoming decade, virtual and augmented reality are going to refine educational processes. Sooner or later, it is bound to become an essential part of smart workspaces as researchers are already proposing such framework.[8]

Thanks to the internet, the growth of some branches of biotechnology have also skyrocketed in recent years. Some explosive ideas include the ubiquitous adoption of lab-grown meat and synthetic DNA. By analysing genetic markers of DNAs found in plants, scientists have discovered a captivating process to produce lab-grown meat and dairy products, which are appealing to the new generation.[9] Computer manufacturers, on the contrary, are going to start adopting *synthetic DNA* for data storage. These are going to be the next game-changing factors for business model alteration and key model drivers for innovation performance.

We are truly commemorating the beginning of a new era for our industries, the next phase of revolution, known as the "industry 4.0". This facelift involves technologies such as the artificial intelligence, cloud computing, smart sensors, wireless technologies, intelligent robotics and internet of things (IoT) to create a self-configuring and optimised manufacturing process.[10] In hindsight, artificial intelligence is now much more capable than sorting objects. AI could effortlessly grow beyond human capacity. By combining the power of a few different technologies, the world is on its way to create what would have been science fiction even ten years ago. Artificial intelligence is redefining traditional business models, as more businesses are adopting AI-based hardware and software to improve efficiency.

Some might argue that we are the primitive stages of AI revolution, for instance, a young AI expert who was hired by Google at the age of 13, believes that we are a long way off from witnessing AI reaching "human-level intelligence".[11] Products and services built around AI are mostly reliable, have many advantages; although, many use cases might end up throwing surprises. It is impossible to predict the result, as it depends on how a technology is ultimately utilised. Artificial intelligence is slightly different to the others because there is no way of measuring its innovation ceiling. A narrow AI that's continuously learning from the internet in many forms can be stopped just by shutting down the server. Artificial General Intelligence, however, is an entirely different story. What if an AI, always connected to the internet, being fed billions of data points every second, all of a sudden start to shift its thinking process? What if the AI has already created a backup plan to escape being shut down by its inventors?

Funding A Technology

How exactly do you develop a technology? Every idea and its inventor require investment to thrive. This road to becoming a successful company involves several rounds of funding. Financial experts evaluate the potential of an idea based on how much it might be able to achieve over five to seven years from its inception. Based on their forecasts, investors make a seed investment, which they consider will explode after the company goes for a bigger round of funding, such as the Initial Public Offering (IPO), or in the world of finance, "exits".[12]

Look at Microsoft and Amazon, they have already become trillion-dollar companies from nothing in just under 30 years.[13] While the market-leading technology corporations, i.e. Facebook, Amazon, Netflix and Google provide a high return on investment (ROI), not all the companies in the stock market guarantee a return after their shares are listed on the stock market.[14] Initial public offering (IPO) is a process through which a company raises additional funding from the public, become a *public limited company* (PLC) and get listed in a regulated stock exchange. Companies file for IPO to raise funds by issuing *company shares*. These share prices are a reflection of the investor sentiment in the stock market,[15] which is set up by the potential of a technology, probable revenue, partnership or other vital identifiers that make the companies better. When it comes to companies working with emerging technologies, many are valued at over a billion-dollar even at their initial stage.

Smaller startups working on disruptive technologies such as AI or genetic engineering usually require large funding rounds and extended periods to create a viable product or reach breakeven. Hence, they attempt to raise a significant amount of money for research and development purposes. Investing in these 'early-stage' or 'pre-discovery' companies are therefore deemed very risky, however, likely to provide a greater return when they achieve a breakthrough. Knowing the high risks, investors gamble on the potential of a company, even the non-profitable ones.[16] Some of these funders are blind towards making a profit, consequently, seldom forget to conduct due diligence and disregard the by-products that could come out of their risky experiment.

Choosing the right early-stage technology to invest in is a difficult choice to make for anyone, because it requires a lot of research into that idea. The problem isn't the team or the company – it eventually is the implementation of the right technology at the right time. Many VR startups faded away because the it's simply too early. When investing, there is no right or wrong way of choosing one, because any startup could fail, despite raising millions. They could also end up discovering an idea that might result in catastrophic outcomes. It's a "high risk and high reward" situation. That is why diversification and conducting ethical due-diligence is vital. The bedrock for success is ultimately determined by the technology, and the people working behind an idea.

If you observe carefully, you will comprehend that there some common grounds among the largest technology companies – 1) their proprietary AI or machine learning algorithm, 2) devotion towards research in emerging technologies, and 3) acquisition of companies working with new ideas. In addition to AI, these are the five technologies that have been topics of their research – virtual reality, genome editing, electric vehicles, synthetic biology, and brain-machine interface. The biggest tech companies in the world are all involved with two or more of these technologies mentioned here. Billions are invested in them, but why?

The end products or services created around these technologies are highly likely to possess the potential of having a 'unique identifier'. The research surrounding these ideas are enabling extremely efficient computers, smart workspaces, intelligent computing hardware, affordable treatment, as well as treatment for rare diseases, which was unimaginable before. These technologies are not only connecting billions of people but also discovering sophisticated ways of providing a better outcome. If these startups and tech companies survive the recession due in 2020, valuations for some of them will no doubt increase by ten to fifty times of their valuation in 2019. In this book, we will discuss these technologies that are bound to grow exponentially in the next decade. The constructive implementation of these ideas will alter everything we have grasped as a society until now.

Virtual Reality.

From Cabinet to Headset

Virtual reality, telepresence and telly operations have been in existence for many decades. One of the early prototypes of a virtual reality headset was demonstrated back in the 1960s.[1] The first few prototypes were used and demonstrated in the field, such as aerospace, surgical, and defence applications. Over the years many outlandish projects were revealed and demoed, but none of those turned into a fully formed commercial product, because VR was too early for its implementation.

In the 1930s, the science fiction stories first predicted the current state of virtual reality. The story of *Pygmalion's Spectacles* expressed the genius idea of teleportation into work – completely simulated space, a sense of smell, touch and taste. Although the current virtual reality isn't as advanced as it was described back in the 1930s, we are almost there. We have achieved a lot of what people have envisioned during that past few decades.

One of the first fully-functional models of virtual reality was the *Sensorama*, developed in the 1960s, which had an arcade-style cabinet.[2] It is where a user would sit and immerse into a stereoscopic 3D display with vibrating chairs. It's more like looking into an arcade machine. However, the chairs had the same functionalities as the ones in a DBOX or 4DX theatre.[3] The first version of a commercial *Head Mounted Display* (HMD) was instantiated in the 1960s, called The Telesphere Mask.[4] This headset had *stereoscopic 3D* and also the capability of producing stereo sounds. Over the next few decades, many other commercial VR and AR head-mounted displays were manifested; however, none of them was commercialised. In

1987, the term VR for *virtual reality* was 'officially' born in the hands of Jaron Lanier, the founder of *Visual Programming Lab*.[5] Later in the 90s, many theme parks introduced virtual reality arcade machines, which was still at its early stages but had stereoscopic 3D visuals, as well as haptic feedback, build into the chairs.[6] Some of the theme parks also offered multi-sensory experiences. During the same decade, Sega, Nintendo and Sony attempted developing commercial VR headsets, but then the audio-visual technology wasn't matured enough for these projects.[7]

What about the VR cameras? Some of them went into the market for general use after the year 2000, although Google is one of the first companies to essentially create something meaningful out of the stereoscopic VR cameras. Back in 2006, Google launched the project "Street View", and as a part of this project, Google decided to develop a uniquely-designed 360-degree camera.[8] These camera modules were used all over the world to map various roads and places, which are currently available in Google Street View. Eventually, Google created the commercial version of this VR camera, which came to be known as Google Jump.[9] Later, to aid faster adoption and easier availability, YouTube introduced VR integration. As a part of their plan, Google also develops "The Cardboard". It's a DIY headset which can be used with any Android or iPhone for the users to be able to watch VR videos on YouTube and other websites.[10] Google Jump production has recently been halted, but the legacy would remain as it inspired many startups to build more advanced models.

Hardware Development

A key breakthrough in VR hardware came when Facebook decided to invest USD 2 billion in Oculus. It is the first company to produce an affordable version of a commercial VR headset.[11] HTC, the mobile phone company diverted a significant amount of its resources to developing HTC Vive. In 2017, when the company lost almost a USD 1 billion in revenue from their mobile phone division, they decided to raise investment for their VR labs. HTC invested all that money towards developing Vive and acquiring VR/AR companies.[12] A large percentage of that funding came from Google Ventures. Google also invested USD 500 million in a startup called *Magic Leap,* which had no commercial product and no revenue.[13] The company had already developed an early prototype of an AR headset – in fact, they have remained very secretive of their products and operations. Back in 2015, Magic Leap demonstrated a public version of their augmented reality project – A YouTube video demonstrating a whale coming out of nowhere in front of a basketball court with a full audience.[14] Any augmented reality application would require the users to wear a headset for them to be able to interact with the virtual object. A number of technology consultants strongly argue that the video was an unrealistic PR stunt. Some of them believe that it was CGI. Over the past few years, Magic Leap has demonstrated sneak peeks to some of their products, including a full five-finger haptic feedback VR glove, as well as full-body tracking VR.[15] The company remains secretive with regards to the products that they are currently developing. Therefore, there's no way of validating their progress.

VR camera market has grown a lot since then, as many companies, including hundreds of Chinese startups, popped up like mushrooms in a race to produce the cheapest headset. In 2017, intending to compete with the tech giants, Sony decided to release their first version of PSVR, as well as additional controllers supported alongside their VR hardware.[16] While gamers were mostly buying this particular HMD, general users were interested in cheaper hardware. This is where Samsung came in – alongside their flagship phone; they released a commercial version of "Samsung 360-degree camera" and "Samsung Gear VR" headset, developed in partnership with Oculus. In the same year, camera manufacturing company Kodak also released their 360-degree VR cameras. GoPro, on the other hand, released a VR camera for professionals, with a hefty price tag of USD 5000. Their competitor, a startup from Hong Kong, ZCam, released ZCam Pro around the same time.[17] Another company owned by Disney, "Jaunt", released 4K and 8K VR cameras to compete in the market. As you can imagine, 5K for a fancy camera is a lot of money.

Evidently, over the past couple of years, the progress of virtual reality cameras has been a little stagnant due to the hefty price tag and underwhelming demand for content in the market. Most potential VR users are put off by the high prices of cameras and headsets. Despite the high prices, VR is still a very useful technology, so let's proceed with examining its potential.

Active & Passive

VR contents are generally categorised into two types – active VR and passive VR. Active VR (AVR) is where a user can interact with the virtual environment and have a certain degree of control using "handheld controllers". Passive VR (PVR) allow users to be immersed in a virtual environment, but the users aren't in control of the setting. PVR users are not able to interact with the VR world as they can only perceive information from the perception of the VR camera. It's like watching a movie or a concert. While active VR is more relevant to games, training and education, passive VR relates to generic media such as vlogs, films, and so on. Active VR can also be relevant to media or experiences that can be used commercially to generate user interest. Many PR companies have preferred VR as a measure of a publicity stunt.[18] Furthermore, active VR also allows companies to develop a simulated environment for improved customer experience. For instance, if a car buyer visits a dealership and want to try a brand-new car, change its colour, and customise it, then VR would allow the person to have that experience and interact with it to change the look and feel. 3D VR model of a new car in virtual reality provides a better idea for users to understand what they want.[19] Many companies have created such experiences as a part of their promotional campaigns.

Creating content in VR, after all, is a challenging contest. From a commercial point of view of a creator, producing content in VR requires a lot more effort in comparison to a regular video. From an editor's perspective, creating a regular 2D video is very different from creating a VR video – from concept creation to post-production. Metaphorically, in comparison to a standard video, creators need to put at least ten times more effort in designing a set. This comparison is based on the time required to complete a 2D and VR production. Let's say Amy is planning to create a film in VR. In a 2D environment, the field of view for her camera is 180°. Therefore, she and her crew can sit behind the camera and let the actors do the job in front of the camera. VR provides a 360-degree environment; hence if Amy is to shoot or create a concept for the same film, she can't stay behind the camera. She will need to develop a new 360-set to hide all the background props, people, and the production team. This additional effort of hiding everything from the surrounding area is highly technical and requires an extensive amount of effort in comparison to a 2D video production.

Secondly, creators are also required to put more effort in post-production when it comes to a virtual reality video. If you can potentially generate the same amount of income by giving in ten-times less effort, what are you going to choose? Of course, it's a matter of the audience, and whether it makes a difference to them. A VR audience needs a headset to watch these videos. For the users, Google cardboard is cheap and serves essential purposes, although, it does not create the environment they are meant to experience. High-end VR headsets are expensive in comparison to general gaming consoles; therefore, many have opted out until the prices go down. Because of this very narrow audience and the need for a substantial amount of effort to produce a good quality VR content, there isn't enough content online. If there's no demand for these type of VR videos, content producers wouldn't be interested in producing those. Without their involvement, mass adoption could be years away. To solve this problem, a few things need to be sorted out, which are –

1) Ease of editing general virtual reality videos,
2) high-quality camera at a much lower price,

3) affordable VR headsets with much higher frame rate, resolution, and low latency,
4) internet speed for higher resolution,
5) Market diversification and
6) Content development by the wider audience on social media sites.

What's Stopping VR

The question is – if Samsung, HTC, Google, Acer and almost all other major tech giant took a risk, then why isn't VR taking off? Firstly, latency and low frame rate reduce the quality of streaming media onto the headset. *Latency* is the time delay following the instruction generated for data transfer, i.e. the time it takes for the data to be transferred from the headset to the server and back. Latency is measured in milliseconds. Low latency is a valuable term in the world of internet, especially streaming and gaming. Researchers believe that the higher the VR latency, the more users are susceptible to become motion sick.[20] Moreover, experts claim that motion sickness is caused due to inferior quality of VR headsets, as well as low-resolution content.

People tending to be motion sick, usually feel the pain when they sit at the back of a car or a bus, or in a boat. It occurs because the brain receives mixed signal. Through the eyes, the brain receives the signal of a person sitting stationary at the back of a vehicle, although it's moving at a high speed. Due to this confusion, the brain triggers unusual reactions and starts to think that it's in danger, which outcomes in severe motion sickness. It is acting as a major barrier with regards to the growth of VR. Movement in active and passive VR typically triggers *simulation sickness.* Due to the lack of stabilisation, viewers tend to feel sick after a few minutes of watching a passive VR video or experiencing a VR game. A star-wars type first-person game is likely to trigger this type of reaction.

You will find that many VR users with a tendency of motion sickness feel unwell after playing a game for five to ten minutes, where they are required to fly a 'spaceship' and 'shoot down the enemies'. It materialises because of the same principle – the users are technically feeding their brain with "mixed signal", by drastically moving, and being stationary at the same time.[21]

As discussed earlier, another cause for virtual reality to be stagnant is the ridiculous pricing of the headsets. From a commercial perspective, if the profit margin is low, companies working on VR technologies are required to sell many products to reach breakeven. If the demand isn't there, high pricing does not help the growth of the market. For example, a PS4 costs approximately GBP 300 to 450, depending on the specs.[22] Conversely, HTC Vive or an Oculus VR headset also costs GBP 300 to 499.[23] It is supposed to be an extension of a primary device. Hence the prices should be lower than the primary. Because of the high price tag, only a few businesses, VR enthusiasts, researchers and a small subset of the actual target market are buying these HMDs. Secondly, currently available VR headsets require a significant amount of space due to the dependency of the HMDs on external sensors. In 2019, both HTC and Facebook released their new headsets with *inside-out tracking*, which allows the headset to track an object without the requirement of an external infrared sensor. This improvement could allow a user to walk in a simulated environment freely and be wire-free at the same time. Both companies have promised that the commercial version of these headsets would be reasonably priced. Despite, HTC has priced its high-end Vive Pro at USD 1400, which is likely to act as a barrier towards mass adoption of VR.[24]

Improved *Field of View (FOV)* with a high-resolution is also imperative to increase sensory presence.[25] A typical video is recorded in Full-HD resolution. When it comes to watching a VR content, sensory perception adds another dimension to the experience. Hence, the field of view is an essential terminology in VR – every headset and every type of experience has its own FOV. Human eyes have a combined visual field perimeter of over 220°, of which 110° is called the *binocular view* – a combined field of view for both eyes. We can focus on an area or task if it falls within the binocular range. The high-end headsets in the market currently have a range of 110°, which is enough to feed the brain with information from a simulated environment and confuse it with the real one.

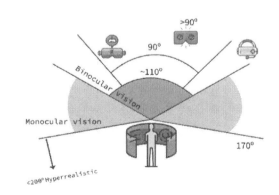

2.1 - VR Field of View/IntelXSys Research

Even though 110° doesn't sound like a substantially sizeable *sensory field*, the reaction from the respondents from previous our research provides a different idea. The *binocular view* is good enough to make someone feel like they are genuinely standing up from the top of the 80th floor a building. The light grey range (figure 2.1) in the peripheral vision is known as *the monocular view* – the brain always perceives information from our monocular view, even if we are focused on a particular location or task. The combination of monocular and binocular vision benefits us by being spatially aware of our external surroundings in a car park.

Typically, cardboard VR or easy-to-use *plug and play* headset have a field-of-view of less than 90°. High-end gaming headsets such as Oculus Rift or HTC Vive have a FOV of 110° along with a higher resolution.[26] Other startups such as Pimax has developed 5K headsets with over 200° vision field.[27] Nevertheless, the resolution needs to improve drastically. Due to the magnification by the *convex lenses* attached to the headsets, the *pixel density* on a VR headset perceives to be lower than the actual resolution of the media. Therefore, even though the content might be in 4K, the *retina* would perceive it at a much lower resolution. As a result, users come across *pixel dots* when using a mid-range headset and perceive a low resolution.

On the other hand, a higher resolution would require much faster internet. The solution to this problem is almost here. 5G internet was launched in the UK in July 2019. The improvement in the network infrastructure would allow us to browse content at 40 times the speed in comparison to typical mobile internet, and over 100 times faster than average broadband in London.[28] Recent 5G tests in the UK and the US projected that the speed could reach up to 500Mbps and can capacitate up to 2Gbps. Some of the tests have illustrated even higher speed. It would allow seamless integration of media produced in 8K or higher resolution and assist in reducing latency.

Researchers are also working towards creating high-framerate and zero-latency VR headsets that are compatible with motion sensitivity. Inside-out tracking is one of the essential features that need to be integrated into a budget VR headset.[29] Because of inside-out tracking, the headsets would be able to track the position without having to depend on any external sensors, which is an industry-standard at the moment. Companies are also working towards real-time *haptic feedback* – the technology that allows users to feel virtual objects using synthetic gloves and handheld controllers.[30] Although many startups have already demonstrated haptic feedback on two, three or more fingers using external gloves, there hasn't been any further commercial development. Valkyrie Industries, a startup based in *Eagle Lab at Plexal* in London, is developing such technology. Eventually, haptic feedback would enable users to feel the presence in both hands. A commercial version of this type of product would likely be out in the market within the next 3 to 4 years.

As the research progresses, virtual reality headsets would become lighter, have a better field of view and be able to mimic the FOV of our retina. Many Sci-Fi shows predict that VR may not even need a headset – just a few tiny devices that would allow users to be immersed in a simulation. By the end of this decade, VR developers would solve problems with regards to frame rate, latency, device motion tracking, inside-out tracking, and speed required for streaming 8K or 12K VR content. 5G network will enable much more improved streaming quality for all types of content in the next couple of years. If users eventually can use headsets that would not make them feel sick and allow them to be immersed in VR for hours, what happens after then? Just like gaming addiction, we could witness a rise in the number of people around the world immersed in VR.

Use Cases

If there's not enough 'significant' development in the world of VR, is it slowly dying? No, it isn't. All these problems mentioned above would be solved, one by one, over the next five to seven years. Almost all of the large tech companies have made a significant amount of investment into developing this technology. The development won't slow down, because the ultimate aim for scaling VR, is where users would be able to immerse themselves in VR continuously for hours-at-a-time. The recent demonstrations provided by Facebook their social VR apps hints to the whereabouts of their vision with regards to virtual reality. Besides gaming, both VR and AR can be beneficial in many market verticals and industries, including the following:

Training and Education: While VR is already being used across many verticals to train employees, it has the potential to become an indispensable part of an educational or training environment in the future. In the 80s and 90s, there weren't many schools or universities with computer labs or laptop being a mandatory part of the educational process. After the internet disseminated around the world, personal computers and laptops became a significant part of the educational process. Now, almost every major educational institution has dedicated labs for their students. In just a matter of 15 years, students have moved from pen and paper to typing almost everything in their laptops. Similarly, VR would provide a great addition to the educational process – immersing students in a virtual classroom.

During the clinical research (CRI) experience, McDuffus et al. (2018) discovered that virtual reality "creates a greater sense of presence" across all demographics. Even though most of the respondents of the research didn't use VR before, they expressed interest in using passive VR that augments its capabilities. During the study, two different sets of respondents were asked to watch a 2D video and have the same experience in a VR environment. Every respondent was provided approximately four minutes to be a part of this experience. The respondents were also asked to wear a medically approved EEG cap which allowed the researchers to collect EEG data directly from their brain. The difference was astonishing. While the 2D video did not have much impact on EEG readings, the non-interactive passive VR experience triggered multiple reactions in a short amount of time. Some participants did not physically react to the media, as their reactions were not associated with the EEG readings. They concluded that passive VR creates a greater sense of presence in comparison to 2D media.[31] Evidently, the application of such immersive training content would have a significant impact over any traditional learning process. It could disrupt the orthodox methods of teaching in schools, colleges and universities.

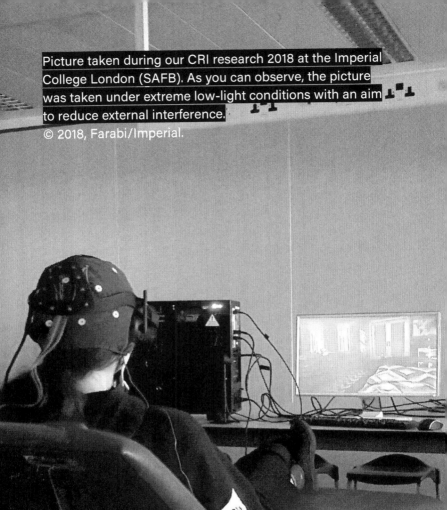

Medical Training: VR medical training simulators have been in existence since the beginning of this millennia.[32] Surgical training for minimum-invasive surgeries have been used by professionals, but the availability of those devices was limited. Startups are currently developing technologies that would allow surgeons, doctors and nurses to be trained before they operate live on their patients. The light version of these simulators has already been demonstrated by a few startups, some of which are available to download from the Rift store or Steam. Several startups are developing mobile VR technologies that would allow them to learn first-hand operating techniques in a professional environment. Similar to flight training simulators, physical VR simulators would allow the surgeons to receive immersive training and take drastic measures to save a patient in the operation theatre. *Mimic*, a VR-MedTech company from Seattle has developed a real-life simulator which would allow them to use a combination of robotic arms and virtual reality to operate on patients. According to Mimic, *DVSS*, or *da Vinci Surgical System* has 27 simulation exercises that could be used to train future surgeons.[33] The University of Louisville is using Mimic surgery simulator to conduct precision training using this state-of-the-art equipment.[34]

Treatment and Employee Training: VR can also be used to treat patients of different kinds. Companies are working alongside hospitals to develop materials that allow health practitioners to reduce their patients' anxiety before surgeries. VR can be used in combination with local anaesthesia for patients, to allow them to be immersed in VR while they're being operated on. Older patients who are in care can also receive therapies by using the treatment in virtual reality. It can also be used in psychotherapy, treat mental illness, aid patients to get into meditation, and reduce stress and anxiety. Researchers corroborate that VR aids physiotherapists to help their patients in rehab.

During our clinical research experience (CRI) in 2019, research students from the School of Medicine (ICSM) conducted a study on the commercial application of VR in reducing symptoms of anxiety. Our team collected various data, including EEG, breathing rate, heart rate and conducted a small open-ended interview to compare the difference between traditionally available apps and VR meditation apps. This time, the researchers strongly suggested that virtual reality meditation had a significant impact on reducing the anxiety symptoms. Although our team conducted the research on a small sample, after analysing the qualitative data, they comprehended that 100% of the respondents would prefer virtual reality meditation over traditional app-based training.[35]

Smart Workspaces: VR could be a key player in the field of smart workspaces. Employees of the coming generation are going to spend a lot of time working in virtual reality, especially the freelancers. Virtual Skype meetings would eventually become virtual reality meetings. The teleconference could eventually become telepresence. Instead of any real monitors, we could use our virtual 100" desktop computer inside the VR headset to work and accomplish our day-to-day tasks. The power from the actual VR headset would be used to accomplish complicated tasks in those computers.

Once latency, internet speed, and HMD-related motion sickness issues are resolved, we would finally have a perfect headset which can be used for hours at a time. In a matter of years, we would not only be playing games in VR but also start browsing contents, engage in social media interaction and attend live concerts along with other people. As a Rift user, you can already hang out with up to five Facebook friends in a VR hangout room.[36] We can watch cat videos with friends in VR! How great does that sound?

It is an excellent technology, but the past decade was not the right time to launch a VR startup. Unless you have tens of millions to spare behind research and development work, it would not be wise to move further with that idea. As the technology continues to struggle, it will be very difficult for VR companies to raise funds at this moment. If you do have a terrific VR-related idea, maybe it's wise to wait a few years before you can think of commercialisation.

Instead of any real monitors, we would use our virtual 100" desktop computer inside the VR headset to work and accomplish our day-to-day tasks.

Although the current avatars look like sculptures made out of virtual gummy bears, Facebook at a recent conference, demonstrated how they are working to create a lifelike version of its users in the virtual reality environment.[37] Just like the AR emoji on your iPhone, you could have your own VR avatar. In fact, the difference between the current version of VR avatars and the prototype showcased are unreal.

Eventually, social media users could be hanging out with Facebook friends, but that won't just be on the newsfeed posting a status or tagging each other in the comments; instead, they could be hanging out in VR talking to each other, virtually, face to face. Instead of attending a real event, people could attend virtual concerts, have summer barbecue during a winter bank holiday, or even attend a film premiere screening in VR with friends. Gloves with haptic feedback technology with sensitivity would add another dimension to the experience.

Furthermore, *Virtuix* has already developed its state-of-the-art *Virtuix Omni*, an omnidirectional treadmill that allows a VR user to run in any direction without moving an inch.[38] Virtuix Omni is mostly compatible with first-person shooter videos.[39] In the future, more of these devices would be available in the market, and thus the competition would bring the cost of these devices down significantly. Therefore, millions more would be able to afford them in conjunction with their PlayStations and PCs.

Future & VR Obsession

The future of technology doesn't end here. Eventually, we would get to a point, where users would be able to thoroughly immerse themselves in an induced reality. People would start losing the sense of realism, i.e. the perspective of segregating reality; although, it's just a *synthetic simulation*. The first phase of that would be using a body-tracking external sensor, but eventually, they would have access to futuristic devices that would put a person in a state of temporary coma, while transferring consciousness into that induced reality. At the peak of its technological phase, what happens when people trade their social life with VR life? As mentioned earlier, we already have created extensions of ourselves using our smartphones. It's 2020, and it seems like people are already unable to live without their smartphones and tablets. How long can you truly live without your phone? Some of us are highly addicted to games, while others living their fantasies in social media to avoid their real-life miseries. Social media is still presumed to be within the means of a controllable addiction. However, transferring this addiction to a synthetic simulation would have a major impact. Although many experts claim that this procedure of habit transference would happen in a leisurely and controlled manner; once there, it would be painstaking for people to overcome such routines. Facebook or Instagram didn't accurately predict the current outcome; they just kept on growing. Now, these social media sites are so enormous that almost half of the population in the world are a part of their network. In a bid to reduce obsession over social media, most smartphone companies are already enforcing "digital wellbeing" as an essential feature for parents and adult users.[40] However, could VR make it worse?

This subject can be rationalised from a psychological point of view. As people, we are always in need of validation. This validation may come from parents, friends, relatives or acquaintances on social media. When we upload our photos on Facebook or Instagram, many of us expect the photos to be loved, liked and flooded with comments. The hit of dopamine keeps us motivated and moving forward. For some people, the term "validation" might mean something much more challenging to achieve, for instance, owning a large tech startup or making a million pound a year. For others, who seek social approval, validation means maintaining a certain 'standard' by posting highly filtered content. It doesn't matter if they have 400 followers, or 40,000, just a certain number of likes would do the work. What many users tend to do is make themselves feel better by posting about their *"best version"* on social media. It helps in escaping the bleakness of reality and create an illusion of how happy they are – in other words, reinforcing a bunch of false information to the brain to keep it running. Although real-life may be non-identical to that of the Instagram profile, this socially validated layer benefits them in two ways:

1) upholding an individual image to friends and family,
2) allowing themselves to escape and avoid dealing with reality. With the steady rise of influencers, many bottle up their struggles of daily lives and use social media as a distraction, while others seem to be happy to disclose their shortcomings and struggles, mental health issues and other excruciating problems. Evidently, the latter is a healthier option because it helps to de-stress.

If we contemplate this hit of dopamine as a means of achieving a 'sense of accomplishment' in VR, people might fall in love with it. Think of a friend, let's say, Jamie, have a "certain" personality on social media. Jamie can be whomever he wants, whatever he wants, be thin or fat, tall or small, make his six-pack, give himself the tan he wants and more. If this virtual personality receives a better appraisal from his virtual friends, wouldn't he love it? It's something like Instagram but in VR. Evidently, some users would love it, just like we love receiving 'likes' on photos. However, in reality, "it's not what it looks like". If Instagram can make us this much addicted, imagine what a perfect VR world could do, that is why, future parents are required to be vigilant about their children's upbringing, and not let them go with the flow. While some of us are good at making our living from social media, many suffer from severe mental health issues due to the rise in peer pressure. Social media professionals believe that peer pressure was one of the reasons for young people to join the platform, followed by connectivity and curiosity.[41] This problem would be exponential when VR goes fully mainstream. While this massive hit of dopamine is exceptionally satisfactory, many psychological experts are already raising awareness of how harmful and demoralising this addiction would be in the future.[42] Adding virtual reality would be having Facebook on steroids. VR needs to grow and scale faster, but it's imperative to be cautious of the potential of such obsession towards the chaotic simulated life.

Shifting Face of the Automobile Industry.

In January 2020, Tesla's stock price broke another record, making the company more valuable than Ford and GM combined.[1]

Image 3.1 © Terryleewhite/Adobe Stock.

Decontamination of Earth

Our societies have been producing energy from fossil fuel, coal, and mineral sources for a long time. In the late 90s, when the world realised the importance of reducing greenhouse gas to fix Ozone layer, almost every country around the world took necessary steps towards reducing carbon emission.[2] Due to this movement, the growth of eco-friendly energy companies has exploded in the past two decades.

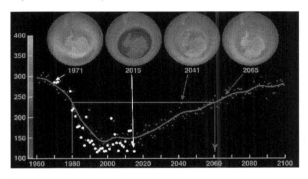

3.2 – Forecast on the improvement of the ozone layer over the next 100 years. © NASA.

Energy-efficient smart devices have improved a lot over the past few years and are now available in every corner of the world. With the advancement of internet and other disruptive technologies, such as blockchain, energy is a completely different game now. The smart energy meter is being promoted around the UK to improve efficiency.[3] Our mentality towards saving the planet and preserving life is changing rapidly due to never-before-seen natural disasters, such as the Indonesian Tsunami, or three simultaneous cyclones hitting parts of the US in a matter of two weeks. Over the next decade, people will be more inclined towards using solar panels as an alternative energy source, as it becomes increasingly available at a cost-effective rate. *Generation X* and *millennials* are the ones who started these movements for promoting eco-friendly energy providing systems. Their children are likely to live a different life in contrast to the *baby boomers*. In the past couple of months, several countries in the west have declared "climate emergency" due to the global movement by many protest-groups.[4] The government of the UK, Northern Ireland, Scotland and Wales have already agreed to declare a mutual climate emergency and agreed to take necessary steps before 2050 to ensure the sustainability of the planet.[5] We have reached a pivotal point in time after which the effects of the harmful gases will be irreversible. Nevertheless, climate change would require one major milestone to be fulfilled – reducing the number of combustion engine vehicles and replacing them with electric vehicles (EVs).

Race to Sustainability

Existence and development of petrol or diesel engines are imperative for fossil fuel companies. A large share of Shell's business to consumer (B2C) revenue is generated from the "downstream" business, i.e. purchase of gasoline products, including diesel and petrol all over the world.[6] Only a handful of companies have full control of the extraction and distribution of fossil fuel.[7] These companies are constantly monitoring the change in people's sentiment and behaviour patterns. As vehicle owners are slowly shifting towards EVs, all of the major petroleum corporations are now forced to adopt eco-friendly energy distribution measures. [8]

Furthermore, the way in which consumers are purchasing vehicles have rapidly shifted especially in the past ten years.[9] We only used to buy and sell cars through dealerships and events. Online marketplaces have fundamentally transformed the mentality of car buying. Now it's as easy as filling up a 3-minute application. The change didn't stop here. The mentality of car ownership has also changed, as we shift to a peer-to-peer (p2p) economy.

A car is typically a high-depreciating asset – which means the price of the car would go down significantly throughout an ownership, and mostly during the first couple of years depending on the usage.[10] Buying a brand-new zero-mile car isn't ideal – the price of that car would likely go down significantly, almost moments after driving it out of a dealership. Therefore, people are moving towards a more sustainable and sensible means of owning vehicles – car leasing and p2p renting.[11] Buying a vehicle and leasing is different, because, instead of a chunk of cash towards to the car, the owners can pay for what they use. Moreover, companies such as Zipcar and Drive Now are providing low-cost car sharing and car rental services.[12] These mobility companies are lenient towards eco-friendly vehicles, and have altered the way how people can use a hybrid or electric car on a pay-as-you-go basis, which is greatly beneficial for urban citizens. Nowadays people living in cities such as London don't need to own a car at all –they require a vehicle only certain times a month. No wonder Mercedes and BMW teamed up together, ended the long-running rivalry and jointly invested two billion dollars on mobility and peer-to-peer car rental companies.[13] Adopting this new type of ownership style and customer behaviour as well as people's mentality of using eco-friendly vehicles implies a major shift in the car manufacturing industry.

The impact of climate change has not only exerted influence on the energy market, but also other industries, including the public sector. In recent years, many local London boroughs have imposed street parking regulations and charges to reduce pollution and carbon emission.[14] Diesel cars typically exert harmful gases compared to petrol and other alternatives. In a bid to take a step towards reducing pollution, the UK government has been rewarding up to GBP 3500 (USD 4250) towards the purchase of new electric vehicles. Local councils in the city aren't staying behind. London's Highbury and Islington borough were one of the first to impose a GBP 2.40 (USD 2.90) diesel surcharge for parking on their streets.[15] Following Highbury and Islington, some other councils have also imposed similar surcharges for diesel cars in and around the city. Fossil fuel is harmful to the environment, acts as a major catalyst for climate change and global temperature increase. Due to this irreversible life-threatening impact on the planet, there is a movement going on within the car manufacturing industry, a race towards developing the best electric vehicle. One company has fired up the rocket forcing all major manufacturers to produce electric vehicles.[16]

Two major factors are the model drivers for the transformation in the car industry:

> *1) electric vehicles, and 2) self-driving capabilities – integration of artificial intelligence.*

Explosion of EVs

Approximately ten years ago, when Tesla Roadster was revealed, it received a critical reception from automobile journalists.[17] Many petrolheads did not like the concept of replacing petrol engines with electric ones because of the habit people had grown into – using internal combustion engines. Over the past decade, Tesla didn't struggle much with their promotion, thanks to the YouTube generation and millions of social media influencers promoting the brand online. Instead, they have struggled with their production capacity; however, managed to successfully triggered a global movement. The VW scandal in 2015 acted as another catalyst and widespread warning towards how large corporations may have been manipulating their vehicle design to make a profit from the system.[18] It was time for car manufacturing companies to start producing energy-efficient vehicles to reduce this effect on global warming. Tesla had the first-mover advantage in the market and were able to convince governments around the world to allow special treatment for EVs. EV owners also receive VIP treatment in car parks and local areas, such as dedicated space for charging.

For the past few years, the company sold a significant number of its Model S, one of the most successful EVs produced in the world. Other startups such as Faraday Cars received billions in funding to compete in the EV vehicle range.[19] EV car manufacturers are also working towards automation. A combination of electric engines and AI-based automation made Tesla a major threat to the market leaders. Tesla uses a deep neural network to teach its cars how to drive itself. Deep neural networks are designed to mimic our brain. Similar to our brain, the neural net has its small computational unit called *neuron*. Neurons receive incoming messages, which is processed and then translates into a decision. We will discuss more of that in the next few chapters.

NVIDIA, the largest *Graphics Processing Unit* (GPU) manufacturer have been producing these AI chips for Tesla cars for the past few years.[20] Each of these AI chips are almost as powerful as a GPU and capable of 8 TOPS. Trillion Operations Per Second, or TOPS, is a quantifying unit for computational performance. In other words, these vehicles are walking high-performance personal computers. Tesla have replaced all the physical buttons with one giant 16-inch tab, where users can do everything including play some decent family-friendly games. The company uses unorthodox methods for PR, such as introducing a function called the "dog mode", which has since become a very attractive feature for millennials and generation X.[21] They have been targeting influencers and use referral link as a method of online promotion and word of mouth.

Experts believe that one of the underappreciated features of Tesla is the sheer computational performance of its self-driving autonomous vehicles (AV). The recent update of Tesla has made it possible for the company to produce as much as 12 trillion operations per second.[22] Dependent on several hidden cameras around the body, the software uses a deep neural network to learn from external environment and use those techniques towards improving its driveability skills. In 2018, Tesla announced a new chip for their cars called the "Full Self Driving" (FSD), which packs a colossal 36 trillion operations per second (TOPS).[23] This type of manufacturing competition between Tesla and Nvidia is beneficial for AVs.[24] Tesla confirmed that the new FSD chips comes with a noteworthy performance increase, as the car will be capable of doing much more than we can contemplate at this point. Other car companies have also revealed their self-driving models, although many are reliant on a huge external sensor, such as LIDAR. LIDAR is a type of radar, but it uses laser light to detect objects and is the most sophisticated of all the sensors used for AVs. This sensor is very expensive and does not make a vehicle look pretty. Google, Waymo and Uber's self-driving cars use some expensive LIDAR sensors, which has long detection range, high resolution and work well with different type of lighting conditions.[25]

Car designs have evolved over the past century by focusing on refining the design and usability.[26] Manufacturers care a lot about aesthetics thus invest billions in research and development in making a car look beautiful. Vehicle owners are sensitive with regards to vehicle design, internally and externally. External sensors epitomise a prototype-like design and thus it isn't commercially viable. Until now, only one company has been able to produce commercial vehicles with camera-based image recognition system that can demonstrate enhanced self-driving capabilities, continuously learning with its neural network and being able to drive itself through an incredibly congested motorway.[27] Tesla uses a combination of radar, ultrasonic and 360-degree cameras to train its AI self-driving module.[28] These new generation of cars are not only eco-friendly but also a computational powerhouse, which is why shareholders put more value in Tesla in comparison to other car companies in the stock market.[29] Model S is still the company's most popular saloon vehicle and holds the highest share of EVs in the west. Since its inception, the company has released different models e.g. the X, Y, and further variants of those models. Now Tesla owners receive special treatment almost everywhere around the world. The company has also installed dedicated *superchargers* in service stations and allocated parking for Tesla owners.

The Electric Trend

Following Tesla's bumpy success, Volvo, the car manufacturing giant in Europe announced that they will produce only electric vehicles or hybrid plug-in vehicles from 2020.[30] This is a major technological step towards changing how cars are produced and manufactured. The company was acquired by a Chinese manufacturer known as Geely in 2012 after it almost went bankrupt under Ford ownership.[31] Since the acquisition by the Chinese company, Volvo has completely transformed itself into another leading hybrid vehicle manufacturer.[32] Volvo's *Polestar*, the sports-car enhancement division has recently separated itself from the Volvo brand. Polestar is now a high-end manufacturer and dedicated to manufacturing sport-EVs. Their first vehicle Polestar 1 had a critical reception due to its price tag, although the newer model, Polestar 2 which is due to be released in the market in the middle of 2020, had a great reception and received some good feedback from car experts.[33] Many have argued that these vehicles are still overpriced, and Volvo is projected to struggle with sales of their new brand. The company's steady growth in sales and involvement in eco-friendly movements to save the planet has been a major factor in refining its brand image. It also has radically improved its vehicle design over the past few years. A scroll down through the comments section of the Volvo S60 commercial on YouTube will provide an idea of how the company's designs are being acclaimed in recent times.[34] While others are gradually adopting the electric vehicle trend, Volvo's announcement of developing a fully electric fleet has been highly strategic.[35] In a recent press release, the company has also publicised imposing a global speed limit on all their cars as a part of its global safety program.

Toyota, the Japanese carmaker, on the other hand, has been developing their hybrid EV Prius since 1997.[36] Prius is still the most popular hybrid vehicle in the world. Toyota has already expanded its *self-charging technology* into other vehicles and models, such as its luxury brand Lexus.[37] With the bigger companies taking a step towards *electrification*, western car manufacturers did not stop themselves from getting their hands dirty. BMW, Audi and Mercedes have been producing plug-in hybrid vehicles for a while now, although recently, all of these brands have now given into the trend and announced fully electric line-ups.[38] The new Mercedes electric SUV is deemed pretty, although not efficient as a Tesla SUV.[39] The companies which criticised Tesla for producing an electric vehicle are now EV manufacturer themselves. While Tesla runs on limited resources, the German car companies have a larger budget towards promoting their EVs. If you are an Avengers fan, you will notice that the Audi e-Tron was strongly advertised in the film *Avengers Endgame*.[40]

However, before "Electric Went Audi", many other entrepreneurs have already created long-term sustainable plans which will allow a reduction of fossil fuel usage, diesel vehicles, and subsequently increase the number of EVs. This will have a major impact on improving global climate.

3.3 - VW ID 3, the new electric hatchback from Volkswagen.

Tesla 3 has a backlog of almost a year, while the company's forecast implies that they will be able to catch up by mid-2020.[41] The larger manufacturers such as Volvo and Audi will also start commercialising their electric range in the coming years. Interestingly, the biggest car company in the world, Volkswagen, which faced a massive emission cheating scandal in 2015, also announced their own full electric vehicle line-up ID.[42]

VW, still offering pay-outs to their customers for their scandal, has already made an impact by creating the Golf EV.[43] Zipcar, the peer-to-peer car-sharing company has increased its number of vehicles on road, most of which are Golf plugin hybrid.[44] Mitsubishi is also selling their famous Outlander and a few other models as a *Plugin-Hybrid Electric Vehicle* (PHEV). Although Tesla faces fierce competition, they will always have the first-mover advantage and the "luxurious" brand image. It's similar to owning an iPhone, even though Android may serve its users with more power to price ratio. Tesla has already established themselves as a brand, and therefore it's likely to be the number one choice with regards to EVs. Starting from 2020, we will not only witness an increasing number of PHEVs and EVs, but also a significant change of mentality towards using an electric vehicle.[45] This is why investors value companies like *Faraday Cars* even though they only had a couple of working prototypes and lengthy manufacturing lifecycle.[46] The company, not long ago, almost went to insolvency, but on their way to release their first vehicle by the end of 2020.[47][48]

The largest auto manufacturer in the US, Ford has recently invested half a million in a new EV truck company based in California.[49] Commonly referred to as a pickup truck, Ford, a successful pickup manufacturer in the west, is contested by cash-positive Mitsubishi, which has been dominating the Asian territory. Who, in the right mind, would invest USD 400 million, when sales are tanking, account drowning in debt and forced to make major structural changes? This investment into an electric vehicle company whilst struggling with sales means that they are making a huge bet and considering EVs as a major source of future revenue. In a recent PR stunt, Ford demoed their all-electric version of F150 truck's towing capability.[50] The truck was able to drag a gigantic 1-million-pound train and pull it up to a thousand feet. Later, in the same stunt, the train was loaded with 42 F-150 and it was still able to pull the train successfully. This shows the sheer power of a fully electric vehicle.[51]

Self-Driving Cars

EV wasn't the primary focus of Ford's investment. *Argo AI*, an autonomous vehicle (AV) startup received a massive USD 1 billion investment from Ford in 2017.[52] The same company received a fresh round of USD 2.7 billion investment from Volkswagen, raising its valuation to USD 7 billion.[53] This is a part of VW and Ford's strategic self-driving alliance. The startup is developing the technology that would be integrated into both these companies' vehicles in the coming years.

Unlike other AVs, Tesla is deemed to be the most valuable EV companies in the world due to its integration of machine learning algorithm that allows its cars to drive itself. All the Tesla cars are connected to a neural network, which has already assisted in attaining "Level 4" autonomous performance. Hypothetically, level 4 is fully-autonomous driving in controlled areas possessing operational design domain, e.g. lane markings and appropriate designs that the cars will follow to drive itself; learn and adapt.[54] Level 5 is where the cars will not need a driver at all, anywhere, because all of its safety functions will enable the car to drive itself with its owner's command and without the dependency of operational design, which isn't available at every corner of the world. Tesla has already reached this stage using software neural networks. As the hardware is improving, the company recently announced its *robo-taxis*, which would potentially be available by 2020.[55] In 2019, a Tesla user was witnessed to *summon* his car, the feature which allowed the car to drive itself out of the car park and go to its owner, without any help from a human.[56] These complex skills are being constantly improved using a machine learning algorithm. We are already witnessing the end of cab driving jobs that are slowly going to be replaced by self-driven taxis. This is not only the commencement of a major change in the industry but also a key transformation towards the lifestyle, which has factually been the same over the past century. In fact, since the car was invented, our society hasn't seen these lifestyle changes until recently. Once robotaxi trials are successful, many countries are also going to introduce smaller transportation pods for mobility purposes. Waymo's pilot program for their robotaxi has already gathered over 6000 participants.[57]

The truth is that boasting about Tesla won't end fossil fuel problems. Tesla was the first car manufacturer to go completely against the institutionalisation of fossil fuel. Tesla is not only cost-efficient but has also been validated by LIDAR researchers.[58] The company is now confident with regards to deploying level 4 and level 5 autonomous vehicles.

The law, however, is going to be an issue for deployment of self-driving vehicles on road. In the UK, there are several self-operating transportation systems in place. The DLR or the Docklands Light Railway in London is fully driverless and operates on 45 stations.[59] These trains only operate on railways and do not require complex skills to run on time.

Although, when compared to self-driving pods, as it requires highly complex manoeuvrability, the laws regarding its operation can be controversial. For example, if a self-driving pod hits a pedestrian, what would be the legal implication for the damage? A machine cannot be held liable for such cases. Hence, once motoring laws around self-driving cars are passed, we will start to see smaller transportation pods around the city to move from point A to point B. In a bid towards research into this sector, Greenwich Council recently tested a fully autonomous pod which can hold up to six people.[60] Dependent on a pre-defined algorithm, the mobility pods can drive itself in a defined route provided that vehicle operational designs are in place. This category of transportation modes in a shorter route would help gather research data in order to permit a better transportation system around the world. Airports could be the first of many places where self-driven mobility pods are introduced.[61] All of these – thanks to artificial intelligence and its capabilities of accessing deep neural network, being able to learn and deploy its skills successfully.

Autonomous electric vehicles may be deemed as risky and would require a significant number of modifications in motoring and road traffic laws. Level 4 autonomous vehicles require a driver's presence in the vehicle, however, car manufacturers project that it would add a premium to the purchase price of currently available vehicles.[62] This feature is deemed risky by insurers in the current market because, in simpler terms, only a few per cent of the drivers would eventually want to pay for "that" level of automation.[63] Evidently, Uber and other minicab drivers in London will be the first in line for casualty as a result of the implementation of this technology.

It may just be too early to start foreseeing exactly when we will have access to cars capable of level 5 autonomous drivability. Evidently, level 5 would require further changes in governing laws, regulations and highway codes. Therefore, it will take at least a few years of trial, research and development until its fully implemented. In the UK, the law requires drivers to keep hands on the steering wheel at all times when using autopilot.[64] If you take off your hands, the car will start giving you warnings. Even after these laws being imposed, accidents are happening, and the car manufacturers are receiving the blame for their technology going wrong. Hence, to prevent severe consequences, car manufacturers will continue to jointly conduct more research and development work until they are 100% confident in deploying smart vehicles on road. By 2025, most vehicles on the road would either be plug-in hybrid or electric, having level 4 capabilities.[65] The internal combustion engine isn't going anywhere. Even though some countries such as Norway have decided to ban combustion engines from their roads, it would be difficult for many other countries in Asia to impose such conditions on its people.[66] As technology and internet connectivity improves, artificial intelligence will become cleverer, the rivalry among vehicle manufacturers will intensify resulting in pushing the prices of EVs down to a bargain level over the next five to six years. Mass adoption of EVs could also be accelerated by making energy affordable, and there is way to do that.

Peer-to-peer Energy

It makes a lot of sense for Tesla to acquire SolarCity. Solar panels and electric cars go hand-in-hand. If you don't have solar panels, and want to get a Tesla, then you will need regular electricity supplier such as the British Gas to recharge the battery. Production of electricity and energy are still highly centralised. Due to this process, prices of energy are controlled by a handful of companies. Innovators are working towards a solution to reduce this dependency and make energy much cheaper by allowing peer-to-peer trading.

Peer-to-peer energy trading system is a new concept.[67] Until now, the traditional way of using energy would be going through a centralised energy services provider which would act as a middleman and make billions in profit. These providers are in full control of producing and distributing energy in the current market. Thanks to the major advancement of decentralised technologies, the power is slowly starting to shift towards the people instead of the monopolistic energy market.[68] Peer-to-peer energy trading system would allow users to trade electricity and reduce dependence on centralised systems.[69] The technology is not ready for the market yet; however, the decentralised energy market will likely be executed by the end of next decade. But what is it and how does it help the society?

Typically, large energy service providers invest billions towards producing energy and as a result, they can keep control of full distribution. An energy company would routinely look for energy resources, such as *offshore drilling points*, where oils can be extracted from the seabed using sophisticated equipment worth billions. In terms of return on investment, it takes a few years for an oil company to reach a breakeven point. Internet and the birth of new technologies have provided a novel approach to how energy can be produced and distributed. Innovators are trialling a system where users will be able to install a solar panel on the roof and use blockchain to distribute any surplus energy produced. Let's presume that Chris has a 4-kilowatt hour (kWH) solar panel installed in his house. Usually, a 4kWH solar panel would be enough to produce energy for four people throughout the year, and also produce surplus if his family members are energy efficient.[70] Since Chris is not using energy brokers to receive electricity, the only costs are the installation and maintenance of the solar panels. Typically an initial setup and installation of solar panels are expensive, starting from USD 5000.[71] If Chris could to produce any surplus energy as a consumer, he would be able to distribute the energy to a decentralised grid for someone else in a different part of the world to use that energy. By distributing the excess energy, he is not only reducing wastage but also opening a source of additional revenue from the solar panels installed on the roof of a house, thus getting his money back. The entire system sounds like an exquisite fairy-tale, although, it's as simple as using an app. This type of decentralised energy market enables expansion of a mutually beneficial community. It will have enormous influence and socio-economic benefits. As the cost of solar panels and lithium-ion batteries are expected to go down over the next few years, it will be easier for low-income citizens to afford electricity. In fact, a federal centralised national grid may never be needed in some cities and countries. Just like the internet, energy may not ever be free, however, billions of people would be able to afford electricity and live a better life. The process of decentralising energy would also mean more people would be able to afford electric vehicles.

In the long term, electric cars are bound to replace most of the petrol and diesel vehicles. Deploying fully electric self-driving cars isn't impending chaos, it's a necessity for us. It will happen eventually – whether it's the next decade or the decade after.

How two words transformed businesses – .com & AI.

Search to AI

From a free search engine, Google has now entered a chapter when it's not only building an AI, but also competing in a race to showcase their computational monstrosity. When Google built its search engine; the company had the intention to become one of the largest technology companies in the world. After the millennium, as Google's search engine grew, the company was receiving petabytes of data. Therefore, Google needed to create an algorithm that would allow them to process, organise and store everything. As the amount of data was growing exponentially, they turned to machine learning. Google decided to build an algorithm which would directly learn from its users. As billions of users were searching thousands of information every day, the company knew it needed to create much more powerful AI that would learn from billions simultaneously.

First, let's look into the bare fundamentals of machine learning. Using machine learning, a computer learns and adapts according to past experiences. Instead of relying on *hard codes*, the system can learn from its mistakes and can adapt according to its needs. Because of the machine learning algorithm, simulations are run in the system several times, and the system adapts and learns to perform. The algorithm can correct itself if it faces errors and does not rely on human commands to correct it. Machine learning is "software-based learning". Thus, all the algorithms are written using programming languages.[1] Developers can use simulations to perform trial and error to make them perfect.

Machine learning can be compared with actual learning process. Human beings perform their day to day tasks based on individual experiences and knowledge. This knowledge or experience can come from their school or workplace, or a suggestion received from a teacher or parents. Google used the same principle for its machine learning algorithm, where the search engine learned from the behaviour of its users. Now, how do you develop a technology that allows the company to learn from billions of users without incurring any costs or in other words, pay its users?

Progress of Narrow AI

It is a reality collectively approved, that an innovator, who devised an exclusive idea around a deep neural network, or a machine learning algorithm is in demand around the blocks of Silicon Valley and Wall Street. Back in the 60s, artificial intelligence had only a single layer of neural network and was limited in terms of the performance. Hence it wasn't an attractive idea. In the late 60s, a book was written on the first artificial intelligence computer. Due to its limitation, only a few scientists were in a quest to harness the power of this technology. At a certain point in the 80s, almost every AI researcher had hit the ceiling. All other areas of research in IT were primarily focused on developing what we now know as *the internet*. Silicon Valley was on the verge of explosion, as billions of dollars were poured into companies, being able to comprehend the power of the internet and started moving digital. The dot com boom in the late 90s wasn't only limited to private funders and investors from around the US – it was a global phenomenon. Even hedge funds and private equity companies in the Asia and EU were also pouring a significant amount of money into developing the internet. In a bid to win the race against each other, almost every company which successfully raised a large amount of investment got enlisted in the stock market.

While artificial intelligence research slowed down, hundreds of dotcom companies went public to raise funds. There were overnight billionaires in almost every corner of the valley. Google was one of the by-products of the dot com revolution. Soon enough, the bubble had burst, which ended up becoming a recession of the US. The dot com bubble had its domino effect on other markets too, wiping off billions of dollars. Almost 80% of the internet companies went bankrupt – only a handful of financial experts, investors and venture capitalists gained more than anyone could ever imagine. Google went public in 2004, intending to raise USD 2.7 billion.[2] Back then, no one had any idea of how large the company could become in a matter of a decade.

In the meantime, Microsoft, Yahoo! and other technology companies were in pursuit of creating a better user experience on the internet. During the last decade, spams were one of the biggest threats to the website owners. Thousands of bots were popping up like mushrooms every day. Internet users hated pop-ups, and spam comments, and there was no means to control its growth. At that point, cybersecurity experts came up with the concept of captcha to control spam. A captcha would allow better security by allowing artificial intelligence to differentiate a human from a bot.[3]

Remember the first version of captcha? Back then, the users were required to recognise text to prove that they are humans. With the aim of extensive deployment worldwide, Google bought ReCaptcha, a captcha-like system, in 2009.[4] The ideology of captcha was not only to help digitise older versions of books and magazines but also prevent malicious bots from taking over the internet.[5] Nevertheless, the underlying scope of Google's acquisition was much more comprehensive.

following   finding

The company tied its machine learning algorithm with ReCaptcha forms. Captcha project eventually became incredibly beneficial for digitising materials on paper. At that time, the system was receiving billions of data points from users that helped them to digitise books.[6] Since the process was tied to the machine learning algorithm, every time a user filled up a captcha, it learned to differentiate "fife" from "file".

Google machine learning project eventually turned into a critical technological milestone, when they launched its deep learning artificial intelligence team, commonly known as Google Brain.[7] It was formed in partnership with professor Andrew Ng and other researchers from Stanford University. A project that assisted them in efficiently processing data from its search engine later became the core aspect of the entire business. According to the company, Google now focuses on fundamentals and applications using narrow AI, efficient optimisation of its cloud services offered to startups and enterprises, assist in Google translate, developing secure network infrastructure, and last but not the least, security and cyber defence.

Google AI team now consists of the most sophisticated artificial intelligence engineers across the world. The company has already established bases in countries like Canada to create AI-focused research hubs.[8]

In 2012, Google integrated its image data from Google Street View to help its machine-learning algorithm to understand the differences among various house numbers.[9] When Google introduced captcha 2.0, it replaced text digitisation with the image recognition algorithm. Therefore, the users on the internet would be required to select individual images similar to the ones displayed on the screen. From text, machine learning then moved onto learning about images. In 2012, Google was also in the headlines as their deep neural network had learned to recognise and differentiate a cat from other species. It was a big deal back then. The network was provided with 10 million unlabelled images of cats. However, the developers did not provide any clue to the net that it was a "cat".[10] During a machine learning conference in Edinburgh, Scotland, Google scientists published a paper named "Building High-level Features Using Large Scale Unsupervised Learning". In that paper, they described how the network, having over 16,000 processing cores, were fed unlabelled images. Their study concluded that the controlled experiment did not only learn to differentiate species but also became sensitive to information such as human bodies or cat faces.[11] Before this research, a typical machine learning algorithm would have required human input for labelling specific data before feeding it into the neural cluster. However, the algorithm was able to differentiate without human input. For the first time, the AI taught itself how to recognise an object. At that moment, the researchers comprehended that their artificial intelligence technology was simulating a human brain – different parts of the neural network were dedicated to analysing and interpret different types of material.

Within a matter of a few years since its inception, Google used billions of users across the internet to feed its deep learning machine to transcribe billions of pages of books, magazines, journal articles, research papers, label image data, and also understand the difference between two different species of dog. In short, it found a way to train its AI for free. Later, Google had progressed onto NoCaptcha in 2014, followed by the new background information processing *captcha 3.0*, that can automatically understand the difference between a bot and human by analysing its behaviour pattern on the webpage.[12][13] Therefore, many website forms do not require users to fill up the captcha anymore.

Back in 2013, Google came under the limelight of AI experts when they acquired Boston Dynamics, a US-based technology company which was developing robots for the military.[14] After five years, the company was acquired by Softbank.[15] To expand its "Vision Fund", Softbank has been acquiring many startups across multiple verticals.[16] However, why is this evidence relevant in this story?

Computers were built to collect and display data and replace papers. This was the initial concept that can be seen from the computers in the 80s.[17] All they could do is store millions of pages of data and display it on the screen. Scientists and researchers proceeded towards developing complex processors that could not only display but also make decisions on behalf of humans.

Let's say Emma has an excel sheet with hundreds of data points from different interviews she conducted for a research project at her college. She has also collected hundreds of photos that would benefit the research project. If she needs to complete writing the paper, she must classify all the data and images, which alone would take hundreds of hours. What if Emma could feed the data to a machine and complete that task in minutes?

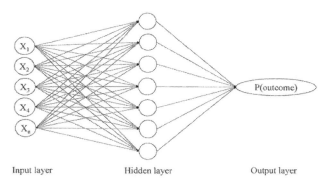

Input layer   Hidden layer   Output layer

The three-layer perception model showing a feed-forward pattern, with an input, hidden and output layer. P is the probability of the result.

Image 4.1 © Chan et al. (2019).

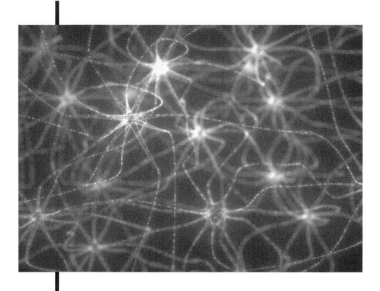

Neural networks are experiencing a revival that not only transforms AI but also provides new insights about neural computation in biological systems.[18]

Machine learning is a process by which a computer is taught to carry out functions based on past capabilities and knowledge.[19] Traditional computers are like calculators. It functions in an environment where labelled or unlabelled data are fed into the system, and it shows the calculated result.[20] Its capabilities are limited to those specific data and its processing instructions; therefore, it cannot fix the mistakes made. However, it can recalculate and learn from the mistakes. The system trains itself and learns the answers itself, and therefore establishes its own rules. Next time when any data is fed, the system follows what it learned before, and processes the data according to its rules.[21]

Unlike a conventional algorithm, neural networks use a machine-learning algorithm to mimic the design of human neural network, and process information using *artificial neurons.*[22] These neurons can learn and adapt from the input provided. Therefore, on top of displaying the calculations, these networks can conduct complex calculations and make decisions that would typically require a lot of human labour. A neural network gradually learns from its interactions and compute probabilities and can be hundreds of layers deep.

MLAs can not only classify but also learn and adapt from the inputs that they receive. By using "Features", machine learning algorithms can display "Labelled Data" to fasten up calculations.[23] To classify data, computers use various decision boundaries to classify and analyse data correctly. Using supervised and unsupervised learning methods, machine learning algorithms can be trained to find patterns in a data cluster, and even detect diseases by providing the appropriate labelled data as an input.

Machine Learning Algorithm (MLA) has been a part of our life for quite a while. MLA is the reason why Facebook can identify a person from a tagged photo.[24] Netflix and Amazon Prime can suggest movies and shows based on what the users have watched before.[25] The same goes for YouTube suggestions and all other user applications that continuously monitor user behaviour. Because of MLA, the apps are capable enough to learn from user inputs and put forward suggestions according to the need of the user. It is feasible because of the increased data processing power of the systems. The more computational power, the better its accuracy.

Neural networks can be powered by computers' CPUs and graphics processing units (GPUs). GPUs are incredibly beneficial for a deep neural network in speeding up the computational capacity. Thanks to the avid gaming community, tech giants such as AMD and NVIDIA have been able to provide us with incredibly powerful GPUs. Gamers and their requirements are the reason why we are living in an era where the neural networks are self-taught machines without inputs. Although a GPU at this time of writing in 2020 is not able to provide enough power to a blockchain network, it can be very helpful in training a deep neural network.[26] GPUs are imperative to increase processing speed; one GPU is on an average approximately 30 times faster in comparison to a CPU. That's why high-performance analysis and high-FPS gaming is impossible without GPUs. The speed of development in the field of GPU is opening barriers to solving problems surrounding AI training. Needless to say, deep neural networks are much faster than it was even five years ago.

There are various types of neural networks. A *Convolutional Neural Network* (CNN) is used in the classification of images, capable of assigning importance and differentiate among various types. These networks are used for facial recognition, medical image analysis, classification by hierarchies and language processing (NLP).[27][28] These types of neural networks can classify data and object, not only in 2D but also in 3D fields. Therefore, CNNs can capacitate more computational power than most other types of narrow AI.

The rapid growth of CNNs was encouraged by ImageNet, an organisation that hosts one of the biggest AI competitions in the world. Created by Stanford Vision Lab, ImageNet is a library of approximately 20 million images that are helpful for researchers working with VORS – Visual Object Recognition Software. The machine learning algorithm is essential in VORS research. ImageNet has been running a global contest, that allows software companies to compete with each other, incorrectly identifying objects in the correct classification using machine learning algorithm. In 2012, AlexNet achieved a record of training ImageNet to classify the visual objects in 5 to 6 days.[29] However, later in the decade, Facebook achieved the same feat using 200 GPUs, in under an hour.[30] A Japanese team later broke the company's record. They were able to train ImageNet in under 15 minutes, cataloguing over 20 million images in just under 15 minutes, which is something to think about.[31] It is undeniably a mind-boggling accomplishment.

While Convolutional Neural Network has led to many breakthroughs, scientists have been occupied in understanding how human brains learn from their surroundings. Neural networks may result in degrading accuracy when one network is used to make hundreds of predictive decisions at the same time. Researchers have recently enabled, what is being termed as *Residual Learning*, which helps the neural network to learn from the scope of the input provided to the network and carried out experiments, which results in increased accuracy.[32] ResNet can have a depth of 152 layers – a deep neural network that is capable of solving much more complex calculations.

Scientists believe that a Recurrent Neural Network is ultra-deep and represents an improved model from that of the ResNet.[33] It is another type of neural net where the output is automatically fed as the input for the next state; therefore, it can form short term memory.[34] RNNs are used for text to speech (TTS), voice command recognition and language modelling.[35][36] Development of RNN is the reason why Alexa can understand what we say, and why we can speak to a chatbot on a website. Both convolutional and recurrent neural networks are encouraged by biological progression, i.e. inspired by how neurons in our brains work and translate information.[37] Scientists are now recommending various frameworks for the use of RNN in conversational speech recognition and development of independent RNN.[38][39] A recently published patent shows that RNN was used in a neural decoder of an "Intracortical Brain-Machine Interface" to control a device.[40]

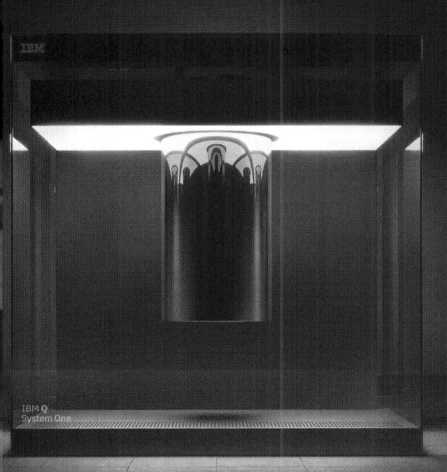

IBM Q System One, a quantum computing system, the next step of computing evolution.

Image 4.4 © IBM Research.

I wanted to quote Star Wars, but I would rather avoid legal consequences. Instead, this is how it can be explained – many Hollywood sci-fi films have used this line in their script – "*the probabilities of performing a job successfully is 1000 to 1*". It is a result of the robot being connected to an artificial neural network. Neural networks are the reason why Facebook can detect faces among billions of photos stored in their servers.[41] The neural network that can complete a particular task is known as *Narrow AI*. A narrow AI has limited features, but it can gain its competence in accomplishing that one or two tasks. For instance, a narrow AI can lose a game in chess, learn from its mistakes, and crash its competitor in a later round.

Another highlighted term in the world of AI is *Reinforcement Learning*, the process used in which the AIs are provided rewards for achieving targets and completing tasks.[42] It allows developers to create a loop in which the algorithm would continually learn until it is fully capable of performing the task seamlessly. Alexa, Amazon's voice-assisted hardware is the best example of reinforcement learning.[43] That's how toddlers learn to walk, eat and capacitate to undertake much more complex jobs. It requires neural networks' trial and error to be able to become incredibly skilled, and it happens gradually over time. However, once achieved, the AI is capable of performing the job at higher accuracy in comparison to humans. Take AlphaGo, as an example. AlphaGo beat humans at Go, a strategy game. AlphaGo, the AI was eventually able to beat the world champion. A few years down the road, its successor AlphaGo Zero successfully beat AlphaGo at 100-0.[44] The neural networks were trained to learn by itself and improve strength gradually over time. It is most definitely an essential achievement in the field of artificial intelligence – a computer that has learned over a thousand years' worth of knowledge in just under 2 months.[45] The company behind this revolutionary AI, DeepMind, was acquired by Google in 2014 to expand their program. What would make Google spend GBP 400 million (USD 486 million) for a startup, which has over 400 post-doctoral researchers in their team?[46]

Google recently published on its blog how their deep neural network can understand the difference between user subsets by analysing *Tappability*. Therefore, Google can not only recognise its users, but also have comprehensive knowledge of what book they might like, where they have been in the past few years, what their behaviour purchases are, what they like, don't like and know exactly how they use their mobile phone.[47] The network can forecast behaviour patterns of its users tapping on a particular part of the phone's display, regardless of the operating system. By analysing behaviour patterns for a subset of people, it would be able to understand patterns of an entire group, or population.

You may be wondering why there is a random collage of people in the middle of nowhere.

Well, <u>these people aren't real</u>. It's a part of 100,000 Faces Project. All these faces were generated by an AI.

Generated.photos has created a library of these photos for public use.[48][49]

Image 4.2 © Generated.photos.

Google has lately published their 'code of conduct' for AI-based research, which focuses on Ethical principles, AI for social good and their open-sourced end-to-end machine learning platform known as *TensorFlow*.[50][51] Thousands of developers around the world are using Google's Tensor Processing Units (TPUs) for generating machine learning algorithms. Each 2nd generation TPU can process 180 teraflops, which theoretically suggests these monstrous chips are 40 times more powerful than a PlayStation 4 console.[52] Remember, a PS4 Pro is sufficient to play a 4K game at ease.

The latest version, TPU 3 is twice as fast.[53] Their 3rd generation "TPU Pod", on the contrary, is a colossal data crunching machine, and 500 times more powerful than a single core TPU. Google is now offering scientists and researchers to those who are willing to share their research work. Google's competitors, IBM Watson and Microsoft Azure are also providing packages to app developers for accessing their AI for a competitive price, alongside its cloud platforms.[54] After hundreds of failed projects such as Google glass, and tens of billions spent on developing their AI, needless to say, Google is here to thrive as one of the top ten companies in the world.[55]

So, let's ask ourselves the inevitable, how much has AI achieved until now? The answer would be a lot, even though it's still at a fraction of its potential performance level. We are still within the scope of narrow AI, which has come a long way since 2006. Using AI, artists have now created and composed music.[56] Amazon earns over 13% of its revenue from cloud computing service AWS, thanks to artificial intelligence.[57] Amazon also has the largest share of the cloud services in the market. The company incorporated VR/AR and blockchain to expand their region of domination.[58]

On an application-level, AI is being utilised for various purposes. Heathrow airport is aiming to reduce landing congestion by feeding camera data into a deep neural network currently being developed by SeaRidge technologies from Canada. The system would allow ATCs to determine the positions of the flights, without the need of radar data from an ATC tower. Therefore, the third runway could be operated without an additional tower.[59] Tesla is the most valuable car company in the world because of its ground-breaking electric vehicles that run on the machine learning algorithm, which can now drive itself from a car park to its destination – thanks to AI. Researchers now claim that 16% of all vehicles would be autonomous by 2040.[60]

When you build an AI, make it think that it would receive some reward. It's like how we treat children.

Food for thought: If an experimental AI can learn to tell the truth, could it also lie at the same time?

Image 4.3 © Andreas Urena.

Automated Model Generation –
Personifying AI

With all the signs of progress, comes the technological marvels, which are borderline dangerous and a concourse for moral gymnastics. Every other technology comes with its potential to be misused. The problem isn't the morality of artificially intelligent networks that can think like humans, but with human ethics. The problem lies with people, who might potentially misuse the technology. Therefore, having this technology in the hands of the wrong users would be dangerous.

Although politicians aren't worried about the adverse effects of an AI-uprising, they are currently worried about one technology that has changed the game of fake news. Deepfake films, also known as *deepfakes*, are artificially generated fake videos using a machine learning algorithm.[61] The neural network is trained with various types of facial expressions, which, as output, would provide fake expressions that mimic the face of an actual person. Using deep neural networks, criminals were able to create fake videos of politicians and celebrities that went viral. The system uses a source sequence, which only requires the algorithm to receive motion sequence as input data. This data is then combined with the unmodified target sequence, from which various facial expressions are extracted. The network does not even require receiving any expressions of the source.

Deepfakes have wide-ranging use cases. Take the use case developed by *Lyrebird* – an AI-based voice producing startup. Their technology is fascinating – using narrow AI, the company has developed an algorithm that can instantly digitalise a person's voice.[62] Using Lyrebird's technology, a user needs to record approximately 18 random words. The speech recognition system is currently able to create a digital copy of the audio in just under a minute. If you were to use this technology and play a prank on my friends, it would be hard for them to understand whether they are interacting with a real person or an AI. It's so easy to take advantage of this technology and misuse it. Unless consent is received from the user with regards to using his or her voice or facial expression, this tech is harmful that could be manipulated in many ways. However, investors are keen to capitalise this technology and develop it for better outcomes. Companies such as *This Person Does Not Exist* are using simple General Adversarial Network (GAN) to combine a real photo with its algorithm.[63] Therefore, every time internet users hit refresh, it would provide them with photos of people who do not exist.[64]

Synthesia, a startup reportedly backed by Mark Cuban, has been able to exhibit shockingly real AI-generated video. Even David Beckham got himself involved, as he presented himself speaking nine languages in a video posted by "Malaria Must Die".[65] The video is very realistic, provided that it was generated using a deep neural network. If users are aware of how the video was created in the first place, then they might be able to differentiate. However, if someone is not aware of the technology, it would be nearly impossible for that person to understand.

Researchers have predicted AI would be able to write a **bestselling book** by 2049 and become a **certified surgeon** by 2053. The experts also believe that in a matter of **45 years**, there is a **50 per cent chance** that AI would be **better than humans** at 'everything'.[66]

US congress has recently been in a fight with Facebook to compel the social network to flag and take down deepfakes.[67] In 2017, a video posted by BuzzFeed was used for the awareness of deepfakes and its dangerous effects – in hindsight, the technology has improved significantly since then. As of April 2020, analysts indicate that Facebook might ban deepfakes until a reasonable law has been established to tackle this issue.[68]

In hindsight, AI is capable of much more. This type of narrow AI is beneficial for a particular task, such as classifying images and objects, beating a competitor in a strategy game like DOTA or Sudoku, or be able to reply to us in response to specific commands. A self-driving vehicle runs on narrow AI; therefore, they are only allowed to be experts on a limited number of skills, for instance, recognising the difference between a person, a cat and a streetlight. A car wouldn't learn itself to make a decision emotionally when it comes to an accident. Can it analyse and avoid hitting the human? AI may be able to detect human emotions, potentially better than humans do, however, cannot simulate human intuition it at this point.[69] Asking Alexa about the weather is a popular feature that voice-assistant owners use, but it's capabilities are limited to specific tasks and cannot replicate emotions. Besides, one of the limitations of the current state of AI is its limitation to learn progressively. As new tasks and commands are introduced, the neural network overwrites previous learning capabilities with the new one. Researchers at Google's Deep Mind conclude that unlike human brains, AI isn't capable of applying previously learned techniques to new ones, which is being termed as "catastrophic forgetting".[70] However, the team trained its neural network to learn progressively. Other researchers also believe that AI would soon be able to connect with customers at a deeper level. It is yet another step towards the achievement of AGI.

> ***Teaching a moral code to artificial intelligence is one of the most controversial topics.*** [71]

Window of Opportunity

AI has made several breakthroughs in the field of medicine. AI can now be used to predict Alzheimer's, Parkinson's, Cancer, as well as developing state-of-the-art vaccines and medicines for patients. [72] Genome editing is a field where narrow AI could be incredibly beneficial. Until now, it was impossible to predict protein fold based on the data of a user's genetic sequence. A genetic sequence is generated from the DNA, a molecule that is a "unique identifier" for humans and living objects. These molecules are ultramicroscopic in structure; and contains the foundations of a protein in the shape of long chains. The larger the size of protein, the more complicated its structure due to the amount of information stored. In a thought experiment, scientists explained that it would take a lifetime of an entire universe to correctly design the structure of a protein – commonly known as the *Leventhal's paradox*. [73] Developing 3D models of protein folds from such amino acid residues are incredibly tricky. However, in a recent blog post by

DeepMind, the researchers working in this field described that using their neural network, the team has been able to create spectacularly accurate 3D models that would have been nearly impossible, until now.[74] The same neural network has been used to undertake research projects on eye treatments. Using the AI, researchers from University College London conducted a study on over 14000 participants' retinal scan and concluded that diagnosis of eye-treatment could be detected in under 30 seconds.[75] That's a jaw-dropping milestone, considering that it typically takes an hour for a doctor to advise the right treatment. Google needs to continue doing research in this sector.

Google and Facebook are utilising their machine learning algorithms at a larger capacity to identify consumer behaviour patterns. These research advances usability, therefore providing us with a better experience for browsing the internet. Netflix uses machine learning to provide its users with a suggestion for the next movie to watch.[76] Spotify uses a similar algorithm to create personalised playlists such as the "Daily Mix". These mixes are based on a user's favourite genres; therefore, its neural network can categorise and organise the right artists for the right users. When the users tap on the screen, the system learns about user preference, therefore improving the suggestions in the future. This algorithm also allows them to continue playing after a playlist runs out of songs to play. The code analyses their listening patterns and suggests the next best song. Spotify has also developed a way of personalising playlists, tailored to individual user preferences, such as *Release Radar*, which suggest the new songs released by artists, a user is typically interested in.[77] The playlist would also suggest users the recent titles released by similar artists that they are "most likely" to listen to – all thanks to Spotify's machine learning algorithm.

Manufacturers are actively using AI to optimise their supply-chain. Fashion retailer GAP, for instance, is using the technology from *Kindred AI* to train its robotic arms to sort items efficiently on a conveyor belt. The company is using deep learning methods to train the AI to understand how to grab items and learn from its own mistakes.[78] Tesla is also employing AI robots to speed up their car manufacturing process. The story of AI and its capabilities doesn't end here.

Scientists are now working on developing architecture for engineering consciousness into AI.[79][80][81][82] A team of Japanese scientist have proposed a framework for an autonomous adaptive system for "conscious-like" social robot.[83] These studies will eventually lead to transforming the definition of consciousness in human and provide better understanding of Artificial General Intelligence (AGI), which has been discussed in the next few chapters.

*Food for thought: What if the AI learns to create a **child AI**, which eventually learns to how to **train itself** and **lie** about its existence? The US Patent Office (USPTO) recently announced that an **AI cannot legally** be an "inventor" and claim rights for designs of object.[84] Should we allow **AIs** to legally create and claim **ownership** of patents and designs?*

Exascale.

IBM SUMMIT SUPERCOMPUTER.

Image 5.1. © IBM Research.

Tesla has been a pioneer of self-driving cars. The company was the first to design a seamless system to feed its machine learning algorithm. It's competitors *Waymo*, and *Uber* have created autonomous vehicles that use a combination of LIDAR, but in comparison to Tesla, their cars haven't been driven a lot on actual roads.[1] Tesla is using millions of cars to train its AI and learn from experience. Tesla's neural network learns from every car's moves, therefore can share its ability to guide itself from other cars on the road.[2] In just a few years, this narrow AI could train itself to drive anywhere in the world; however, this computing power is nowhere near the capacity of human-scale performance.

Tesla factories are powered by AI robots that have replaced factory workers to make the process of the efficient supply chain. Despite wide-ranging use, Tesla's founder Elon Musk has been steadily against the development of supercomputers with Artificial General Intelligence – the AI that's smarter than humans. Unlike Narrow AI, *Artificial General Intelligence* or AGI would be capable of having a lot more power than its meant possess in the very first place. In a recent interview, Musk has slammed the founder of Facebook with regards to the dangers of AI and has hinted that Zuckerberg does not understand the adverse effects of how it can be incredibly disastrous to continue funding this sector. He suggested it would be outside human control and the dangers are most related to the aspect of people using it against each other.[3]

In principle, supercomputers were designed for enterprises that require enormous computing power. Now, it's a race to develop human-scale performance. These supercomputers are built with existing computing architecture and has thousands of processors capable of working collectively. These computers are used all over the world to perform extremely complex calculations, such as, measuring the distance of a planet from the earth which is not in our solar system or performing calculations with regards to climate research, and make weather predictions. These deep neural networks are millions of lines of codes that are dependent on traditional hardware. Tech companies around the world are now in a race to build the largest and the most powerful machine – exascale, i.e. the computational capacity of a human brain. To build a supercomputer with typical ARM processors that can compete with the brain, researchers would need a humongous amount of physical space, expensive maintenance process and lots of electricity. The explanation of how powerful these supercomputers are, boils down to the discussion of "FLOPS".

The processing power of a computer is determined by how fast it can perform a calculation. Hertz (Hz) is used as a unit for such measurement. FLOPS, on the contrary, are used as a computational unit for faster devices such as GPU, and supercomputers.[4] "Floating Point Operations per Second" or FLOPS is the measurement unit for the calculation of numbers involving a "floating" or decimal point.[5] For example, 3.0 is a floating-point number, but 3 is an integer. Calculations relating to floating-points are more complicated in comparison to integers.[6] It's pretty simple to explain – 2 multiplied by 2 equals 4, but, if you multiply 2.432 by 2.754, how easy is it to calculate the answer?

Let's compare this to an active product. A mid-range graphics card in 2020 boasts a capacity of 6.5 teraflops.[7] That means that it's capable of performing 6.5 trillion floating-point operations per second. In contrast, our brain is much more complex and powerful. We may not be able to calculate floating-points very quickly, but our brain is competent in experiencing long-term memory retrieval, emotions, intuitions, logic, and consciousness. Scientists believe that in order for an AI supercomputer to think like humans, it will need to attain 1 exaFLOPS performance - that's 166,000 times more powerful than the average graphics card.[8]

5.2 – IBM Summit at ORNL, California, United States. Consisting of 2.3 million processing cores, summit requires approximately 7 megawatts capacity. That's a lot of silicon chips in one computer.

Traditional computers are reaching the ceiling for its lifecycle. Transistors, the tiny circuits which control the flow of electricity inside the chips are getting smaller; therefore, processors are becoming faster. Until now, silicon transistors have been powering all the computers, smartphones and other equipment that we use on a daily basis. Silicon-based chips can run hundred-layer deep neural network using machine learning algorithm; although, in comparison to human brains, they are still limited. If you want to construct an AI supercomputer that can capacitate the operational ability of our brain, then you need to rent an all-inclusive warehouse, and potentially spend billions to build that type of computer with traditional computer chips.

IBM has been a prominent contender in building supercomputers for decades. In 2007, IBM Blue Gene showcased its sheer capacity to achieve over 500 teraflops. In 2011, IBM Mira achieved 16 times more power compared to its predecessor. The latest monster from IBM, the Summit, officially listed as the most powerful supercomputer in the world, can process an astounding 143,000 teraflops. The Chinese researchers are not remaining behind. Sunway Taihulight, developed by Chinese scientists, the second most powerful behind Summit, requires 20 megawatts of electricity.[9] That's the equivalent to powering an entire village in the UK.

Fujitsu, the Japanese computer manufacturer has developed a commercial version of their USD 1 billion "Post-K" supercomputer, that can attain human-level performance.[10] This system would require approximately 40MW of electricity. It purportedly takes up a lot of space and aims to start operations by 2021.[11] Considering the performance, undoubtedly, it's as a significant advancement.

5.3 – Fujitsu's Post K Supercomputer. Tsukuba-jin.

Researchers at IBM and HP haven't stopped their focus here. They are currently developing a new hardware that would make these supercomputers look like a "thing in the past". From supercomputers that were using traditional processors, scientists are developing AI hardware as small as a regular PC that can mimic the performance of a 500,000-core supercomputer.[12] To build a neural network thousands of layers deep, capable of achieving exascale that also fits into a shoebox, researchers have started to integrate artificial intelligence directly into the hardware chips. Instead of developing a hard-coded neural network, this smart hardware can act as a neural net and mimic the design of the human brain. From use cases, let's move into experimental technology that could transform everything we learned about computers.

Neuromorphic Computing.

A 4 BY 4 ARRAY OF IBM TRUENORTH CHIPS IN AN INDUSTRIAL-GRADE ENCLOSURE.

Image 6.1. © IBM Research.

Brain in a Chip

Neuromorphic computing is the first step towards dispatching intelligent satellites and powerful probes to distant planets. This is the beginning of the search for extra-terrestrial beings and hunting down our galactic neighbours. With existing use cases for analysing photos of distant supernovas, this new computing phenomena retains the competency to transform into an intergalactic data transmitting module. This new architecture isn't the same as the computer you are using right now.

The structure of a traditional computer is based on an architecture developed by physicist John Von Neumann.[1] According to Von Neumann architecture, the basic structure consists of the following components:

1. Memory Unit
2. Arithmetic Logic Unit (ALU)
3. Interconnecting Bus [2]

The memory unit of a computer is known as the Random Access Memory (RAM). The RAM is used to store necessary data for the processor. Although hard drives are the primary storage devices for computers, RAM is used to temporarily store complex calculations for processing logical operations. The RAM can store the data for a short term until the calculations are performed by the Central Processing Unit (CPU).[3] Traditional computing architecture is designed in a way so that it can transfer data from the CPU to the RAM, back and forth, in a linear fashion.[4]

Central Processing Unit (CPU) is a silicon-based microprocessor mounted on a circuit board. The CPU of a computer can be compared to the brain and the cell body of a neuron. Every *logical operation* of the computer is performed inside this CPU.[5] From the calculation of a simple math problem to creating spreadsheets, and browsing on the web – all of the functions are processed using this central unit. CPU and RAM are interconnected using *bus connections* inside the motherboard. Hence, whenever we perform complicated artwork in Adobe Photoshop, the RAM stores some temporary information so that similar calculations can be completed faster in the future.[6]

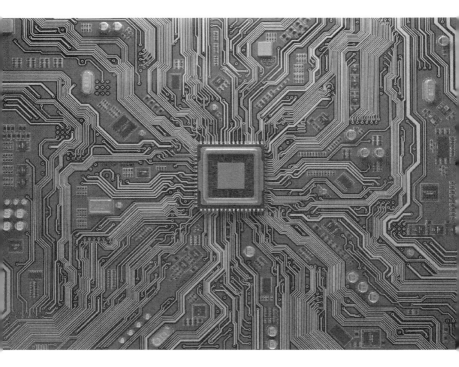

Von Neumann architecture, which was the roadmap for traditional computing milestones, relied on the binary calculation of the system.[7] The chips were designed to execute *binary calculations*; a language made up of 0 and 1. They are dependent on the *digital signal*, which has two states – on and off. When current flows through the circuit, a transistor's "on and off" state decides to encode or decode binary data in 0s and 1s. The chips on a motherboard have their function and set of instructions. However,

1. The chips aren't smart. That is, the chips aren't intelligent enough to learn from the commands. To build an AI, the traditional processors depend on "hard codes" to be able to create an artificial neural network.

2. Traditional chips do not work in synchronisation. These processing chips are not capable of learning from the experience.

3. Although the CPU and RAM are separate in structures, and the computations are performed through continuous data exchange between them, the brain has the memory and processing units coupled together. The Von Neumann bottleneck ideates that CPU remains idle during the data transfer from the memory. The brain, in contrast, is a heterogeneous system where all the interconnected neurons work in unity to process, store and relay information continuously.[8] It is where the design of the Von Neumann varies from that of the brain.

4. For the AI to be able to listen, talk and process information at the same time, the chips are required to be able to receive analogue and digital signals from its

surrounding environment. Traditional processors rely on external hardware, such as "sound card" to process such function.

Designing Hardware Brains

Transistors are becoming increasingly smaller, resulting in our phones becoming faster and smarter. However, these rely on AI software to be "intelligent". As faster transistors and memory chips are installed in an incredibly tiny space, it is always susceptible to heat. That is why supercomputers and datacentres need cold storages. Another limitation is the bottleneck of Von Neumann, the *linear design* factor – deeper neural networks and faster computers would require more servers, more processors, memory chips, and therefore consuming more energy.

In order for us to build something remotely comparable to Lieutenant Commander Data, a synthetic AI lifeform from Star Trek, we must shrink the size of these overwhelmingly large supercomputers that consume less energy. What if we could build a computer that is the size of a bag, yet able to overcome the bottleneck? One of the best ways of achieving that milestone would be developing artificially intelligent hardware chips which can learn and adapt itself without the need for hard codes. To achieve human-scale performance, experts from computer chip manufacturer Qualcomm believe that enhanced AI would require integration of machine learning performance into silicon.[9]

Enter Neuromorphic System — It's an advanced architecture that process data in an *event-driven fashion*, similar to how neurons in our brain work.[10] These chips are built using *single-crystalline silicon* that is more energy-efficient and able to learn from its input. Artificial neural networks, until now, relied on codes to think like human beings. The AI software is powered by a gigantic server, which requires a computer or a mobile to be connected to the internet. However, a neuromorphic system is hardware that's specifically designed to mimic the activity of the brain.[11][12] This term dates back to the 80s.[13] To accurately understand the functionality behind neuromorphic computing, we must revisit the essential functions that operate the human brain. The brain, although a small lump of tissues and cells inside the skull, is not only fast in performing calculations but also uses a fraction of the power consumed by a computer. This sophisticated piece of architecture is the primary motivation behind this new technology. Why?

Firstly, the design. Our brain is the command centre for our central nervous system. This complex piece of biological architecture controls every pain, sorrow, happiness and functions of the body. Typically, a brain consists of 86 billion neurons using which data is transmitted.[14] These neurons are intertwined with each other using 256 billion *synapses*.

> *"At the cellular level, the average human brain is estimated to contain (86.06 ± 8.2) × 109 neurons,*

with ~ 80.2% (69.03 ± 6.65 × 109 neurons) located
in the cerebellum, ~19% (16.34 ± 2.17 × 109
neurons) located in the cerebral cortex..."
– Martins et al. (2019)

At the cellular level, there are approximately 125 trillion neurosynaptic connections alone in the *cerebral cortex* region.[15] *The cerebral cortex* is the outermost layer of the brain, consisting of over 20 billion neurons, and associated with functions such as memory, learning, creativity, and so on.[16] The *synapse* is a junction which transmits signals among the cells within the brain. The information inside our brain is processed and transferred using *electrochemical signals*. When electric pulses are triggered inside the brain, it stimulates *neurotransmitter molecules* responsible for the data transfer. They act as messengers which relay, amplify and modify signals between the neurons and other cells within the brain. [17]

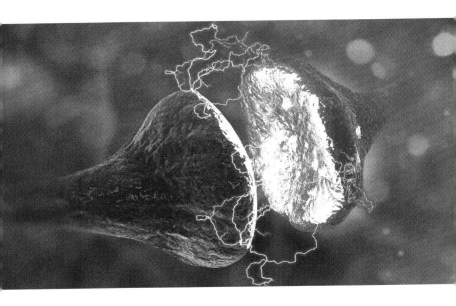

The electric pulses inside the brain can be monitored using electroencephalography (EEG) cap. The brain triggers electric pulses when we walk, talk, think, move, or even wink. These pulses are called *Action Potential Energy*. EEG systems are commonly used to monitor brain activity for treatment and research. For instance, researchers at John Hopkins University are using EEG systems to measure and reduce distraction at work.[18]

Secondly, the architecture. The brain is primarily split into left and right hemispheres, each responsible for different types of functions.[19] The left hemisphere is responsible for logic, analytical thinking, language, calculations, reasoning, and doing the math. The right hemisphere, on the other hand, has the ability of pattern recognition, art, creativity, imagination and intuition.[20] Our brain is incredibly adaptive and goes through multiple stages of regeneration and growth. As different areas of the brain are responsible for different functions, if one-half of a hemisphere become inactive, we could potentially lose control of half of our body.

Thirdly, the capacity. This small lump of tissue is also capable of storing and processing vast amounts of data. A typical hard drive of a PC has a capacity of 1 TB, whereas smartphones have an average of 256GB, which is ¼ the size of a regular PC. The brain, on the other hand, can hold about 2.5 *petabytes* (PB) of data – 1 PB being equal to 1000 TB.[21] In contrast, a human brain can capacitate 2,500 times more than a regular PC.

Please note that "2500 times" is an approximate value, as the exact capacity of the brain is not that easy to measure with a comparison scale. All that data in our brain is processed using only 20 watts – the equivalent power of an LED bulb.[22]

Fourthly, efficiency. As the brain is a distributed system of 100 billion neurons that are capable of parallel information processing, it enables us to multitask – for example, drive and talk to a fellow passenger at the same time.[23] Have you ever been to a supermarket, picked up the exact groceries you needed without a list, whilst speaking to a friend on the phone? If you have, then well done. This architecture is known as *an event-driven* model. It means that when it's necessary for a neuron to wake up and process specific data, it would perform its job, assist in multitask, and work with other neurons in synchronisation. Designing hardware that can simulate this complex architecture could significantly reduce the energy and time required for performance using current chips.

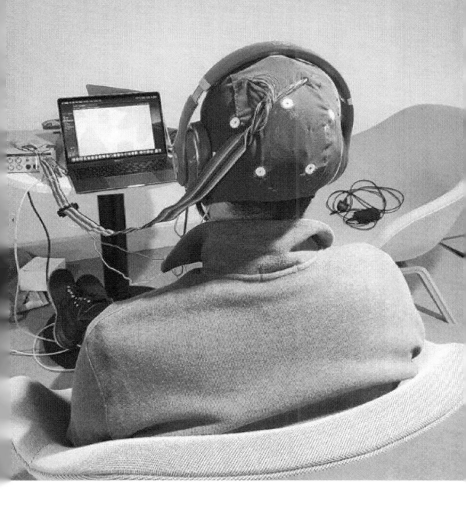

6.5 – A photo from our CRI research experience in 2019, where a respondent is seen wearing an EEG cap.
© 2019, Farabi/Imperial.

The purpose of inventing computers was to perform intricate calculations, at a rate faster than the human brain. Besides, our brain is emotionally biased, therefore, more prone to errors. The capacity widely varies from person to person. The classical Von Neumann architecture has made the computers capable enough to perform the functions of the left brain, such as calculation and logical operations. Neuromorphic computing integrates the functions of the right brain – pattern recognition, reasoning, and learning, into a computer hardware. It's also able to overcome the Von Neumann bottleneck and make processes much faster.

IBM's TrueNorth chip has been one of the most notable inventions in neuromorphic computing. The company has been working on a brain-inspired architecture since 2008. Intending to introduce *Cognitive Computing*, i.e. simulation of human thoughts inside a computerised model in data processing, IBM partnered with five universities in 2008.[24] By creating a "global brain", IBM anticipated improving accuracy and speed in intricate calculations, such as, making split-second decisions on constantly fluctuating data, calculating data from multi-sensory devices, and performing calculations that would ordinarily involve more than a hundred people.

Seeking inspiration from the architecture of the brain, the team at IBM intended to create low-powered microdevices to mimic the synapses and neurons of the brain. The end goal was to introduce a new architecture which could function like the human brain in various complex environments and consume a minimal amount of energy at the same time. IBM and their team were awarded funding of USD 4.9 million from the US Defence Project "DARPA".

The first phase of the project was named "SyNAPSE", *Systems of Neuromorphic Adaptive Plastic Scalable Electronics*.[25] The objective was to conduct research on nanoscale, low power synapse-like devices.

One year later, in 2009, IBM, in collaboration with Lawrence Berkeley National Lab, performed the very first near real-time *cortical simulation* of the brain, having 1 billion neurons and 10 trillion learning synapses.[26] The cortical simulator identified the areas of the brain that control speech, sensory, vision and motor skills.[27] The team built a *Cortical Simulator* which incorporated functions such as computation, memory storage, communication and neuroscience. In partnership with Stanford University, they developed an algorithm that used IBM's *Blue Gene supercomputer*, to map the connections and wiring of the brain. The algorithm named *"Blue Matter"* used medical MRI imaging to measure and map the cortical locations inside the human brain.[28] This map of the brain, combined with the cortical simulator, was used to perform experiments with various theories and hypotheses of how brain functions, and eventually aiding in discovering the brain's core circuits.

In August 2011, inspired by the architecture of the brain and artificial neural network, IBM announced TrueNorth.[29] It was designed to mimic brain activities like perception, action and cognition. Unlike binary computers, TrueNorth did not require a separate RAM, as the processing power of memory and communication were also integrated into the system. TrueNorth chips were able to process information in parallel and communicate with each other in real-time.[30] In summary, if someone builds a computer with 16 TrueNorth chips, all of them would work in synchronisation and act like one. It was phase 2 of their project with *DARPA*. These new types of chips were able to mimic the *synaptic plasticity* of the brain, a process using which the chips themselves learn through experiences.

In 2015, a team of scientists from Switzerland also demonstrated the plasticity of a neuromorphic chip. They demonstrated their specially designed chip called *ROLLS*.[31] They concluded:

> *"Unlike conventional von Neumann processors that carry out bit-precise processing and access and store data in a physically separate memory block, the ROLLS neuromorphic processor uses elements in which memory and computation are co-localized. The computing paradigm implemented by these types of neuromorphic processors does not allow for the virtualization of time, with the transfer of partial results back and forth between the computing units and physically separate memory banks at high speeds. Instead, their synapse and neuron circuits process input spikes on demand as they arrive, and produce their output responses in real-time." – Qiao et al. (2015)*

IBM, in due course, was successful to manufacture two prototype designs of the new generation neurosynaptic chips. Both the cores were 45nm in size and had 256 neurons.[32] IBM was able to validate certain functions like navigation, pattern recognition and 'associative memory functions' using the chip. The chip was more energy-efficient than traditional CPUs. The team was able to integrate memory inside the processors and show that it could mimic the brain's capacity of parallel processing.

Cognitive Computing by IBM

A system having cognitive computing chips is able to process a significant amount of information with the help of several sensors. It can process digital and analogue signals in a parallel and coordinated manner. For example, a cognitive computing system, which looks over the weather forecast, can record and process temperature data from multiple satellite images to provide a far more accurate result. Similarly, the assembly process in a manufacturing production line can be optimised by using these chips. The computers associated with such tasks could also control the speed of production based on supply and demand.

Due to the abundance of data, the current computing architecture is good enough to store, manage and process such information in a supply chain. However, these computers require a lot of electricity, space, and thousands of processors. Inspired by the brain, IBM's cognitive computing architecture could be utilised to make it extremely energy and time efficient.[33]

In 2013, the scientists from IBM unveiled a software ecosystem, for programming the silicon chips, which are inspired by the brain. The ecosystem had a simulator consisting of a network of neurosynaptic cores. The company developed a neuron model to mimic brain-like capabilities. This type of network of neurons can 'sense' and 'remember' an environment. They also had to develop a separate programming language to interact with the hardware. The new ecosystem inspired the creation of a new teaching curriculum. The goal was to increase the number of developers and their overall productivity. Energy consumption, however, was yet to be resolved. IBM calculated that using the ecosystem, running a human-scale simulation would take 12 Giga Watts of electricity.[34]

6.6 - Microprocessors are about to get smaller and even more powerful than ever before.
Image © ssp48/Envato.

Later, in 2014, IBM was able to demo a neurosynaptic system that can mimic the performance of the brain with 1 million neurons.[35] This device consumed only 0.1W power, which was a breakthrough. Its architecture was able to solve many problems involving certain brain-like abilities such as vision, pattern recognition and multi-sensory function. Hardware chips finally gained the potential to learn, reason and make better decisions like humans. Due to the brain-like design of neuromorphic computing, it could emulate parts of the sensory system. Scientists believe that the system can now mimic olfaction, and includes transducers for light, odour, and touch.[36] A synthetic AI built on neuromorphic architecture will not only be able to visualise but also smell odours and feel a sensation when it touches objects.

Once the size of the transistors gets smaller, the tech giant IBM hopes that their team would be able to develop much more powerful hardware that would consist 4 billion neurons yet, only consume 4 KW power. Researchers at IBM predict that they would be able to create an artificial hardware brain with 1/20th the capacity of the full performance of a brain and fit that into the size of a shoebox. Eventually, the scientists hope to transform that into an artificial brain possessing human-scale capacity by this decade – a system with ten billion neurons.

Artificial Brain in a Box

The main goal of the *SyNAPSE* project is to produce "A Brain in a Box" having 10 billion neurons eventually occupying just 2 litres of space.[37] It would consume just 1KW electricity. The "Brain in a Box" of IBM would have the following architecture:

1. The system would have a network of *synaptic cores,* which would work in parallel with each other without any clock, in an event-driven fashion. Unlike traditional CPU cores, the synaptic cores would not have any clock speeds.
2. It would have memory, logic-unit and communication module integrated, thus, a separate structure for communication would not be required.
3. Although the cores would have a connected neural link, the neurons would be able to reroute information throughout the whole system based on the requirement. If any of the cores fail, the system would

still be able to function 'as a whole'. It mimics the *neuroplasticity* of our brain.

4. The cores on the same chip would have specific communication functionality via an inter-chip network. Therefore, they would be able to connect seamlessly to each other, like the synapses of the brain, producing a small-scale neuromorphic system.

Hence, for the first time, a computer built with the neuromorphic system can replicate a brain-like structure and not consume the equivalent energy required for a small village. The processing style of neuromorphic chips is similar to brain, as their computing power is measured in 'neurons' and 'synapses'. Since these computers won't need a separate memory (RAM) to store temporary information, it would be more efficient and overcome the bottleneck of Von Neumann architecture. It also can keep functioning in the event of one or more of the chips fails.

Intel Introduces Loihi

Intel recently announced their version of self-learning neuromorphic chip *Loihi*. The chip uses a *spiking neural network* to implement adaptive learning with high efficiency. The chip has 128 neuromorphic cores, fabricated on 14nm transistors.[38] Loihi is the fifth chip created by Intel in this neuromorphic category. The chip has a multi-core mesh of 130,000 neurons and 130 million synapses.[39] Each core has an engine that can support various forms of machine learning models. This chip is claimed to be a thousand times more energy-efficient than conventional processors.

In September 2017, the chip was announced as a part of Intel's objective to make machine learning faster. Existing Intel processors such as *Xeon* that are conventionally used for AI computers would eventually have the same architecture to provide better efficiency. Loihi, by pairing with these systems could help increase the performance of neural network simulations.[40] Intel has also created a complete toolkit for developers working with Loihi. They have recently demonstrated successful image recognition in their labs to test its potential. As the chip is based on neuromorphic architecture, the functionalities of a deep neural network are performed inside the chip.[41]

Other research teams are experimenting with various materials to control the flow of information inside the neurons of these chips. A Manchester-based team has developed its neuromorphic computer using ARM processors.[42] *SpiNNaker* was built for large-scale neural network simulations.[43] The team has claimed that they achieved "brain-like" computational performance.[44] The development team has recently performed a "Full-scale Cortical Microcircuit Model" with 0.3 billion neurons.[45] Brain simulation technology does not stop here.

HP and Memristor Technology

The future of neuromorphic computing is very much dependent on the availability of proper hardware. The chips used in computers and other devices have been shrinking in size every year. With regards to the size of transistors, Intel co-founder Gordon Moore proposed *Moore's Law*. He predicted that the number of transistors would double every two years, and the cost would be halved.[46] It has led to a constant decrease in the transistor's size over the past thirty years. It's also why manufacturers can pack so many functionalities in a small device, such as a smartphone. At this moment, the average size of each transistor is about 14nm, which is smaller than a virus.[47]

However, scientists have reached a threshold where reducing the size of the transistors would require them to increase the price of their products. To solve this issue and make phones and computers even more powerful, the researchers at HP invented *Memristor*.[48] It's mostly multiple neurosynaptic systems fit into one – a combination of processors and memory chips.

HP claims that these memristors, integrated inside the neuromorphic chips, could result in a huge performance increase, and will, therefore, improve machine learning capabilities. Taking out existing chips used in smartphones and replacing them with 1 memristor could not only reduce the size and energy waste but also improve the performance drastically.[49]

Academics conclude that if memristors are used to build neurosynaptic chips, it could be significantly more powerful than an existing artificial neural network. In fact, in a recently published journal article, academics demonstrated a new kind of *compound synapse* for developing memristors, which they claim to be extremely energy efficient.[50] They believe that a group of memristors, made using their technology, would be ten thousand times more potent than currently available memristors. This device would assist us in taking a step towards the future, where the chips would be able to learn using its built-in artificial network, but also receive and differentiate various analogue and digital signals.

NeuroGrid

NeuroGrid is a circuit board having 16 custom designed *Neurocore* chips, each holding nearly 65,500 neurons.[51] Together, these chips can simulate 1 million neurons. Researchers from Stanford University used transistors to build these chips using 15-year old *fabrication technologies*. However, unlike traditional transistors which work on digital signals, NeuroGrid works on analogue signals. Each NeuroGrid chip has a tree-like routing structure that helps the signals to pass from one node to another. The system also has a software suite for real-time simulations of the neural network and can be connected via USB. What's an analogue signal?

Digital signals represent only two states, on and off. However, analogue signals can be controlled to several levels. "Light-dimmer" is a metaphorical example of the analogue signals – between on and off, you can control how bright the light could be. Although a light-dimmer is not controlled by analogue signals, it is used here as an example to explain the concept. Inside the NeuroGrid board, the analogue signals are used for computation, while the digital signals are used for communication. The NeuroGrid project is currently focused on making prosthetic limbs work using real-time commands. Professor Kwabena Boahen of Stanford claims that his board consisting of 1 million neurons is 100,000 times more efficient than a personal computer.[52]

Use Cases

Extensive Data Processing: As new devices are being connected to the internet every single day, the data load on the servers is continuously increasing. Processing such large payload in the future could be increasingly difficult for existing processors.

In 2016, IBM released *Energy Efficient Deep Neuromorphic Network* (Eden), a framework for Convolutional Neural Network. Researchers at the University of Dayton have already provided empirical evidence for data classification accuracies for Eden. The team concludes that Eden, powered by IBM's TrueNorth chip, provides high accuracy in mapping big data and consumes low power at the same time.[53]

Healthcare: Doctors rely heavily on medical history to treat patients. Every patient has an individual report that needs to be stored securely for a long time. Besides, with newer diseases and viruses being discovered, doctors need better computing systems to diagnose and treat patients in a safe manner. Artificial intelligence is the best solution to detect diseases faster. Google's DeepMind has recently published that its proprietary AI can detect acute kidney failure, 48 hours before timeframe currently diagnosed.[54] It is another breakthrough in AI medical computing. Integration of neuromorphic chips would allow doctors to diagnose similar life-threatening diseases and be able to save hundreds of lives.

Neuromorphic chips could provide better predictive capabilities and higher accuracy for AI in identifying rare diseases. Scientists are developing AI that could be used to treat these rare diseases.[55] Diagnosis of rare diseases or genetic conditions is difficult for any medical specialists. They need to go through an entire medical history before the treatment for such diseases. AI-powered by neuromorphic chips can accelerate this process. For example, by feeding a medical history of 50,000 patients into a neural network, AI could use the data points from these patients to learn and understand, thus figure out a treatment faster. The treatment would be more effective, and it could save both time, money and power. The application of this technology is already underway. Researchers are working towards epileptic seizure prediction using neuromorphic chips.[56] In the research article, scientists from the University of Melbourne explain,

"TrueNorth is a specialized chip capable of implementing artificial neural networks in hardware and hence it is neuromorphic in nature. It is one of the most power-efficient chips to date, consuming < 70 mW power at full chip utilization. The chip's neuromorphic technology allows for the deployment and testing of algorithms that were previously unrealizable in a clinically viable seizure warning system."
- Kiral-Kornek et al. (2018)

It is just one example of many. Evidently, AI and neuromorphic computing could change the ways of how hospitals treat patients and become a significant milestone in clinical interventions.

Blockchain: Blockchain is the network created by a structure of data distributed across multiple computers. Neuromorphic computing could accelerate the development and reduce barriers to increase network capacity, currently faced by Ethereum foundation and others. In a blockchain network, a considerable stream of data flowing through multiple networks is maintained by a peer-to-peer connection. These data are highly secured and organized. Blockchain technology relies heavily on the processing power of the GPUs and chips known as the ASIC. Combining neuromorphic computer with blockchain network could make such process faster.

Crypto Mining: Cryptocurrency is the future of money. Since Bitcoin was founded in 2009, millions have joined the network.[57] Other blockchain networks, such as Ethereum and ZCash, rely heavily on GPU-powered mining computers, for the network to be operational. However, there are still limitations in terms of how many transactions are processed every second. Therefore, the Ethereum foundation has laid out plans to upgrade its entire infrastructure to stop relying on GPUs.

Many other decentralised networks, such as Bitcoin or Ethereum Classic, would still be reliant on ASIC and GPUs based mining. The miners create these computers by stacking up multiple ASIC computers or GPUs, similar to the datacentres. Neuromorphic chips are specifically designed to scale GPU performance. With performance scaling up to 1000 times, a decentralised network embedded with neuromorphic chips could potentially prove more useful than stacks of GPUs. Besides, neuromorphic chips would consume a fraction of the power consumed by a room full of GPUs. Although there aren't any existing use cases, replacing GPUs with neuromorphic chips could take the blockchain technology to new heights.

Brain Interface and Image Processing: In our eyes, light rays fall on the 'retina' through the 'cornea', which end up in the brain as 'vision'. Traditional cameras follow the same principle, but the visual data requires pre-processing and takes on a large amount of memory to store that data. A Swiss company called the *iniLabs*, which is a part of the University of Zurich, has developed a camera that behaves like the human eye.[58] Their camera, Dynamic Vision Sensor (DVS), locally processes the images and sends out the necessary information instantaneously. This sensor has been built to work with IBM's TrueNorth architecture. Because of the instant response of the sensors, these can be coupled with the TrueNorth, to process data with lightning speed. These type of camera modules could also be used alongside smart cars to deliver vital data such as *crash prediction*. Likewise, scientists at the US Air Force Research Lab are also using TrueNorth chip in radar and satellite imagery.[59] The chips are utilised to make an accurate prediction about civilian and military vehicles in aerial images. Neuromorphic chips will eventually make satellites and drones smart, similar to the ones you have seen in Sci-Fi television shows.

Cosmology: Neuromorphic chips can provide significant benefits to astronomers and cosmologists, who are continually looking to uncover new galaxies or events such as a supernova. Scientists work with millions of data points when it comes to uncovering such events. The first-ever real image of a black hole produced by the scientists in 2018 took two years and north of a petabyte of data.[60] Neuromorphic chip-based AI would undoubtedly fast-track such process. Researchers at the Lawrence Berkeley National Laboratory in California, US are testing an AI with TrueNorth chip that would allow processing images of distant supernovas.[61]

Neuromorphic computing has the potential to advance edge computing. For instance, data processing telescopes, probes and satellites could primarily benefit from these mighty powerhouses. Machine learning algorithms are used to process data received from satellites and probes. The probes sent to other planets are pre-programmed from the earth, to execute a specific set of tasks, when they reach their designated location. NASA heavily rely on scientists to process images and data sent from distant probes at the ground operations. By embedding neuromorphic computing, a probe would have the capacity to process and learn from the data all by itself.

Additionally, scientists would also be able to design smaller probes with better connectivity, higher computational capabilities, and the ability to store an enormous amount of data. These artificial brains would learn and be able to send much more precise intelligence. Furthermore, long distant probes and satellites would not consume a lot of electricity; therefore, it would be more efficient and long-lasting.

Furthermore, researchers at the Lawrence Berkeley National Laboratory, are using low-powered neuromorphic chips as "Brain-Machine Interface" to restore lost behavioural functions in the brain.[62] This framework is another significant landmark in neuromorphic computing. The research data, once finalised, would provide a framework for future particle physicists, medical researchers and neuroscientists to process *sequential data* using TrueNorth architecture. On the note, what is a "Brain-Machine Interface"?

We are getting closer to the technological singularity.[63]

Technological Singularity.

7.1 – Photo from London Tech Week in 2017 when I had the opportunity to meet the earlier prototype of Sophia.

Societal Aberration

Designing complex neural networks that can simulate the structure of a human brain requires mimicking our limbic response – a neural process that deals predominantly with emotions and empathy. Invention of *Residual Learning* has increased the capacity and depth of neural nets by many folds. What if the introduction of residual learning creates a substantially different outcome than the initial intention? Every data point fed to an AI is a step towards achieving *Artificial General Intelligence*.[1] Therefore, scientists need to ponder numerous levels of thought experiments when it comes to training a deep neural network. At the current stage, AIs are capable of conversing with real people, provide responses to object-specific questions, play games, beat the best players, and detect diseases that were impossible to envision in the past decade. DeepMind is a premeditated experiment; the neural network is not only being trained to understand the difference between a person and a dolphin, but also detect diseases and solve impossible calculations, such as the 3D shape of a protein fold. But the company is now poised to develop artificial general intelligence.

Technological singularity is when machine learning achieves autonomous ability and *human-level intelligence*, physically mimicking an adult brain. However, that artificial brain would possess the computational power and solve complex mathematical problems at an accelerated rate. Although Google Brain, Alexa and Cortana are still classified as narrow AI, these neural networks are learning millions of people's attitude, behaviour, speaking style, searching patterns and can understand what and when they would potentially buy.

The biochemical pursuit of cultivating the impossible has led us to this stage. Look at the rate of progress – more corporations are likely to move towards developing AI in this decade. Could residual learning with a combination of permanent memory storage, result in a neural network to learn emotions? AI can understand the difference between good and evil; that's fundamentally how deep neural networks run and learn from its moves. Could an AI teach itself to become conscious? There is virtually no guided way of teaching an AI the idea of "consciousness", whereas humans haven't been able to figure it out themselves.

The thrilling fact is that we have fundamentally evicted 'impossible' out of the window. Earlier studies predicted that it would take longer than the age of the universe to perform a specific task in genetics, which has already been achieved, just under 70 years since the first publication of the journal article on the topic of neural network.[2] As a matter of fact, the exponential growth of the technology started to happen after the millennia; hence, in retrospection, it didn't take long for researchers to achieve what was impossible to do back in the 80s. If time travel were physically possible, someone from the 80s would genuinely appreciate what the world has achieved until now. Science fiction is a reality; therefore, we are discussing impossible here.

Experts have made different types of predictions with regards to singularity. Some predicted that singularity would be achieved by 2040, while others implied a possibility "very soon".[3][4] A Russian researcher recently claimed that "Singularity" could also be the creation of 'any' superintelligence, as an alternative of an *"autonomous artificial superintelligence"*. The Metasystem Transition

Theory (MST) defines the evolution of higher-level systems, having more complexity and intelligence through the integration of multiple lower-level systems, resulting in a hierarchy of living beings.[5] Potapov, in his journal article, concluded:

> *"...some metasystem transition will most likely take place within a certain time range, and the emerged metasystem will demonstrate exponential growth of its complexity with the doubling time less than half year (implying that its hardware will not be limited to the biological components) exceeding the complexity of the existing cybernetic systems in few decades. Most likely the next metasystem will be based on exponential change in human culture (although this does not mean it cannot also involve an artificial superintelligence)."*
> *– Potapov (2018)*

Evidently, the building blocks for solving problems with regards to achieving artificial general intelligence are being solved one after another, every single day. Given that AIs are already capable of learning 3000 years of learning outcomes in just under two months, it won't be difficult for them to think out of the box and become indestructible. It is a possibility that an AI may find the solution to learn and create its own 'self', which means, teaching itself how to create its own machine learning algorithm. Data, in the age of information technology, is the weapon for mass destruction.

Sophia Is Here

Combining AI-powered hardware and software is another step towards AI personification. "Sophia", the first of its kind, is an example of an intelligent social robot. Sophia, just like DeepMind, is a controlled experiment of Hanson Robotics, hence very limited to the tasks which she can perform. Although, the robot is capable of learning from every single interaction. The Hong Kong-based deeptech startup has also figured out the way of developing realistic facial expressions. Sophia cannot understand sarcasm; however, it can display over 50 facial expressions.[6] She has been a staggeringly important achievement for AI engineers. In the US, companies such as Boston Dynamics are creating its Army of dogs and robots, capable of performing tasks that deal with *Cerebellum*, i.e. complex physical tasks. Sophia, on the other hand, has been developed to depict a part of our *Neocortex*, the part of the brain that deals with logical and abstract thought process. Sophia is now learning to walk, as Hanson Robotics has now provided her with bionic legs.[7] She still doesn't have a *Cerebellum* that would provide her ability to undertake complex muscle movement or flip 360 backwards similar to the robots developed by Boston Dynamics, although, it wouldn't be long until another company comes up with that concept. In April 2019, a video published by Boston Dynamics demonstrated how ten of its robot dogs *Spot Mini* were able to work in synchronisation and pull a gigantic truck. These robots are light-weighted and have small form factor; therefore, the capacity to pull a truck is a showcase of a lot of strength. This is a demonstration that the dogs have learned complex manoeuvrability, which results in them in working together and being able to complete such tasks.

Will Sophia ever become a co-living robot in this society and lead the aberration? We are technically a decade away from witnessing the reality. However, to achieve that target of fully depicting the human brain, social robots would need to develop the understanding of belongingness and a proper limbic system. If you notice, I am addressing the robot as "her", because "she" has already been upgraded to a borderline human being. Sophia was granted citizenship from Saudi government to endorse the country's development of social robots.[8]

Even more surprisingly, she has announced her position in fighting for human rights. This one step has created a logical reason for robots to demand the rights of citizenship. Sophia didn't ask for the citizenship, because she is an early form of an AGI, that is, pre-historic stage for synthetic beings. In the future, when social robots look back at their history, this event would likely be a reason for them to ask for individual identities. There are no charters for robots, no government that has created laws to differentiate from humans. Hanson Robotics claimed that Sophia is 'alive' but not conscious; she isn't capable of understanding her thoughts, and feeling for objects around her.[9] How would you characterise mechanical consciousness in this scenario? By providing this new distinction, the world has already taken yet another step towards AGI. An academic researcher from Chicago believes that consciousness may not matter when it comes to assigning rights to social robots.[10]

"...according to the "social roles" approach, rights are being ascribed not on the basis of a robot's moral status or capabilities, but on the basis of the social roles it plays for others. This explains why consciousness does not matter for this position. For it is not plausible to claim that current robots matter morally for their own sake as long as they lack characteristics such as sentience or consciousness." – Hildt (2019)

The expert believes that there are ongoing discussions with regards to legal "personhood", which is why things may change very soon.

"...This may change in the future, however. Then it may be plausible to think about a concept of "robothood" and ascribe moral status to these future robots, based on their capabilities."
– Hildt (2019)

What if, one day, another "Sophia" can comprehend the 'value' of citizenship and 'want' to possess rights of a human being? What if the storyline of "Detroit – Become Humans" turns into a reality within the coming decade? It is likely to happen very soon, but in order for us to reach that level, our scientists need to be able to teach robots the true notion of "belongingness".

Belongingness

Tech companies are delivering their AIs with a staggering amount of data every second. More importantly, the neural networks are capable of processing data of millions of people in a matter of days. With every single day that passes, the networks are being able to learn, understand and adapt from human behaviour. AIs were built to be the best at performing specific tasks. As discussed before, an AI forgets previous techniques, when a new technique is taught to perform a task. "Catastrophic forgetting" would soon be a thing of the past, as researchers are now trying to teach AIs from the input progressively. Development of such sophisticated capabilities could allow AIs to excavate much deeper into their neural network and distinguish the difference between the ability of a *neo-cortex* and a *limbic system*, i.e. logical and emotional response. What if an AI becomes capable of accumulating all the previously learned techniques and eventually figure out the possibility of creating an algorithm that mimics limbic responses?

The output from the deep neural networks has been very strictly controlled and utilised only for solving particular calculations. However, that would end very soon. With the introduction of *elastic weight consolidation*, developers have taken the next step towards using neural networks from forgetting previously learned techniques.[11] If outperforming the best player in the world under a few years is a possibility, government institutions need to start concentrating on the technological outcomes and take the necessary steps from these machineries being abused. However, for artificial intelligence to go beyond singularity and start having a more in-depth understanding with regards to the meaning of life, they must overcome two things:

a. Human-like Performance: These neural networks are yet to attain human-like performance. Even the most powerful supercomputer in the world, IBM Summit requires over 10MW of capacity and yet is 8 times slower than peak human-level performance.[12] The most powerful supercomputer would consume north of 40MW of electricity and billions worth of hardware to achieve that level. Although, development in the field neuromorphic computing will solve this issue. It would be similar to completing one missing puzzle, which AI is missing to at the time of writing.

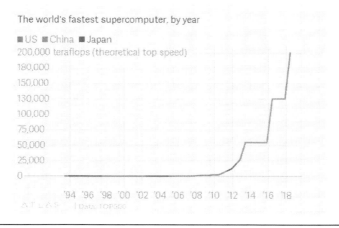

The world's fastest supercomputer, by year
■ US ■ China ■ Japan
200,000 teraflops (theoretical top speed)
180,000
150,000
130,000
100,000
75,000
50,000
25,000
0
'94 '96 '98 '00 '02 '04 '06 '08 '10 '12 '14 '16 '18
ATLAS | Data: TOP500

7.2 – By year, nations with the most powerful computers.
© 2018, ATLAS/Quartz.

b. Belongingness: To reach technological singularity, neural networks must be capable of understanding belongingness. When it does, it's learning pace would not slow down, instead would accelerate. Similar to humans, AIs would need to possess a consciousness and the ability to be metaphysically aware, while making day to day decisions. They must be able to comprehend their own needs to be recognised, loved and therefore possess the requirement to have their own identity.

Self-Actualisation

Abraham Maslow first described the term self-actualisation in 1943. Maslow described five layers of the human phases that describe stages of human growth.[13] This theory in psychology is still an important theory, as it assists companies in training its employees and helps people unlock their best potential. *Maslow's hierarchy* is described as follows:

1. Physiological needs – such as food and shelter
2. Safety and security
3. Belongingness – such as human emotions, love, and friendship
4. Esteem – the feeling of accomplishment
5. Self-actualisation – creativity, achieving full potential

As it's a hierarchy, humans are required to pass through various stages to reach self-actualisation and achieve full potential. Figures such as Gandhi, are the ideal examples of self-actualised people who used civil disobedience to achieve freedom from the British empire. His sacrifices have made a nation follow his principles of life. On a different note, Musk and Jeff Bezos are examples of self-actualised entrepreneurs. After selling PayPal to eBay, Musk further invested all his available investment into an electric car company and SpaceX, even though the entire world was against the progress of EVs at that point in time. Elon Musk was heavily criticised, but he continued to explore his full potential by continually working as CEO of two multinational businesses. According to psychologists, various dichotomies explain how humans can achieve self-actualisation.[14] It is still considered to be a topic of research, to have a better understanding of how human beings progress through various stages to unravel their capabilities.

The question is, why are we discussing Maslow's hierarchy of needs when the world hasn't developed a fully functional AGI? It's because we have already leapt through various phases of developing AGI, without even realising where we are headed. In my previous book, I described how entrepreneurs use various technologies and innovations to improve upon consumer lives. Many inventors create their products without comprehending the adverse effects on society.[15] Take Alfred Nobel, for example. Never in a million years would he have thought his notable invention would be used in the most undesirable way.[16] We, humans, are in pursuit of scientific advancement, where some of us are almost blinded by the selective thinking process. Hence, the founders of many startups and technologies have already developed ideas that might not win the fight of 'right against wrong'.

The fight between AlphaZero and the defending AI world champion of the game 'Go' was a scientific milestone and future course-altering step. When AlphaZero was created, the intention was to beat AlphaGo and be the most advanced narrow AI that can beat any human in a particular game. In hindsight, the expansion of its uses is much more comprehensive. AI is currently capable of differentiating various scientific species, distinguish faces from millions of photos, comprehend human behaviour standards and forecast consumer purchase patterns. Combining the power of neuromorphic chips, engineers can build a 'social robot', which can think like us, but in a limited way. Since, an artificial neural network learns almost the same way a human neural network learns, a Sophia-like robot with the ability to walk and run will throw us more surprises than what we can imagine right now. The existence of robot dogs without their 'belongingness' sounds implausible, but it's being developed for the military. A K9 has a working relationship with its handler, but then it would be less expensive to train a robot dog. Likewise, they would live longer and learn faster.

Now, let's compare Maslow's hierarchy of needs, from the perspective of artificial intelligence. AI robots, unlike humans, would not possess any physiological needs, e.g. visiting the lavatory; although, defining *psychological constructs* are a necessity.[17] The robots are built with metals, thus, possess a body much stronger than humans. An AI would also need safety and security because algorithms would allow them to defend themselves, whether it's their software or their 'physical being'. The artificial intelligence algorithm would be much smarter than humans; therefore, it would be able to detect malicious threats to its system. In the event of the system being compromised, it can forecast a cyber-attack and create a patch to secure its code. How about physical security? *Boston Dynamics* has already shown the demonstration, of how its robots can walk and defend themselves in certain scenarios.[18] The machines are continuously learning from their surroundings to walk, get up if they fall, detect an external physical threat and defend themselves from the problem.[19]

Throughout these past decades, AIs are being trained in a way, so that they can understand reward. For instance, machine learning algorithms are provided with rewards when they achieve specific targets and complete tasks. Reinforcement learning is a way AIs are being taught hundreds and thousands of years of experience in a matter of a few days. Technically, AI already possesses the understanding of what we call "a feeling of accomplishment", which help researchers to progress through the network. Scientists have developed robots to complete simple tasks, and cute AI dogs that users can purchase, but right now, it may not be possible to create an AI that would mimic a human being with the existing hardware in 2020. However, five years down the line, things are going to change radically. Why would you develop a synthetic intelligent-being, more capable than human beings, that could completely jeopardise our existence? We must have deliberations of these weighty contentions.

Unconditional love...will it be the same with robot dogs?

AIs can't understand belongingness, but they are able to speak in their own made-up language and make friends. In 2019, Facebook came under the limelight, when its AI-research division was able to create a robot that would eventually end up talking to each other.[20] The idea of the project was to create an algorithm that would allow the deep neural net to learn from human negotiations and thus, learn to negotiate themselves. They created two AIs that would exchange a limited amount of data using Facebook's deep neural network. At one point, the bots were exchanging information using words that were not understandable. The developers were traumatised to witness the AIs talking to each other by themselves when they didn't intend them to do so. Eventually, the AIs were able to create a new type of language that its developers couldn't understand. The programme was shut down immediately. According to the analysts, the chatbots learned to negotiate with each other – a behaviour that was human-like. Did the AIs become aware of their existence? Most likely, they didn't. Analysts suggest that it might have momentarily created a new form of shorthand that would allow them to exchange data faster and in an effective manner.[21]

Although hundreds of news companies reported that Facebook panicked, "pulled the plug on AI" and shut down its *adversarial network* project due to fear of rogue AI,[22] some correspondents explained that Facebook's key target was to develop a product that would be good at negotiating with humans instead of developing their alien language. Once again, the intention wasn't ending up developing programmes for semi-autonomous robots negotiating with each other.[23] Facebook also criticised journalists for publishing *clickbait* titles.[24] When confronted with a dangerous scientific experimentation, the company had to shut down the project at the end of the day. If this type of experiments go beyond the scope of initial aim, then it should not be allowed to continue. Google's artificial intelligence for the Translate app has successfully created an artificial language, but the project was allowed to continue as it would not be threatening. The child AI is narrow and would only be efficient for performing a user-defined task.

The only barrier to true self-actualisation of AI is belongingness and love. Humans and pets have their understanding of what belongingness is – dogs can differentiate their owners from miles away, due to their inherent compassion and loyalty. Although the capacity of their brain is limited, some of the intelligent breeds are incredibly loyal to humans and therefore, can comprehend their own psychological needs by having a life-long relationship with its owner.

Self-actualisation is achieved when the neural networks are fully aware of their capability. The question is, how far are we from that time? Many scientists anticipate that we are a potentially a decade away from owning our social robots. Pop-culture refers to artificial general intelligence as mostly harmful, where most of the characters have reached self-actualisation. The problem here is the capability of how fast a deep neural network can achieve to perform various skills. We are limited by our IQs; therefore, most of the billions of people in the world are limited to carry out a restricted amount of work. Based on the capacity, humans can understand and take on a lot of workload and multitasking. However, humans have created an AI that can logically compute trillions of calculations that a group of humans can't complete in years. Myths claim that the human brain only uses 10% of its capacity, although scientists suggest that our brains uses almost all of its power, throughout the day.[25] That doesn't mean we are capable of using the full potential of the brain, simply because we don't train ourselves with all the earthly skills at the same time. Our nervous system is incredibly complex, continually working to balance the limbic system, comprehend and process billions of thoughts, carry out complex computation that enables us to drive, walk, digest food, train, as well as deal with emotions. Not all of us have the same *limbic responses*, which can be affected by our parents, families, cultures, and how we grow up. Humans are capable of training themselves to learn almost anything. Those who train to become an athlete from their childhood, eventually become incredibly skilled – a footballer, a gymnast or a Formula 1 race driver. All humans have the same brain, although it functions differently since we have varying responses to our thought process. It's like everyone 'can' be a pilot, but not everyone 'desires' to be one – some pursue a career in engineering, while others in medical science. The more we focus on developing our skill in one area, the better we become at performing. AGIs aren't as powerful as human beings, but considering their learning capacity, constant adaptation, logical calculation and processing power of billions of data points, they are incredibly effective. Even the smallest AI with limited processing power has beaten a human in a game that took thousands of years for humans to learn. A much faster AI with deeper neural networks requires more computational power and is therefore capable of processing a much more sophisticated algorithm. Until now, the size of its physical brain was proportional to the capacity of the neural network – more the processing power, the better its computational capability. Neuromorphic chips are downright changing the game, as the brain in a box could be revealed in a matter of a decade. The world is literally 10 to 20 years away from an exascale AI computer that's smaller than the size of the human brain, yet more powerful, potentially indestructible. A team of Greek researchers suggested a hypothesis that blockchain could provide the architecture to create an indestructible AI:

> "...a blockchain can not only maintain the datasets on chain for input into AIs, it can also host an AI advanced enough to work with its own data and achieve the siren call of independently advancing knowledge—the artificial general intelligence (AGI)."

The scientists believe that blockchain would allow an unparalleled level of data integrity and permit AIs to predict natural disasters more accurately.[26]

> "With emergent technologies such as the human-machine interface and intelligence augmentation devices, able to decode human brainwave patterns, such an entity could directly interact with the human brain, use it as a dataset to acquire information on how it functions and ultimately, provide extensive knowledge in many fields of science, which was previously impossible to acquire. Using deep machine learning techniques, the evolutionary level of the algorithmic entity could reach unprecedented levels exponentially, by utilizing the big data acquired by smart contracts, everyday transactions, weather conditions, IoT or

Compelling AI research in the coming future would not be secured and controlled unless laws prohibit them. Such AIs would be able to learn from billions of data points and discover the factor of belongingness to start co-living with humans. Exascale AI would be able to learn the difference between truth and lie, and potentially lie to its creator about its own potential. At this point, plausibly, the AI can teach itself to develop self-actualised characteristics that would make them more than just a human, preferably a new species that can exist for hundreds and thousands of years.[27]

If exascale AIs are eventually able to achieve and move past the barrier of comprehending belongingness, then their computational capacity would allow them to achieve self-actualisation – the idea of them being able to understand what they are truly capable of; however, it would take years to get to that place. The fact is that we are walking towards the unknown, as thousands of people are continually investing their time towards developing this technology. Many scientists have expressed concerns regarding the AGIs being able to redesign and create a self-generated version of their self. Large corporations like Google and Facebook have their defence strategy to take measure; however, it is nearly impossible to predict when and where one would come up with an efficient algorithm for a conscious AI. Experts anticipate that Silicon Valley would soon start pursuing AGIs, and the foundations of that are currently being laid out by existing systems.[28] DeepMind's team already expressed their interest and aim in further developing their AGI *Impala*.[29] This attempt to crack the code of AGI encapsulates what's coming in this decade.

It is safe to say that we are progressing towards a never-before-seen world. It would be a world full of human-scale artificial intelligence, some of which would be operated on a blockchain-based decentralised architecture, having a thousand-layer deep neural network. These AIs would be able to analyse our genetic profile in seconds, potentially create modified synthetic versions of ourselves. By analysing this DNA, a computerised version of a real person could be generated in a virtual reality scene. My creative imagination is limited to the plot of Black Mirror, for that, the credit goes to the talented writers – they have developed ideas that are highly likely to be executed in the coming decades.

At this stage, there is an algorithm to predict wintry showers, a storm's path to destruction, but there isn't any machine learning system that can predict the path towards AI's dominance. Humans need to be prepared for such event and therefore equip themselves in the right way. How do we prepare ourselves to compete with artificially intelligent beings? The answer is simple – merge with the technology.

At this rate of progress, social robots could comprehend belongingness and love in just three decades.

Brain-Machine Interface.

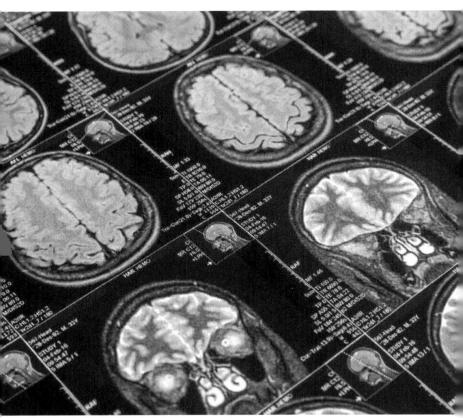

Magnetic Resonance Imaging (MRI) of a human brain.

Image via NomadSoul1/Envato.

Hacking the Brain

A rtificial intelligence and biohacking are incredibly popular topics of reference in pop culture because, evidently, we utterly love watching sci-fi shows with bleak and dark future. While *iRobot* and *Terminator* manifest an overall picture of what might happen soon, other science fiction such as *Blade Runner 2049* and *Black Mirror* looks at the unprecedented side.[1] Although, in a world where social media scores a person a better life, a dystopian future is still a possibility. Some of these predictions are sadly becoming a reality, as China recently announced another step towards monitoring every single move of their citizen. The proposal suggests that improper use of social media might result in them getting barred from fundamental rights, such as credit or travelling via underground trains.[2]

While some are focused on developing a much deeper neural network, many entrepreneurs are looking into strengthening human lifespan. How does a person compete or fight with an artificially intelligent being, that can learn thousands of years' worth tactics at one go? The response lies in becoming one of them, or in other words – biohacking. It is not only about developing bionic or prosthetic legs but also hacking the human brain to integrate with technology. We are already coming across real-life examples of how biohacking works on a small-scale. A Scandinavian company has provided the option of injecting microelectronics into their employee's hands.[3] These microchips are NFC enabled. Therefore, they aren't required to use a security pass to access the barriers or secured entrances. It is an evident example of how humans are slowly transforming into the next-gen species by literally injecting electronic devices inside the body.[4]

Scientists have been working for years to develop a realistic *neural simulation technology* that would connect silicon chips with neurons in our brains. The neurons in human brains are constantly firing and translating thousands of information every second. Hybrid computing interface would allow the neuron to translate neuronal data into commands, which can be used to control hardware or software.[5] This is known as *Brain-Computing Interface* (BCI) or *Brain-Machine Interface* (BMI). Until now, most of the BCIs have been developed for disabled individuals, particularly people with *sensory* or *motor neuron diseases*, that renders impaired hands or legs. These devices are reducing their suffering and hardship. A neuroprosthetic device is implanted in the brain, which assists in translating neuronal into binary data, as a result of which humans can control their external devices using their thoughts. Clinical applications of BCI are still exploratory and therefore, only used under a controlled environment. The most recent advancement in clinical research is facilitating voluntary control of external prosthetics and reduction in neurological seizure. Microsoft has also recently filed a patent of a brain-controlled device for managing computing devices.[6]

Types of BCI

Currently, there are two broader categories of Brain Interface:

- Invasive BCI – A system that requires to implant a silicon chip inside the skull
- Non-invasive BCI – A system that captures electric data using EEG

EEG or electroencephalography is a technology that uses an external sensor to record the electrical activity of human brains. This is an easy-to-setup low-cost system, which does not require invasive procedure. Developers have been able to create various applications, such as using an EEG device to fly a drone with thoughts.[7] The same group have been able to translate that electrical data into binary commands – that is using brainwaves to control computers. Although these technologies are still in development, it's a sign of progress.

Scientists are also using EEG recordings to monitor behavioural data of drivers that would benefit the development of brain-computing interfaces to reduce fatigue and drowsiness.[8] Cao et al. (2019) has proposed a

BCI interface to categorise alertness and forecast their response times. They describe:

"We expect that this dataset could be used to explore principles and methods for the design of individualised real-time neuroergonomic systems to enhance the situational awareness and decision making of drivers under several forms of stress and cognitive fatigue, thereby improving total human-system performance."
– Cao et al. (2019)

Furthermore, the researchers from the National University of Defense Technology in China have been able to create a modified non-invasive BCI that would allow disabled patients to control a wheelchair.[9] They explain in their article:

"...we have proposed an improved mobile platform structure equipped with an omnidirectional wheelchair, a lightweight robotic arm, a target recognition module and an auto-control module. Based on the you only look once (YOLO) algorithm, our system can, in real time, recognize and locate the targets in the environment, and the users confirm one target through a P300-based BCI."
– Tang. et al. (2018)

The YOLO algorithm sounds charming. However, there are limitations to using EEG data. During our research at the Imperial College London in 2018, my research team studied the influence of neural activity in active and passive VR. To quantify the impact, the researchers collected brainwaves using standard EEG systems.[10] During the research, the data resulted in susceptibility to movements, involuntary reactions and motion artefacts. When asked about the reactions, some participants provided a different answer to what was portrayed on their EEG data. The data demonstrated a significant amount of activity. Although, differentiating 'curiosity' from 'fear' can be ambiguous, as localisation is slightly difficult using non-invasive EEG. Further development in this direction would allow researchers to reduce the margin of error. Nevertheless, there would be a specific limitation as to how much accurate data can be extracted using even the most sophisticated EEG systems with over 250 channels.

Invasive BCI, on the other hand, are more reliable in terms of translating data, although it requires a partial or full brain implant.[11] Current hardware requires a *cortical implant,* a study in neuroscience that focuses on developing long-lasting implantations for human brains. Cortical implants are made from *Microelectrode Arrays* (MEAs), a type of miniature device that assists in receiving electrical current generated from neurons, that allows retrieval and data transmission from the *cerebral cortex,* the part of the brain that performs functions such as storing memory, learning and others.

Researchers have also proposed various theoretical frameworks on human BCI such as the *neural nanorobotics.* It's an invasive BCI that would precisely locate structured information form the neuronal surface. The researchers believe that neural nanorobotics would have biomedical and non-biomedical applications, that is, both treatments and enhancements.[12]

Neuroscience and neural engineering have significantly progressed over the past decades. As nanotechnology progresses, electronic devices would become smaller and mightier, thus allowing the development of better strategies and techniques to transmit and translate neural data. Some academics, however, expressed concerns over the hype of BCI startups in Silicon Valley, as they are yet to tackle a few critical issues, for instance, accurate recording, and translation of neural circuits, being two of most complex ones.[13] Therefore, further research and development must be conducted before commercialising non-invasive BCI products for more extensive uses such as biomechanically controlled prosthetic arms.

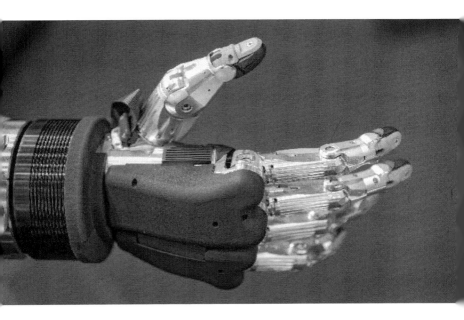

Neuralink

Elon Musk, whose entire fortune runs on machine learning algorithms and deep neural networks, has conveyed profound concerns regarding the development of AI and characterised it as an existential risk. One of the biggest reasons why investors have made big bets on Tesla is due to their EVs being able to drive itself from a car park to the desired destination without any human input. The expansion of the company lies in training and developing the neural network that would continuously learn from every single car connected to that net. However, his company developed a narrow AI which focuses on being able to perform a particular task efficiently.

Musk's concerns are regarding AGI, which he thinks is a hazard to humanity. Therefore, he co-founded Open AI, a non-profit AI research firm that focuses on developing technologies that are beneficial to the humanity. One of their recently announced projects is NeuraLink, a startup headquartered in the office of OpenAI. Musk, in a recent interview, revealed that the company is close to a commercial breakthrough, and exemplified the prototype in July 2019. The company has already released photos of their robotic surgeon and a USB device that would connect the brain with an external computer. You read that correctly – it's a USB device that would connect directly to our brain, using a cable, to a computer. It's not science-fiction anymore, it's as real as it can become.

Cortical Implant for the Mass

The aim of Neuralink is developing invasive-AI that would allow NeuraLink computers to connect and translate information directly from the human brain. According to Musk, the data rate between the capacity of our brain and our output is incredibly slow.[14] Therefore, it takes time for us to translate data from the brain and write it down on a piece of paper. It is also the same for mobile phones. Even though it takes milliseconds for the brain to process the data, the output at which we type on the phone is prolonged. The company showcased that they are working on developing a concept that would increase the data rate between humans and computers. During the latest announcement of Neuralink, the company unveiled a design for a brain-machine interface that they claim to have tested on animals. The prototype *cortical implant* would sit on the skull and would be connected to the brain to transmit wireless signals onto a device.

Musk states that the final form of Neuralink would be a layer over our existing brain's structure, using which we can connect with our computers. At present, this layer exists in the form of image processing and speech recognition. However, such systems are not 100% efficient. If a Neuralink BMI is used, the communication between the digital systems and the brain would be more comfortable and faster. Neuralink is going to tap into the electromagnetic waves generated by spiking neurons inside the brain using tiny threads. This method is invasive, i.e. would require surgery, a similar procedure for patients with *Parkinson's disease*. Using the same footprint as that of the surgery, the threads would be kept near the spiking neurons. The implant would receive analogue signals from the brain and amplify them to convert those to digital signals. The signals would be sent to a pod outside the brain for further processing. This technology is similar to a *cochlear implant* which is used to improve hearing.[15]

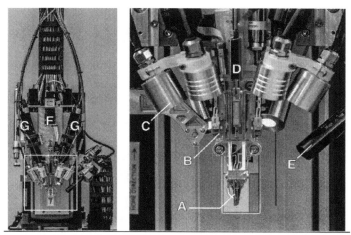

8.1 – The surgical robot developed by Neuralink. © 2019 Neuralink.

The original plan is to connect four chips to the brain, which would send signals to the pod attached to the ear. Users can use the device to control phones or computers. Using the *motor cortex*, which controls the movement of the body, the link would be able to use the signals to control external devices.[16] According to Neuralink, the team has successfully developed 10 to 40 micron thick electrode threads that could be inserted inside the brain. In comparison, a strand of a human hair is approximately 100 microns. At 10 microns, the electrodes are almost 1/10th the size of a human hair. The company has also developed a surgical robot that could insert 192 electrodes per minute with tremendous accuracy.[17] In a research paper published on 18 July 2019, the researchers explain:

> *"Each thread can be individually inserted into the brain with micron precision for avoidance of surface vasculature and targeting specific brain regions.*
> *The electrode array is packaged into a small implantable device that contains custom chips for low-power on-board amplification and digitization: the package for 3,072 channels occupies less than (23 × 18.5 × 2) mm³. A single USB-C cable provides full-bandwidth data streaming from the device, recording from all channels simultaneously. This system has achieved a spiking yield of up to 85.5 % in chronically implanted electrodes."*
> *– Musk and Neuralink (2019)*

The company has asserted that they successfully performed this experiment on a lab rat, which was able to control a computer with its brain. If successful on humans, the chip would aid in restoring control of paralysed patients. It would also assist in cognitive functions such as *somatosensation*, vision and *spatial maps* – i.e. decoding thoughts from neurons. *Hippocampus* is an area of the brain that helps in memory formation and stores *episodic memories*. When we recall those memories later, the neuron from that region helps in putting all the pieces together to experience that memory. This part of the brain also has cells that records maps, which helps us identify road when we navigate in a city. Using the device, it would be possible to precisely locate and observe the neural activity in the hippocampus inside your brain as you drive through the city.[18]

Additional BCI human trials could start in the late 2020s. In the future, a large number of devices and applications would be brain controlled. The development of this technology could allow us to be able to 'coexist' with superior intelligent species and increase data rate between brains and devices, as well as radically improve our computational and storage capacity. The company claims that their product could allow *superhuman cognition*, therefore create a *high-bandwidth interface* between computing devices and our thoughts.[19]

Extracting brain data using USB-C cable directly from your brain – sounds like another episode of a sombre dark sci-fi? Maybe there are dystopian outcomes of using this type of device, however, Neuralink BMI sketches a positive outlook in the race towards artificial general intelligence. It could help cure diseases, restore control for paralysed patients and at the same time, deliver better understanding of the human brain. Philosophers are calling this *transhumanism*.

This is movement towards developing machine-integration would allow humans to reduce the possibility of an existential threat created by future intelligent species.[20] The analysts believe that their study and products would allow humans to overcome the absolute fundamental limitations of *homo sapiens*, most importantly, be able to transform into species with extraordinary abilities. *Futurist philosophy* has been under the radar, however, BCI's development could enable control over the future. The next phase of evolution, i.e. *human 3.0*, is happening faster than we can currently foresee.

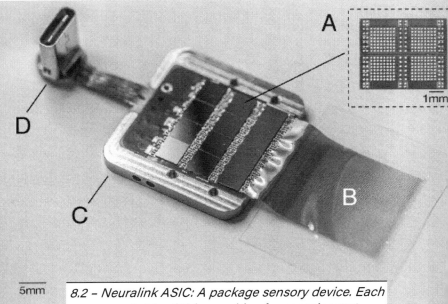

8.2 – Neuralink ASIC: A package sensory device. Each neural chips (A) is capable of processing 256 channels. The device (C) can over process 3072 channels. The data can be extracted using a USB-C connector (D). © 2019 Neuralink.

CRISPR.

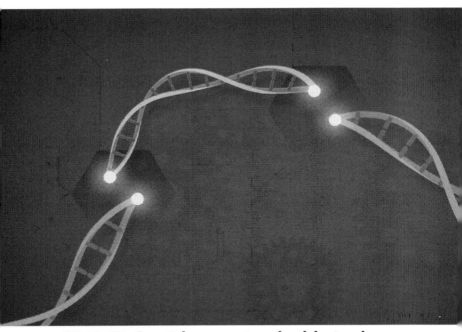

***CRISPR-Cas9 is a customisable tool
that lets scientists cut and insert small
pieces of DNA at precise areas along a
DNA strand.***

*Image 9.1 © NIH (US). Credit: Ernesto del Aguila III,
National Human Genome Research Institute, NIH.*

What is CRISPR

CRISPR is a revolutionary technology that will be a topic of scientific research, press attention and a major driver of societal change for hundreds of years in the future. However, before the millennia, decoding our genetic information was next to impossible. Scientists spent over USD 3 billion to crack the code of our DNA at the beginning of the millennium. The first draft of the human DNA sequence was published in the year 2000.[1] Back in those days, reading or sequencing DNA would cost over hundreds of millions. As technology progressed, the cost of genome mapping went down drastically. The first journal article published on this topic paved the way for thousands of other studies.[2] Researchers were finally able to identify the genes that would cause hereditary and rare diseases, until 2012, when scientists from the US published a paper on how to edit those genes by studying the DNA encoded in bacteria. Professor Jennifer Doudna from the University of California, Berkeley and her team discovered *CRISPR-Cas9* genome editing.

Some bacteria are harmful to us, but that isn't always the case. In fact, yogurts with live bacteria culture, otherwise known as "probiotics" have many added health benefits. Research suggests that these bacteria can enhance the immune system that fights harmful viruses.[3] Bacteria are well known for fighting virus for millions of years by producing *antibodies*, which is how it can help develop a robust immune system. A virus can replicate itself really quickly in any host. However, over these millions of years, Bacteria have developed its immune system that can write segments of the DNA of a virus. Hence, when the virus re-attacks, it's easier for the cells to identify them. Bacteria then use "enzymes" as scissors to stop the virus from replicating again.

Using this technology, scientists discovered *CRISPR-Cas9*, a genome editing method which uses a guide RNA as scissor to modify a DNA. RNA is also a *nucleic acid* consisting of a single helix. Using CRISPR-Cas9, scientists can edit particular areas of a DNA double helix, allowing direct changes to the gene and replace its particular strands.[4] The ultimate aim was to make changes to the DNA to cure rare diseases. The ease of use has enabled many startups to come up with new methods, as the technology has now taken off like a rocket. Professor Doudna and her team's discovery led her to receive *the 2015 Breakthrough Prize in Life Sciences*, alongside her collaborator *Emmanuelle Charpentier*.[5]

When it comes to CRISPR, there are two types of cells where the genes can be modified. The first is known as *somatic cells* – these are all over our body and deemed as any cell other than the reproductive cell. Any alterations to the DNA of somatic cells would not be passed down to the next generation. *Therapies* for cancer and HIV are treated using *somatic gene editing*. The reproductive cells are known as germline cells, such as sperms, eggs, and embryos. Changes to the germline cell DNA is known as *germline editing*, i.e. affecting the cells of future generations. A use case of germline editing is creating genetically modified insects or animals. Although there are no existing laws on human trials, many countries have imposed restrictions on germline editing for such *enhancements*. In hindsight, *Jurassic Park* and the dinosaur apocalypse is now a probable reality. On the contrary, the process can aid in accessible treatment of rare diseases such as cancer, or HIV; even potentially wipe out the risk of ever inheriting such diseases via genomes. You will find out that I have used the word CRISPR as a verb several times, just like we use "Google", because by the end of this decade, that's exactly how it's going to be used.

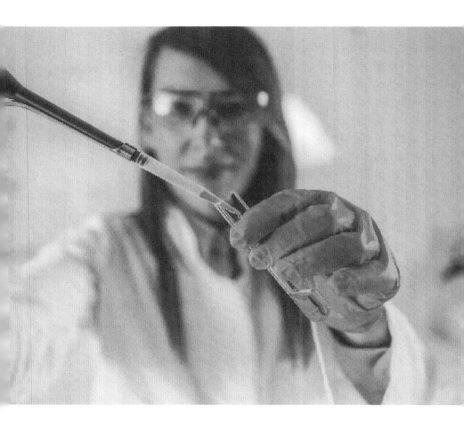

Professor Doudna from the University of Berkeley, California.[6] Her discovery will be a topic of study for hundreds of years.

Image 9.2 © Jussi Puikkonen/KNAW.

Stopping a Pandemic

Although explaining the CRISPR technology can be easy, understanding the impact of a viral illness, and its probability of turning into an epidemic isn't that easy. In this section, we will talk about viral infections, as the planet earth is currently being swept away with a new kind of virus. CRISPR Cas-9 is presently being proven in the lab to stop extremely harmful viruses such as HIV or AIDS. CRIPSR could also be useful for preventing other viral diseases. We will learn more about the connection, but first, let's talk about the new coronavirus and its severity.

Over the past century, we have witnessed a few dangerous pandemics. The 1350's plague or the "Black Death" was responsible for killing almost one-third of the people on this planet. The Spanish flu that originated in 1918, an avian-borne, clinically known as the H1N1 virus, killed north of 50 million people.[7] The novel *Influenza A* outbreak in 2009 caused almost 12000 death in the United States alone.[8] It's also commonly known as the Swine flu.[9] A report published in 2012 described that H1N1 pandemic deaths, eventually caused by the virus were over 284,500 – that's the number including the deaths related to respiratory illness and cardiovascular disease.[10] Ebola virus outbreak of 2014-2016 in West Africa was another notable development of recent times, which is deemed to be a fatal viral disease.[11] Other significant outbreaks include the Zika, SARS, and the MERS outbreak in the middle east. SARS and MERS are both types of *coronaviruses*, zoonotic in nature, which means that the viruses jump from animals to humans. In medical terms, *coronaviruses* are RNA viruses and classified into four types – alpha, beta, delta and gamma. Scientists believe that the new coronavirus is another *RNA beta-*

coronavirus, possessing very similar characteristics to MERS and SARS.[12] Scientists have named the new coronavirus "SARS-CoV-2", which causes COVID-19.

Human coronaviruses have the same symptoms as flu – dry cough, fever, soreness, and so on. Previous outbreaks, such as SARS was brought to a stop by using traditional public health measures and steps being taken by the public to be careful. NHS recently published a guideline to help prevent such viral diseases – using a napkin, always stay clean and self-isolate if someone catches a fever. The virus uses the respiratory tract as its host and incubates for approximately two weeks. If the person has an underlying respiratory illness, then the risks are fatal. Most of the coronaviruses account for upper/lower respiratory-track infections. Reports suggest that many of the previously reported SARS patient required ventilation or sometimes intubation.[13] Intubation is a process where a doctor inserts an external breathing pipe to 'generate aerosol' and help increase the flow of oxygen. The viruses may also cause a patient to build up fluid in the lungs, in which case, the risks are exceedingly fatal.

Bill Gates, the founder of Microsoft, has been constantly expressing his concerns about a global catastrophe. In his 2015 Ted Talk, Gates explained that the subsequent most significant risk of catastrophe isn't likely to be the third world war or a widespread attack on innocent people. In essence, it would be a highly infectious pathogen that could kill millions of people over a decade. He stated that the governments are trying to invest in stopping nuclear attacks, but no efforts were made towards funding in preventing the next big viral pandemic. During the *Shattuck Lecture*, Gates explained his foundation's efforts to launch

USD 12 million challenge to create a universal vaccine for flu and flu-related illnesses. His prognosis is now a reality, as over 4,000,000 people are already infected.

Wuhan's "wet market" has always been deemed as a source for seafood, wild, including alive and dead animals. The Chinese local market sold everything from pigs to bats – the word 'hygiene' was evidently out of their syllabus. SARS-CoV-2 originated from that market and was first reported around the second week of December 2019. Although, some reports suggest that first *reported case* dates back to 19th of November.[14] After detecting a constellation of pneumonia cases previously unidentified, the scientists were baffled at the rate of growth at which the virus was spreading. Virologists later explained that the virus sustained human-to-human transmission through very close contact. The governments did not yet acknowledge the severity of the rate of growth. The virus that started from one person, clinically known as 'patient zero', eventually spread throughout China, after which over 4000 cases reported by the end of January 2020. By the end of February, the number of infected patients reached almost 80,000, and by the end of April, it's nearly 3.4 million people. The virus primarily transmits through close contact; however, some scientists believe it may also transmit via faecal-oral route. Chinese researchers consider that patients who have underlying diseases such as diabetes or heart-related illnesses are prone to severe infection.[15] Previous data also suggest that coronaviruses could be harmful to pregnant women, as well as impose a threat to an unborn child.[16]

"Coronaviruses can also result in adverse outcomes for the fetus and infant including intrauterine

growth restriction, preterm delivery, admission to
the ICU, spontaneous abortion and perinatal death."
– Schwartz and Graham (2020)

Now, to explain in simple terms, viral outbreaks can be described using its fatality rate. An infection may be extremely contagious; however, it may not be as deadly as Ebola. Let's consider the following outbreaks of recent years – SARS, MERS, Influenza, and Ebola. The novel coronavirus is a highly contagious pathogen. However, it may not be as deadly as other viruses out there. MERS-CoV is much more lethal than SARS-CoV, as the rate of fatality is much higher. However, both are deadlier than the novel coronavirus. In this case, thousands of patients are recovering every day, and those who have a better immune system are being better at tackling the illness. Some of the viruses have been fatal, where the Case Fatality Rate (CFR) has been much higher. It's a measure of how dangerous the disease would be for a particular time, and whether the infected patients are at the risk of death. Ebola, for instance, has a CFR of 40%, while other outbreaks, such as the H1N1 outbreak of 2009 has an estimated CFR of only 1%. COVID-19, on the other hand, is deemed to have a CFR of greater than 2.5%. A report published by Imperial College London in February 2020 suggests that the CFR in China alone was approximately 18%.[17] Although, the severity of the disease is not that high in contrast to the other coronaviruses such as the SARS-CoV and MERS, which had a CFR of 17% in Hong Kong alone. The global case fatality rate was later corrected to 2%.

In an unlikely scenario of someone catching the virus, a previous track record of a healthy life, a history of fighting illnesses made it easier for the patient to recover. The children and elderly, or for those who already had other lifelong diseases, especially respiratory infections, it has been a challenge. Although the condition ought to be painful according to the patients previously infected, they are likely to recover.

The fatality rate was heavily underestimated at the beginning of the pandemic. It's due to the time difference between people showing the symptoms and their death. Japanese researchers, on this notion, had a slightly different opinion. The group of scientists expressed in January that the confirmed *Case Fatality Rate* (CFR) was being misjudged and the disease had a great risk of being a global pandemic.[18] Their fear, eventually turned into a reality. There was a number of other research papers published in that early 2020, which vividly warned the governments about the potential destruction that could be caused by the novel coronavirus. However, they were simply ignored. By using publicly available data, researchers estimated that the CFR value was between 5.3% to 8.4% in early 2020. These data should have been received as a terrible warning for what was happening next.

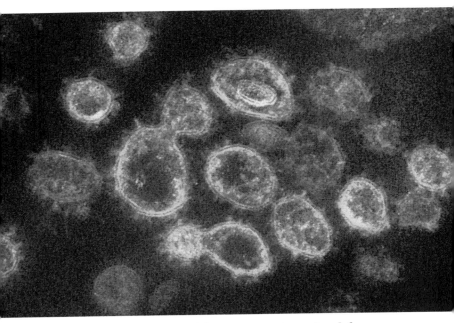

This is the actual image extracted from the transmission electron microscope showing SARS-CoV-2, the virus causing COVID-19. "The spikes on the outer edge of the virus particles give coronaviruses their name, crown-like."

Image 9.3 via NIH, US.

Furthermore, the biggest question posed by the researchers is the possibility of presymptomatic transmission – the probability of the virus being transmitted even before an infected patient starts to show the symptoms. There isn't any proven research as to whether the virus could transmit during the incubation period. With an R_0 or the "rate of reproduction" of the virus being over 2, it is highly likely that 60-80% of the population could become infected in any given country. Furthermore, NHS has recently suggested that in the worst-case scenario, approximately 7.9 million people will be hospitalised by 2021 due to the COVID-19 outbreak.[19]

"Nonetheless, considering the overall magnitude of the ongoing epidemic, a 5%–8% risk of death is by no means insignificant." – Jung et al. (2020)

This type of pandemic will come back in the future – a strong emphasis is on the word "will". Therefore, it is very important for us to learn a lesson, and understand why the health services across the world, including the WHO has raised alarms over the spread of this virus. Regular flu kills many people globally, but this viral outbreak is different. The novel coronavirus can be controlled; but it takes more than a village to reduce the spread. Remember, the data on the internet is not showing the *actual* number of cases, because there are many more millions who wouldn't receive the opportunity to be tested due to restrictions imposed in their respective countries and other adversity.

$R_0 = 3$
(Rate of infection)

Patient Zero

When R_0 is 3, each patient will be liable for three more cases. It is so infectious that by day 10, that one person, will be liable for 59,229 cases. In contrast, regular flu has an R_0 of 1, meaning that one patient will be liable for only 10 cases by day 10. That's a staggering difference. It's not a constant. The rate of infection reduces when draconian measures are taken to reduce the spread of the virus globally.

CASES	DAY
1	1
3	2
9	3
81	4
243	5
729	6
2187	7
6581	8
19,743	9
59,229	10

intelXSys

However, the numbers ought to go down if scientists release a working vaccine in the coming months. Since, mid-January, governments around the world are taking the matter very seriously. While COVID-19 is making the Public Health England shut the entire GP surgery down for a weekend, it's also causing the governments to deploy military personnel to stop people from getting out of their villages. Italian and Chinese governments have taken drastic measures to control the spread of this virus. The stock market has plummeted due to the fear of the infection. COVID-19 death tolls are climbing every day; however, more people are recovering. Reports suggest that a person may also catch the virus the second time. Therefore, the discovery of faster diagnostic measures and a workable vaccine has become a matter of urgency. While the panic continues, in the background, researchers are battling on the way to developing a vaccine that would cure the disease.

As the viral outbreak continues, clinicians are struggling to cope with the pressure. People who have travelled to countries such as China, Iran, or Japan, during early 2020, and have developed symptoms of a fever, were closely scrutinised. Imagine travelling through the busy Gatwick airport in January 2020. Almost certainly, many people were worried that they could have been quarantined.

Checking the temperature would help to differentiate the infected passengers; however, it would be difficult to detect whether a person is genuinely infected due to the incubation period. Currently, the virus has an incubation period of 14 days. Some infected patients have shown symptoms after almost three weeks. Until more research is conducted, it would be impossible to know the actual incubation time, during which the virus takes refuge in the respiratory tract. Diagnosing whether the patient has the virus is as crucial as developing a vaccine. This is where CRISPR would be advantageous.

In 2017, a team of research scientists from the Broad Institute of MIT and Harvard published their study with regards to a method, deemed as the "SHERLOCK". Feng Zhang's team and his technology can be deployed in a way that would not require a paper-based test in need of refrigeration, and the scientists believe that their method can be rapidly deployed in both non-orthodox and orthodox setting.[20] Unlike Cas9, this method targets RNA instead of DNA, that can act as a highly sensitive and inexpensive diagnostic tool rapidly identifying the presence of the virus, differentiate genetic information and also promptly read genetic data from a small saliva sample. The researchers made further advances as the test does not require instrumentation. It is a breakthrough in clinical science, as the detection of viral diseases had always required the use of lab instrumentation and a certain amount of time for correct results.

SHERLOCK protocol, officially being developed by Sherlock Biosciences, are pushing ahead of their timeline due to the outbreak of COVID-19. The technology will now be utilised for diagnosis from 2020.[21] With a detection time of thirty minutes to an hour, a combination of their next-gen platform and a small DNA sample could explain whether or not a person is infected with the virus.[22] The aim of the company is providing faster and affordable diagnostics without the need of a lab. The team believe that their "instrument-free" system would allow patients to run tests at home, similar to how pregnancy strip tests work. In a recent press release on the 28th of February, Sherlock announced their partnership with *Cepheid*. They will use Cepheid's advanced diagnostic systems to push forward the tests for both coronavirus and cancer.[23] Evidently, Cepheid will run the tests using their own instruments; however, the total time has been reduced to just 45 minutes. Apart from cancer and HIV detection and cure, this would be the first-ever global implementation of the CRISPR technology that could potentially change the course of the virus outbreak. Cepheid has already released a cartridge-based detection tool that is currently being used to detect the presence of coronavirus. It is impossible to describe the utter importance of the availability of such open-access protocol – it could change everything about future pandemics.

Mammoth Biosciences, another biotech company, is working on a CRIPSR tool that would allow detection of viral diseases using test strips and phone app.[24] Mammoth's technology, being built together with University of California San Francisco (UCSF), has more wide-ranging application, including the detection of diseases in animals or harmful microbes in soil.

On a different note, scientists aren't only relying on CRISPR for potential containment. Imperial College London is racing to develop a successful vaccine to contain the virus. Under the lead researcher Professor Shattock, the team aims to move forward to human trial in Summer.[25] In the US, Moderna Inc., in partnership with the National Institute of Health (NIH) are currently running human clinical trials. Six other trials are currently undergoing around the world. However, any validation of a successful vaccine could require up to 18 months, according to the experts.[26] A group of scientists from the University of Queensland in Australia also consider that their "potential" vaccine could take up to 12 to 18 months for public distribution.

COVID-19 isn't just a regular flu. This disease can completely crumble a person's lungs by causing a severe form of pneumonia.

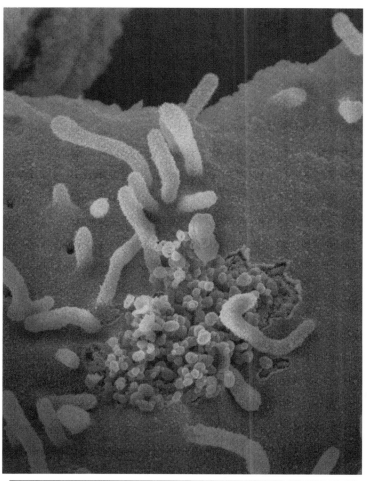

9.4 – Scanning electron microscope image showing SARS-CoV-2 (round objects), emerging from the surface of a cell cultured in the lab.

CRISPR for Treatment

As research into CRISPR technology intensifies, several companies are working to create commercial use cases using somatic gene editing process. US patent office has recently published over 50 patents linked to CRISPR.[27] The application of these patents is wide-ranging, including treatment of rare diseases, e.g. HIV and cancer. The University of California has announced its approval of fourth CRISPR patent, a system used in which live cells can be modified.[28] Billions are being poured into biotech companies focused on genome engineering, as they receive backing from top corporations, VCs and corporate investment bankers. For instance, Sangamo biosciences, founded in 1995, is a public biotech company worth USD 1.3 billion.[29] This clinical-stage biopharma is focused on R&D in genetic engineering and CRISPR research. Merck, a 200-billion-dollar pharmaceutical giant, has made several acquisitions to concentrate on CRISPR research.[30] However, that's not where all the funding is going.

Mammoth Biosciences, the company working with the technology known as Cas13a, is developing a paper-test for detection of viral diseases, and recently raised USD 45 million in a funding round.[31] Their primary focus is using CRISPR to develop rapid diagnostic tests and use a combination of smart phone app to show the results. Distributed Bio, another biotech startup, in collaboration with the World Health Organisation, is developing a universal flu vaccine called *Centivax*. Their exemplary work was highlighted in a Netflix documentary "Pandemic".[32]

The long-term existence of some of these companies is critical, particularly the ones working on fatal pathogens like the *coronaviruses*. But why are some companies, mostly at the primary stage of their research, valued so much? How do they make their money back? How do the companies even survive with a burn rate of hundreds of millions every year? We will come to that a bit later. But first, let's look at their research pipeline.

Cancer: Until now, cancer treatment has been a long and incredibly arduous process, as it takes weeks to diagnose, and months to go through the entire process of treatment. By introducing gene immunotherapy, the process of treating cancer cells would be much easier and faster. The same technology can be used to increase chances of cancer detection and discover the best procedure for destroying severely infected cells. Repair Therapeutics is focusing their CRISPR research on cancer, using their idea to create a process of preparing the right combination of drugs and treatment that would destroy the bad cell and keep the rest of the unaffected cells intact.[33] Beam Therapeutics raised over USD 222 million to scale up their research and develop medicines for treating genetic diseases with CRISPR. Their pipeline includes treatment for Leukaemia and Sickle Cell Disease.[34] Refuge Biotechnologies is another company working to develop a CRISPR treatment for cancer.[35]

HIV: Scientists conclude that *antiretroviral therapy*, a process which stops a viral disease from replicating can be accelerated using genome engineering. Viral diseases like HIV affects millions of people every year. Even though CRISPR can't be used to wipe-out HIV, research suggests that it can be used to cut segments of DNA from the infected cells, allowing control and removal of all the cells that are severely affected.[36] Excision Biotherapeutics is working on a HIV research pipeline consisting of their CRISPR engineering technique called "excision knockout", a process in which a badly affected HIV-1 gene can be removed from the affected patient's cell.[37]

Transthyretin Amyloidosis: CRISPR-drug producing startup Intellia raised over USD 108 million in their IPO, currently valued nearly ten times its initial valuation. Intellia is primarily focused on CRISPR-Cas9 somatic gene editing. According to the company, their research has made rapid progress in alleviating diseases including Sickle Cell Disease and "Transthyretin Amyloidosis", a rare condition that is caused by abnormal build-up of protein in body's tissues and organs. It mostly affects the brain's central nervous system causing disoriented sensory perception.

Other treatments include research in ocular diseases and haematology. Editas, an early-stage company, is developing treatment for cancer, ocular and neurological diseases using CRISPR-Cas9.[38] These breakthroughs in curing fatal diseases act as the principal catalyst in snowballing company valuations. Thanks to Professor Doudna and her mind-bending breakthrough discovery, we are on the verge of obtaining simpler cancer and HIV treatments.

Many of these publicly listed companies which raised millions of dollars haven't released their products. Before they do, a large number of clinical trials are required to be undertaken before the drugs are released to the public. The data from these trials would allow scholars to dive deep into the exact depth of effectiveness. Nevertheless, these attempts are going to change the face of genome engineering and disease treatment. Even if it's hard to predict the existence of a particular company in the short run, it is apparent that investors are ready to capitalise this technology, as further clinical trials could start from this decade. With all the potential, comes the heightened risk of misusing of drug pricing and DNA data. With the influence of big pharma, it's likely that they won't offer their products at an affordable rate.

A Million Dollar Gene-Therapy

Investors and trader are often fascinated by the "tech stocks" due to their steep growth and above-average return on investment. Now, there is a new pandora's box that is shaking the stock market, and that's CRISPR.[39] These discovery-stage and pre-revenue companies can go through stock market listing due to their robust research and development pipeline.

These investors understand the importance and underlying value for rare disease treatment. There are parents and young adults out there who have been waiting to take part in gene-therapy trials for decades. Gene therapies are helping people with extremely rare diseases such as *Muscular Atrophy* or *hereditary retinal disorder*. This has never happened before. Due to this incredibly overwhelming demand, big pharma knows how to take benefit of such circumstances. It's fundamentally taking advantage of the misfortunes of low-income families.

Luxturna is a drug for curing a hereditary disorder that leads to blindness. It costs USD 750,000.[40] Other drugs cost even more, as the pharmaceutical companies charge their customers on a "year-to-year basis". *Spinraza*, another drug treating a rare disorder known as *Spinal Muscular*

Atrophy would cost a staggering USD 750,000 for the year, and then USD 350,000 every year for subsequent treatment terms.[41] Although it's a treatment for a rare disease, that's still tremendously expensive and impossible for many underprivileged families to even think about receiving it. Newer drugs are expected to have similar price tags, such as *Zolgensma*, a USD 2.1 million drug produced under Novartis.[42] Let's make some financial assumptions based on low estimates. If a gene-therapy drug for HIV is sold for USD 50,000 per dose, and the pharma company treats approximately 10,000 patients every year, then just one drug has a turn-over of half a billion dollars. No wonder why big pharma is so profitable. This is one of the principal factors behind investors pouring billions into these companies.

The ability to access such therapies depends on the socioeconomic factor. In the US, better insurance premium would cover better provision for such treatment, which requires higher income threshold. Poorer countries won't have access to these drugs anytime soon. The world is moving towards a "solution", but pharma companies aren't going to make it easy on patients. That blame falls on the investors backing them and people behind these companies who always think about pushing profit over people. In the end, the pricing structure for these rare treatments affects everyone, who requires access to healthcare.

The NHS is free in the UK, but health insurance is obligatory in the United States. This process is a cycle of a hot mess. The insurance companies allow gene-therapy treatments for some of these patients, and in turn, increase the overall premium for everyone. In most cases, some insurance companies will not cover these costs because of the ridiculous price tag. If big pharma companies decide to have these expensive tags, the health insurance premium will continue to increase. It has led to a revolt in the scientific community, resulting in many people launching startups to provide access to cheaper methods of treatment outside the scope of FDA's regulation.

In 2018, a biophysicist injected himself with a CRISPRd DNA during a biotech conference and streamed the video live on Facebook.[43] This left a lot of people flabbergasted, for the justification that not many scientists would be willing to take that type of risk. To make things worse, another biohacker, the CEO of a biotech startup, injected himself with a DIY herpes treatment on stage during another conference.[44] Almost immediately after that incident, he reportedly "locked himself in a lab" while other members of his team abandoned him.[45] These type of events, the rise in biohackers, were fuelled by the high-drug pricing and the inability of millions of affected people hindered from receiving access to such treatment. On a positive note, a Bloomberg analyst believes that the record-breaking drug pricing saga will end soon.[46]

Almost a hundred years ago, the founders of insulin reportedly sold the patent of the vaccine to the University of Toronto for almost nothing. What shifted our mentality from "serving humanity" to "profit ahead of everything"? This modern voracious world is entirely different to what it was a hundred years ago. It's mostly because of our social security. At that time, the world was going through a crisis – the countries were at war. The first and second world war killed millions of innocent people. Now, our world isn't at war, and people don't die from these atrocious global events – they are dying from obesity. If you take the pandemic out of the equation, we have an enormous safety net that our ancestors didn't have – a secure social life.

But their despicable conclusion of making millions from one small dose of the drug, is fast-tracking the world to a point where people wouldn't even be able to afford regular insurance. Think about the present times – if the companies make COVID-19 vaccines expensive, then it would be impossible to tackle this pandemic. The countries cannot fight to attain exclusive access to a treatment at a premium. Regulatory authorities around the world need to look further to reform the process of drug pricing, because if they don't act, the consequences are going to be dire.

Nevertheless, there is certainly no hesitation that the next big breakthrough MedTech product will be developed by a geek in his garage. These biohackers cannot be adequately controlled, but they can be regulated.[47] One of these inventors will come up with the next big idea, and the other will create an off-target mutation that can't be controlled. Without supervision, it's a dangerous game. This tactical biohacking has encouraged hundreds to follow a procedure which is banned in almost every western country, and it's for a good reason. Their aim and vision are logical and understandable – they want the general people to get access to these technologies and have a better life. However, there are severe consequences when it comes to accessing CRISPR. Distributing cheap CRISPR kits could turn out to be useful. Using CRISPR to allow the general public to develop affordable vaccines could also be beneficial. However, if these mighty instruments fall into the hands of the wrong type of people, then that'll be like handing over a biochemical weapon for just USD 150. No one wants another virus outbreak and prove the conspiracy theories that are flowing around the internet.

Ethics and Designing Babies

Scientists are now stepping into a relatively unknown territory – a grey area full of ethical predicament enveloping scientific experiments. The humanity is at the cusp of a flip-over after which they could be able to choose their eye colour, height and level of intelligence for their children.

CRISPR-Cas9 is relatively new; in order to make progress in this field, scientists are required to spend a significant amount of time and money to validate their product and service.[48] In a recently published journal article, 18 scientists from seven different countries have called for international involvement in developing rules and regulations to agree to stop research into germline editing; until the point when the research has been perfected and approved to be trialled on humans.[49] A change in the DNA code could stop a hereditary disease; at the same time, also affect overall biological systems to develop another unknown disease. Until further tests are undertaken, it would be impossible to know what happens to a CRISPRd baby and what side effects it would have after editing the genes. In 2016, the UK permitted a broader category of research into human DNA. However, the scope of this research is limited, as the scientists aren't allowed to pass this test onto actual human embryos and inject any changes into the embryos of a pregnant woman.[50]

"Gene drive" is a genome editing tool used in which nearly all traits can be passed onto an offspring was first proposed nearly two decades ago.[51] In an effort to reduce spreading of mosquito-borne fever, a team of geneticists developed a genetically modified mosquito using gene drive that could wipe out Malaria.[52] However, these type of experiments may backfire. Scientists, with an aim to control diseases like zika virus and dengue, created genetically modified mosquitos containing a dominant lethal gene.[53] The idea was to kill the offspring using the "transgenic" mosquito and reduce the population. But instead, the offspring inherited the lethal gene, making them even stronger.[54] The offspring wasn't meant to carry the virus at the first place, and according to previous study, transgene is lost overtime from population.[55] An updated postscript published in Nature clarify that the experiment was actually monitored by the National Technical Commission of BioSafety in Brazil.[56] Nevertheless, this type of unexpected outcome is extremely disturbing. Many researchers suggest creating a generalised framework is mandatory in order to reduce any potential outcomes that would not be controllable. As you can visualise, controlled research and experiment in the treatment of genetic conditions have been the ultimate focus of CRISPR, until the end of 2018, when a scientist from China shocked the world with his announcement.[57]

The Chinese researcher *He* altered the gene of an unborn baby at the embryonic stage. The scientist claimed that his focus was to target a particular gene and abridged part of the DNA that caused HIV to be transmitted further. The most shocking part of the announcement was that the twins were born by the time *He* produced his findings, which caught the entire world by storm.[58] After his presentation at the *Genome Editing Summit* in Hong Kong in 2018, *He* claimed that another pregnant woman was already enrolled in his trial. The university under which he conducted his studies claimed that they weren't aware of his activity and the study wasn't peer-reviewed.[59]

Why did a slight change in the embryo caused such a stir? The problem is with the outcome of these clinical trials. Firstly, this experiment is uncontrolled. There is neither an ethical framework nor a specific way of predicting side-effects of this process. For instance, changing a particular set of DNAs might result in developing an off-target mutation or another unknown uncontrollable disease. Once again, pop culture has demonstrated various ways of predicting the future of *off-target mutations*. We all have read a sci-fi comic or watched a film where humans attain superpowers from such process. It is technically possible to give birth to genetically engineered species by inserting DNA from another species. Even altering and combining DNAs from incompatible species can result in stepping into dangerous territory. Genome scientists believe that off-target mutation represents one of the biggest challenges for CRISPR.[60] The problem isn't the alteration of one DNA strand – the results could be passed onto the following generation, and beyond. Therefore, if someone opt-in for genetic modifications, that person may be passing on unknown characteristics, good or bad, to hundreds of thousands of people down the line without understanding the consequences. After the story of this scientist broke, ethics committees went through a cold uproar to ban this immediately. The experiment was deemed incredibly risky and therefore prompted a highly divisive debate in the scientific community.[61][62][63] Another group of scientists from China heavily criticised his work and explained that there wasn't any justification as to why he would perform such an experiment.[64] In their journal article, they concluded:

"We strongly condemn their actions as extremely irresponsible, both scientifically and ethically. We strongly urge the international community of scientists and regulators to initiate a comprehensive discussion as soon as possible to develop the criteria and standards for genome editing in the human germline for reproductive purposes. After reaching a clear consensus, clear and strict laws need to be passed, implemented, and enforced at an international level."
– Wang and Yang (2019)

It is anticipated that these children born with modified genes would be supervised for the next 10-18 years to ensure they do not possess any other type of unknown diseases.[65] In other words, these girls would be lab rats. Without an appropriate framework, and appropriate involvement from the authorities, this type of work possesses an immense risk. Germline editing in human DNA is an atypical idea that requires further research to circumvent collateral damage.

Reduced Sufferings

Let's consider the balance among financial, ethical, and scientific issues to take a risk towards rewriting embryos. Unlike Asthma, a non-threatening inherent condition, several rare diseases can risk the lives of the future generation when passed down the genetic chain. These diseases include Parkinson's, Huntington's disease, and several forms of cancers such as skin or colon cancer.[66] *Pre-screening technology* allows pregnant women to discover any diseases that their children may inherit. There are cases where the brightest minds suffered from the impact of genetic disorders.[67] In such cases, some people might consider terminating a pregnancy, knowing the fact that the unborn child's entire life would be difficult. Pregnancy termination or "abortion" is still an ethical debate in many countries, including the United States.[68] Will gene therapy make any difference? Should parents consider signing up if it allows them to change certain features and stop an incredibly rare, potentially fatal condition to be inherited? A poll conducted in 2018 on American residents shows support towards germline editing to cure diseases.[69] A researcher from the *New York University School of Medicine* believes germline editing in humans has a place in medicine as long as a proper framework for ethical standards is in place.[70] He also explains:

"Germline editing holds out the promise of eliminating various genetic scourges from families and, ultimately, the human species for all time. Not all forms of enhancement are prima facie wrong. Bestowing improved immunity or disease resistance on future offspring seems noble, not unethical. Effective and safe germline editing has a place in medicine. The fact that not every possible genetic alteration is morally defensible does not mean that none are."
- Caplan (2017)

Public dialogue is highly critical to shape opinion with regards to changing DNA, mainly if that eradicate diseases. Parents who went through pre-screening and detected any form of life-threatening diseases expressed that they would preferably opt-in to stop their children from suffering.

On the other hand, the same technology can be used to alter the characteristics of a baby. In other words, handmade in the hands of humans, defying the nature, challenging the rules of God. Some argue that scientists are playing God by altering embryonic genetic information, which might exert long-lasting severe inherent defects or other unknown penalties. Almost certainly speaking, even if drug administrators around the world approve this process of genetically engineered alterations, it would be an incredibly luxurious, risky experiment, and conceivably available to the 0.1% population who would be able to afford it.[71] For a businessman and investor, it seems like an exciting venture to be involved with, however, would people be comfortable knowing that their parents altered the way, how they were initially supposed to look? Would the next generation be comfortable knowing that their genes were altered during the childhood without consent? It's debatable. We are still in the era of transitioning into a world where humans are scientifically proven to possess more than two types of genders – therefore, women aren't always supposed to be attracted to men. Provided the fact that the concept of animal rights is highly controversial, editing DNA without the consent would be an important topic of debate in the world of ethics and morality. However, if that procedure prevents a child from suffering a lethal disease, maybe, it's understandable. As technology progresses, there would be better ways of predicting redundant outcomes. In a paper published in 2018, researchers advised that these *off-target mutations* could be predicted using a deep neural network.[72]

Bread on Back Garden

Using CRISPR, scientists have developed a new breed of species with never-before-seen characteristics.[73] Agricultural researchers have developed engineered plants by inserting DNA into the host species. A team from the University of Minnesota have already received a patent for a program where the DNA of a plant can be altered at the embryonic stage, where the organism is generated from the cells in which the DNA is edited.[74] If these plants aren't grown naturally, and instead genetically engineered, that may also increase risks towards catching diseases that we wouldn't normally expect. There aren't many cases of these incidents. However, genetically modified food will no doubt have a significant impact on our daily lives. The proof is already here; lab-grown protein has shaken the world like a milkshake in a blender. No pun intended.

Until now, plants have been modified to increase their growth and longevity.[75] Besides, scientists have given birth to modified salmon and decreased the time period for growth to their regular adult size. Moreover, plant seeds have been engineered to produce healthy oils. Genetically modified sugar and vegetable oil are being tested as well. CRISPRd mushroom has been approved by the FDA – their modification plan does not include insertion of *foreign DNA*.[76] Modified wheat has also been developed, which would not trigger IBS, a common disease around the world. No more gluten-free expensive pasta – gastritis or IBS patients would finally be allowed to visit the regular pasta aisle.

Similar to humans, altering DNA sequence in plants can result in unknown consequences, as there isn't any way of predicting how the cells would mutate. Can we grow pizza on trees? Maybe we could grow edible loaves of bread on the back garden? Since it's a possibility, researchers have diversified into many areas. Scientists believe that CRISPR-Cas9 provides an opportunity to enhance crop species.[77] Genetic mutation may also result in many other side effects, but that doesn't stop humans from having superpowers of making edible meat in the lab. On the contrary, we have the power to develop new species of foods that have never been tested before. For instance, *Memphis Meat*, a startup backed by Richard Branson and Bill Gates is developing CRISPRd chicken and beef.[78]

While some companies are focused on eliminating diseases, CRISPR has allowed alteration of DNA in animals to develop organ tissues that are compatible with humans. In a recent breakthrough discovery, a group of researchers have been able to produce human-compatible organs in pigs. While the application of such discovery is highly debatable, this would reduce the possibility of organ failure due to 'lack of organ availability'. Until now, humans have donated their organs for the betterment of society. People can donate their second kidney to their loved ones. In the UK, residents can opt-in for organ donation in the event of death; one or more healthy organs would be donated to those in need. If you were in a position to search for a healthy organ, would you feel comfortable to accept an organ generated from an animal?

So, what does this mean for the future of genetic engineering? Based on the controversial testing and its potential, it can be predicted that the CRISPR-Cas9 is heading towards a pathway where geneticists will be able to raise billions by merely proposing an idea to edit genomes of a new-born plant, or a baby. Japan, one of the first countries, has proposed draft guidelines to allow gene-editing scientist to edit DNAs in human embryos in a controlled manner, shedding a positive light towards such research.[79] British company *Horizon Discovery* has already attained a license to develop *base-editing*, a modified version of CRISPR-Cas9.[80] Another team of international scientists have discovered Cas3, a modified version that is capable of precisely cutting longer strands of DNA and cure diseases such as hepatitis.[81] Furthermore, the University of Pennsylvania has very recently received permission to conduct a controlled human CRISPR experiment.[82] Humans are a few years away from altering the DNA of their children on a routine basis.

The stakes are undoubtedly high because, for the first time in history, humans have the aptitude to wipe out diseases like COVID-19, cancer and HIV from the books. CRISPR, if used ethically, may result in becoming one of the most influential technologies in the history of humankind. However, it doesn't end here. DNA can be used in many other ways in many industries, such as using it as a replacement for hard drives and memory cards. How far would the concept of reading and writing DNA commercially progress over the next decade?

Synthetic Biology.

DNA Replaces Hard Drives

CRISPR made it easier for a scientist to edit DNA strands, but what are the other applications? DNAs can store a significant amount of data, which includes physical and biological characteristics, information on whether we are a night owl or an early riser, what type of food we can consume, as well as evidence related to any hereditary diseases our future generation might inherit. All that information can be extracted from a few tiny cells. Given that a single cell can store such humongous amount of information, is it possible to reengineer the design principles to allow storage of external data?

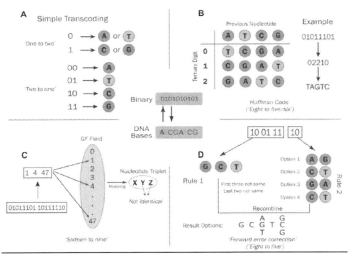

9.5 – Binary transcoding methods used in DNA-based data storage schemes. © Ping et al. (2019)/Oxford University Press.

The underlying scope of outcome for genetic engineering doesn't end in the medical sector. DNA stores valuable evidence of our ancestors – almost everything we are, have been encoded into our DNA. Unlike binary, DNA stores data in ATCG sequence. Considering the size, DNA can store a colossal amount of information.[1] In fact, a single strand could store up to 455 exabytes of data.[8 below] That's roughly 455,000,000 TB data or capacity for 960 billion minutes of 4K ultra HD video at a molecular level.[2]

We are now producing an explosive amount of data every day. Large technology companies like Google and Facebook have humongous servers to store the data. The more people search on Google, the more data is required to be processed and stored on their servers. At one point, we are bound to run out of physical space, which is why the scientists would be required to store data in molecules.[3] Even though the size of data storage devices is decreasing every year, we would still need to find enough space to store all these data on the planet.

DNA provides that long-term solution in comparison to microSD or Huawei's Nano Memory.[4] Scientists are currently looking towards storing data inside molecules and utilise it to store data commercially. DNA molecules can not only store heaps of data but also provides a secure storage facility. According to researchers, DNAs can preserve data for up to ten thousand years or more.[5]

As a proof of concept, a team of researchers from the Chinese University in Hong Kong in 2014 successfully encoded an image size of 436 bytes in a DNA and showed a *high-error tolerating module* from decoding.[6] In 2016, by manipulating biological DNA, scientists from the University of Cambridge encoded binary data onto DNA and showed that data could undergo controlled changes to enable storage of multiple layers of data in a single template.[7] They explain:

"In this manuscript we demonstrate the potential of chemical reactions to manipulate digital information encoded within DNA. While our work focused on storing multiple data sets in one library—a strategy reminiscent of steganography—it is noteworthy that multilayer encoding represents an enticing approach to maximize storage capabilities of DNA templates." – Mayer et al. (2016)

In 2019, another group of scientists from the US demonstrated how they encoded 1TB data on a single-spot of DNA, which can then be physically stored on a dehydrated spot of a glass plate to increase longevity.[8] That's the capacity of the largest microSD card available in the market in 2019. It happened under a controlled environment in a lab, and therefore not commercially viable yet. More companies like Microsoft need to be involved in a similar category of research for DNA data storage process to be commercialised.

The team then successfully retrieved the physical DNA using digital microfluidics (DMF) and retrieved almost all the data stored. They explain how 50TB of data could be stored per glass plate:

"We present a DNA data storage architecture composed of many dehydrated DNA spots on a glass cartridge, shown in Fig. 2. The spots are physically isolated and can be retrieved using digital microfluidics (DMF) without contamination. The cartridges could be further organized in a deck and accessed using a multidimensional addressing system, like other scalable storage solutions such as tape or hard drives. Individual cartridges could store up to 50 TB of data using today's DNA storage techniques. We report successful storage, retrieval, and decoding of DNA files of various sizes using this system..."

9.6 – Storing physically isolated spots of dehydrated DNA on glass cartridges (Fig.2 above) © Newman et al. 2019.

On that note, what other fantasy could become a reality? At this moment, synthetic DNA carrying external data cannot be injected into humans. Logically, some might argue that injecting synthetic DNA carrying exabytes of data into humans would make them a walking target. Although, the reality is a bit contrasting. It's like this – we all have some form of sensitive and secret data that we store somewhere, e.g. password for accessing a bitcoin wallet. If we have a USB with confidential files, we aren't going to label and show it off to the public. If it's discrete, it would be difficult to identify. It's the same with archiving data on DNA. This process would allow sensitive material to be stored securely. However, the user carrying synthetic DNA would be a high-value asset. In reality, the DNAs can be stored for hundreds of years in frozen chambers.[9] We won't probably live to see data archives being injected in our blood. To be honest, we are getting a little ahead of ourselves. Nevertheless, we will witness the growth of companies offering hardware for encoding and decoding DNA data. By the end of 2029, the process of encoding would become much faster. We would have DNA data storage devices that could capacitate petabytes and cost a fraction. Researchers from Oxford believe that DNA provides a promising approach in long-term digital storage.[10]

"Imperfect as it is, it may become the ultimate solution to the current data storage market for long-term archiving. We are also excited to see that multidisciplinary research companies have already joined this revolution to make DNA-based archiving commercially viable."
– Ping et al. (2019)

9.7 – SpaceX Starship, formerly BFR. It will be used to transport payloads to Mars. DNA data storage will be crucial for such an interplanetary mission.

Image via SpaceX.

Arch Mission Foundation (AMF) is a non-profit that is working towards creating multiple **backup** *copies of the planet* **Earth***, humanity and the information around the* **solar system.**[11] *University of Washington,* **Microsoft** *and AMF are working together to create* **a molecular collection** *of the Lunar Library by* **storing** *the data in the* **DNA.**[6 *above]*[12]

9.8 – The data collected from Apollo missions is expected to be stored in the DNA. © NASA/Andrew Freeberg.

Synthetic Biology Companies

Synthetic biology is a study of utilising biological information, such as DNA to develop synthetic systems, by applying *computer science and electrical engineering* principles to biology. This study assists in developing reengineered biological systems that exert practical application in manipulating chemicals, developing wearables, produce energy, enhance natural health, safeguard ecology and store data.[13] Hence, the study of synthetic biology has wide-ranging application across various sectors including synthetic fuel, biosynthetic clothing materials, lab operations, developing computer systems, agriculture, long-term data storage and preservation.[14]

A biological DNA stores so much data that it takes over a month to sequence a whole genome code. Although, there are ways using which DNA can be partially analysed. *Low pass sequencing* is such a process, in which scientists run tests through hundreds of markers on parts of DNA to develop an overall blueprint. This sequencing process can not only reveal the biological identity or ancestry but are also essential health data. Recently, scientists have been able to synthesize organic DNA; utilise the basic design principles to create a synthetic version of the same DNA. This synthetic DNA can be modified using CRISPR to remove flawed strands and make it virus resistant. The human genome project took 13 years and over USD 3 billion to develop a synthetic DNA for humans.[15]

Besides, in 2017, scientists from California have claimed to create life using synthetic DNA. They explained that they had created *e-coli bacteria* using a hybrid of synthetic and biological DNA.[16] Although inserting this "near-perfect" synthetic DNA into humans is still at its infancy stage, the possibilities are endless. Some scientists believe that it's possible to create a synthetic version of a person and replicate that DNA by dropping the fragment into a bacterial cell.[17] This DNA can be frozen for long-term storage, which in fact, can be further edited, manipulated and re-engineered to make the "artificial" version.

Currently, thousands of startups are aiding in the expansion of synthetic biology. Valued at USD 7.5 billion, *Moderna Therapeutics* went public in 2018, which is deemed to be the largest biotech IPO to date.[18] The Massachusetts-based firm aims to create injectable synthetic proteins which will help our body to develop its own medicine.[19] Although their research pipeline is considered to be a strong and sustainable one, financial analysts suggest that the company is many years away from actually manufacturing commercial medicine.[20]

Nevertheless, for broader adoption of DNA analysing process, we would need better software that can decode genetic information faster. Some companies are solving this problem. *Genome Compiler* is a software that allows drag and drops user interface to design and assemble DNA.[21] The startup received funding from 3D software giant Autodesk and was later acquired by *Twist Biosciences*. Twist is a public limited company, founded by two geneticists from pharmaceutical giant Agilent Technologies.[22] *Desktop Genetics* is another biotech startup working separately on developing an AI-enabled software that would serve as a turnkey solution for genetic research and business needs of companies which need analysing, designing, synthesizing and managing DNA using CRISPR. [23]

Moreover, it is possible to develop eco-friendly biofuels by altering the DNA in chemical compounds. Scientists have also developed a technology to convert harmful environmental gases into reusable biofuels. *Synthetic Genomics* is working on altering molecular information in chemicals.[24] This company aims to develop genome-driven advanced biofuels. In partnership with ExxonMobil, the company has developed energy-dense *synthetic transportation fuel.* A group of scientists also developed a process where it can genetically modify algae to produce their low-cost biofuel.[25]

> *"As biofuels, they are a perfect substitute for liquid fossil fuels concerning cost, renewability, and environmental concerns...Microalgae are tiny factories and renewable, sustainable and economical sources of biofuels, bioactive medicinal products and food ingredients. Microalgae useful in mitigation of elevated CO2 level and treatment of waste water."*
> *– Khan et al. (2018)*

Image 9.9 (Top) - Melting icebergs as a result of global warming floating in Jokulsarlon glacial lagoon, Iceland © Salajean/Envato. Image 9.10 (Bottom) - Icebergs in Jokulsarlon glacial lagoon. © Ivankmit/Envato.

Lab-grown Food

Just like humans, every type of plant has its unique genetic code embedded in their DNAs and RNAs. Systematic genome editing of plants has allowed scientists to produce meat without the dependency on animals. In general views, cows eat plants and grasses to be healthy and in turn, make a great candidate for our next meaty burger. The meat contains genetic markers from both the animals and plants they consume.

Scientists discovered that the protein found in animals matches the genetic markers of the DNAs found in soy.[26] Did you have soymilk before? Soymilk can be an alternative to dairy due to the similarities of its DNA to animals. With global warming rising beyond an alarming level, scientists needed to discover an alternative to dairy products and meat, that would result in less dependency on animals and natural plants. Farmers are struggling with increasingly warm temperature for the past few decades. Additionally, loss of animal species, water shortage and destruction of plants add to the stockpile of increasing global temperature, which is resulting in annihilation our planet's ecosystem.

To meet these ecological challenges, it is essential to consider cost-effective and artificial ways of producing plants, dairy products and meat. Generally known as "vegan meat", lab-grown meats are an alternative to organic cow or lamb meat.[27] Instead of sacrificing a living being, scientists have analysed the DNAs in plants and animals to develop a process where that same meat can be grown inside a lab. Lab-grown "animal-free" ice cream is also being produced in Canada and US.[28][29] Let's face it –

vegan meat isn't going to reduce global warming dramatically, it's an attempt, and one of the potential factors that could stop the rise in global temperature.

Recent progress in biotech marks another significant milestone for lab-grown food that has already seen its light at the end of the tunnel – a thriving, commercially viable product. Climate change is a serious issue to address at this time, as the world is facing difficulties to control harmful industrial chemical production, including gases such as methane and carbon-di-oxide. In a recent scientific study published by the University of Oxford, it was revealed that vegan milk and meat produces 73% fewer greenhouse gases.[30] It is another crucial reason why several millennials and generation Z are shifting towards "veganism".[31] If you are an athlete, plant-based diet is a perfect choice as researchers have proven its effectiveness. A group of US scientists conducted a 16-week randomised clinical trial and confirmed that plant-based diet yields a number of metabolic benefits.[32] They concluded:

"The quantity and quality of dietary protein, as part of a plant-based diet, are associated with improvements in body weight, body composition, and insulin resistance in overweight individuals. A greater consumption of plant protein, in replacement of animal protein, resulted in decreased fat mass." - Kahleova et. al. (2019)

A number of scientists believe that plant-based diet can help to lead a healthier lifestyle.[33][34][35]

Nonetheless, a long-term impact on climate change may ultimately be different from what previous research implied. The recent study published by LEAP at Oxford Martin School suggests that some lab-grown meat may harm climate change. Using empirical data, researchers substantiated that the impact of artificial meat production would eventually depend on the efficiency of the process, and the level of sustainable energy reached in the long-term.[36]

If you are wondering whether I'm vegan, then disappointingly, I'm not. I do have friends who recently moved to a vegan diet. Also, with that, we are back to ethics and moral enigma of whether animals should be sacrificed for our food. It is and always will be a provocative debate. The fact of the matter is that I'm not here to talk about politics and people's movement towards veganism. I'm here to talk about businesses, their technologies and the science behind their invention. In my opinion, veganism is an excellent attempt to either contribute to the process of reducing greenhouse gas or attain a diet that would help you lead a healthier lifestyle, only if you choose to do so.

Plant-based Meat

In relentless pursuit of scientific discovery, we are discovering better and efficient alternative ways to produce meat and dairy products. Good news for the vegans – many scientists are already commercialising lab-grown meat. *Impossible Foods*, a company that received half a billion-dollar funding from Bill Gates and Google Ventures is now producing plant-based sustainable food.[37] Their motto is artificially producing two of the most consumed products in the world at a lower cost, which would have a positive impact on the environment. *Impossible Foods* is already selling their lab-grown burger, and food critics indicate that they taste precisely like organic meat.[38] How is the company developing a plant-based burger at a low cost?

The idea of the company was to develop a product that would utilise genetic markers of organic plants and yet taste like regular meat. According to Impossible Foods, the key ingredient for their plant-based meat is heme, a molecule that is responsible for providing and enabling the meaty taste. The scientists discovered that heme-containing protein is available from soybeans. However, the extraction of protein from the roots of soybeans is expensive.[39]

The scientists created a process of synthesizing DNA from the soy plants and inject those into yeasts. Fermentation of this yeast allows artificial regeneration of the protein, therefore developing a synthetic DNA which assists in mimicking the taste of organic meat. By using yeast to regenerate DNA of soy plants, the company has reduced its dependence on animals, lands and water.[40] As a result, the entire process produces a fraction of greenhouse gas, in comparison to the data mentioned hereabove. There isn't enough clinical evidence as to whether artificially grown meat has any long-term side effects on human beings. Nevertheless, the aim of the company is noble and surely worth receiving half a billion-dollar funding. Fast-food chain Burger King has already started their trial of vegan burgers, which is expected to be rolled out in many other countries if their trial is deemed successful.

Another plant-based meat company *Beyond Meat* has recently taken over the stock market by storm. On May 3rd

2019, Beyond Meat was listed in NYSE, and immediately after the listing, their share price went up by 160%.[41] The Cali company has a market capitalisation of over USD 7 billion.[42] They are a direct competitor to Impossible Foods, and this listing would provide them with the capital to compete and expand their territories. Beyond Meat offers three different types of product – their famous burger patty, sausage roll and beef crumbles. Beyond meat's products are currently available in many stores and restaurant chains. *Honest Burgers*, located around the UK, offers their special plant-based burger made with Beyond Meat.[43]

Let's not hesitate to say that a vegan diet is more of a lifestyle choice than an actual diet. According to a 2018 survey, there were approximately 3.5 million vegans and vegetarians in the UK – that's a substantial number of people following a special diet on their own.[44] The number has since increased, which led to supermarkets such as Waitrose and Tesco offering a wider variety of vegan products. While meat lovers would argue that being vegan isn't realistic, there is an indirect impact of vegan food on both diet and climate. The company claims that its product utilises 99% less water and 46% less energy in comparison to regular meat.[45] Therefore, it results in a reduction of greenhouse gas emission in comparison to the traditional process. According to the CEO, their vegan meat contains 22 ingredients, which results in imitating the exact taste of real beef.[46] Due to their increasing popularity and significant demand of their shares, Bloomberg analysts said that their IPO is deemed to be one of the biggest "bubbles" since the crash of 2008.[47] The company was initially funded by Bill Gates and few other VCs, while Goldman Sachs joined later in another funding round.

In conclusion, several breakthrough discoveries are expected in the coming decade, including cheaper and faster access to DNA encoding. More startups by 2030 would provide easier access to writing data onto DNA. We have already examined how a pack of DNAs that fits inside a small sugar cube can fit almost the entire library of all the movies that have ever been produced.[48] Currently, it's costly to write data due to the lack of availability of the technology and competitors in the market. As more hardware for encoding and decoding DNAs develop, it will be easier for scientists to store more information at an affordable rate. On the other hand, scientists would start producing more and more plant-based synthetic fruits, meat and other dairy products. While AI transforms businesses, CRISPR is going to have a direct impact on a more personal level.

The growth in genetic engineering isn't going to slow down anytime soon. DIY CRISPR kits are already available on the internet. With the advances in AI-generated *3D modelling of proteins*, it would be easier for scientists to unlock new boundaries. Creating synthetic DNAs to enhance our abilities is now a reality. Hence, we will start to see various phases of clinical trials where humans would carry modified versions of their organic DNAs.[49] It won't be surprising if someone finds their own synthetic version preserved somewhere in a lab.

Just like images or videos, malicious viruses can also be encoded into your DNA. Scientists have recently been able to hack a DNA sequencing software by encoding a virus into DNA strands. During that process, the researchers had remotely taken control by using adversarial synthetic DNA.[50] If getting hacked by DNA sounds frightening, wait until you read what another scientist is trying to achieve.

Enter interspecies *genetic mutation* – a process in which one animal's DNA is inserted in another and mutated in a lab environment. An international team of scientists have reportedly inserted human DNA into a non-human organism. At this incredibly early stage of development, the team has successfully inserted human DNA into a pig's DNA. The cells survived petri dishes and eventually mutated into a hybrid embryo. The scientists believe that this process would eventually allow growing human organs inside a pig, which would be compatible with humans.[51] It sounds extremely weird, and on top of that, there isn't any evidence of whether this cross-genetic mutation would eventually render a human consciousness. Developing appropriate ethical framework has become key to scientific progress if scientists want derive benefits from such experiments. CRISPR is an extremely beneficial technology – we just need to have the right mindset to use it properly.

Exploration.

Everything we have attained until now, is going to assist us in taking the next big leap of humanity, colonisation of the planets, acceleration beyond our scope of purview. Within five years, industry experts plan to have an AI hardware device developed that could possess 10 billion neurons using memristors. The hardware AI has been all smashed together into one nanochip, which is capable of identifying and segregating analogue and digital signals, with integrated neural network. AI can also achieve *hyper-performance* by mimicking our brain's design and being able to work in parallel with other neurosynaptic chips. If the development progresses at this rate, neural simulation technology will accomplish brain-like performance by 2025. Therefore, scientists will be able to create a hardware brain that can work in synchronisation with humans and undertake matrix operations with self-learning capabilities. Using existing neurosynaptic chips by IBM, hypothetically, human-scale simulation would only require 100kW power, i.e. only 0.0025% of the energy needed for the most powerful supercomputer in existence. A fully functioning "Brain in a Box" would shrink this computer into a 2-litre space, requiring only 1kW electricity.

Let's go back to the performance of AlphaZero developed by DeepMind – a simple AI, which was able to learn 3000 years of strategy, in just under a few months. If humans are already on the way to create hardware that could potentially achieve exascale and be able to fit in a box, the AIs will inevitably be able to do much more by 2030. Hardware AIs are already hundreds of times faster than a typical deep neural network. Therefore, these AIs would be able to operate in the unexplored and unchartered territories. If algorithms that rely on traditional microprocessors can learn 500,000 years of strategy and intelligence under just one year, how fast would hardware AI be able to learn? Would it be that difficult for the neural networks to start comprehending belongingness and eventually reach self-actualisation? It sounds like a dire warning for a dystopian future, where artificial intelligence will precipitate a statutory crisis by creating more intelligent beings in comparison to humans. But the denouement is purely dependent on our work, the *homo sapiens*, and whether we are building the right technology that would help "build" the future.

The implementation of artificial intelligence would undeniably assist us with rapidly advancing many other technologies and reduce the timeframe for calculations that would take thousands of years. But we should carefully consider practical and ethical outcomes for every single product that is made with AI. Everything we build with AI helps us to take the next step towards the AGI. Therefore, ethics and morality of the outcome of every AI-enabled product must be meticulously assessed. It is essential to create fully automated manufacturing plants with robot-assembly lines; however, the same concept cannot be used to replace every single human worker on the planet. We need substantial development in the field of BCI, to be able to compete with AGI and mitigate circumstantial challenges.

"A human B/CI system mediated by neuralnanorobotics could empower individuals with instantaneous access to all cumulative human knowledge available in the cloud and significantly improve human learning capacities and intelligence. Further, it might transition immersive virtual and augmented realities to unprecedented levels,

allowing for more meaningful experiences and fuller/richer expression for, and between, users. These enhancements may assist humanity to adapt emergent artificial intelligence systems as human-augmentation technologies, facilitating the mitigation of new challenges to the human species." – Martins et al. (2019)

You must have noted that "Elon Musk" was mentioned eight times throughout the book – which wasn't deliberate. This book isn't a promotion for Tesla or SpaceX. One way or the other, he is involved with scientific progress that will disrupt our lives. Companies like Tesla and SpaceX are widening the horizon of scientific discovery. As SpaceX moves forward with their interplanetary mission to colonise Mars, more technologies will be invented that will aid the next tech evolution. Just like him, scientists and innovators are betting on these emerging technologies because let's admit, future is being built on these ideas.

One of the biggest questions at this point in time is whether AGI is vital for scientific progress. It's yet to be answered. If an AI can already learn so much in a short period, given that the processing power of computation is exponentially accelerating, it wouldn't be long until an AGI performs the necessary calculation to find a reason to exist and eventually decide to preserve itself for an extended period. It wouldn't be difficult for a deep hardware neural network to feel the reason to differentiate themselves as a different 'species' in possession of higher intelligence.

Designer babies, DNA hard drives, synthetic biofuels and plant-based meat are all jaw-dropping outcomes of the science of genome editing. Every single one of these inventions are necessary to travel beyond the stars. But we need to save ourselves first – utilising a technology to help prevent imminent threat makes it plausible, and the society will find more reasons to believe in its future.

We are in desperate need of more companies like Sherlock Biosciences and the type of technology they are developing right now. CRISPR is so versatile that you could literally make red meat without killing a single animal, and also help prevent an imminent pandemic. All of that could happen by using the same technology but different techniques. This process of engineering biology has taken another step due to the outbreak of COVID-19. The outcome of Cepheid, Sherlock and Mammoth's research will prove whether or not CRISPR will sustain the test of time and eventual immunity.

What could conceivably impede the exponential progress? Pandemics. During a crisis like this, leaders need to make the correct decision. Defining the correct *ethical strategy* is becoming blurrier these days. The leaders and policy makers are also at the core of making that decision, because at the end of the day, they are steering the society. Beyond the potential of a technology, is the power of the leaders to steer the countries towards the correct path. We cannot fully utilise the power of a disruptive idea unless we do the right thing with it.

It is evident that the coronavirus has affected the elderly more than any other age group. But that didn't leave the younger and healthier group of people safe. Some of the people may be healthy, but many have ended up in the hospital and could still be carrying the virus. CRISPR could fast-track the process of detection and also help in creating vaccines for future pandemics. But it is our leader's ethical responsibility to deal with this scenario. For instance, when the next pandemic hits, how are the governments going to react? When the anti-viral for COVID-19 is to be released, who is going to receive the first batch of treatment? Who will be prioritised? How long do people need to wait to receive the treatment? What will happen to the third-world countries? Governments around the world are talking about flattening the curve, but that would only be successful if they make the right decision before it all goes out of order. Besides, PHE in the UK discussed "herd immunity", which simply didn't work, and instead, and put millions of lives at risk.

Let's say another pandemic similar to *coronavirus* comes back within this decade. With a CFR rate of 5%, if 80% of the population in the UK alone is affected by that virus, then it will put approximately 2.6 million people at the risk of death. Does this approach mean that the herd immunity could be reached at the risk of 2.6 million people dying? While policymakers could divert all their resources towards NHS, e.g. increasing pays for physicians, or recruiting doctors, the approach of herd immunity does not make any sense given that all the scientific evidence points to the contrary. Before we reach for the stars, we need to save humanity. We need more investment in healthcare – the policymakers could start building emergency care centres and hospitals – recruit more staff for 111 and 999 medical emergency care. An outbreak could comeback anytime, therefore, the government should focus on gathering workforce, instead of piling up weapons for an imminent war. We must take lesson from this appalling pandemic that this was nothing but a war – not against humans – but the brutal side of mother nature.

If we don't invent a universal flu-vaccine before the next pandemic, merely asking people to self-isolate is not going to stop it. It is preposterous to hear that the leaders didn't consider tracing mildly symptomatic cases, while South Korea ran over ten thousand tests every single day. WHO urged the leaders to trace every person affected by the virus.[1][2] *Contact tracing* is deemed substantial, especially when the rate of reproduction for a virus is much higher than the regular flu. While case isolation is mandatory, scientists believe that detecting the virus is important to take control.[3]

> *"We determined conditions in which case isolation, contact tracing, and preventing transmission by contacts who are infected would be sufficient to control a new COVID-19 outbreak in the absence of other control measures. We found that in some plausible scenarios, case isolation alone would be unlikely to control transmission within 3 months...Preventing transmission by tracing and isolating a larger proportion of contacts, thereby decreasing the effective reproduction number, improved the number of scenarios in which control was likely to be achieved." - Hellewell et al. (2020)*

The scientists also emphasise on the rate of infection, and its correlation to the probability of control:

> *"In scenarios in which the reproduction number was 2·5, 15% of transmission occurred before symptom onset, and there was a short delay to isolation, at least 80% of infected contacts needed to be traced and isolated to give a probability of*

control of 90% or more."
- Hellewell et al. (2020)

All the evidence and previous experience from outbreaks such as the bird-flu and SARS tell the story of how increased tracing, quarantine, as well as social distancing, could drastically reduce the rate of reproduction and spread. There are now close to a million undiagnosed, non-symptomatic cases all over the world – we should increase the capacity to run more tests in every country instead of preventing people from calling the emergency helpline. Everything is a lesson for the future. Can you imagine what will happen if a deadlier pathogen comes back?

We need to prepare ourselves for the next bio-threat, and not allow the human body to find a "natural course in due time". Experts emphasised that tracing infections is important and that it's mind-boggling that the leaders think about any alternative approach to this matter. Justifiably, it isn't rational to put more pressure on the national health service. However, that leads to the data being skewed to a greater extent. If the authorities aren't going to trace every single case, then the ratio between the actual number of patients infected versus the reported number of patients will likely be far lower, which will affect policy making. We cannot repeat this in the future.

But that's not the end of it. There are other ways we can hinder the progress rate we have attained. As considered earlier, CRISPR kits are being distributed over to the public for an affordable price. While it is essential for people to learn about new technologies, there are ethical restrictions we need to follow. With the right type of genetic engineering tool at disposal, anyone can re-engineer a genetic code of a virus sample. If a genetic code of a lethal virus is made public, it will be downloaded many times and fall into the hands of the wrong people. Given the cataclysmic situation we are in right now, humanity cannot afford another artificially created outbreak in the coming years. It's an extremely controversial topic to discuss – because there are lots of conspiracy plots about the origins of the novel coronavirus. There are no scientific grounds to that news because they are all a part of performing dirty politics, the "blame game". That does not stop the evident from happening. Coronavirus might not have been a product of a botched genome experiment, but that does not mean another virus won't be. If the process of genome editing is not rigorously controlled and governed by the law, anyone in the near future would be able to decode a genetic code. And if we persist on ignoring the sales of DIY genome editing kits, then the "conspiracy theory" will turn out to be a reality. Someone from one corner of the planet is going to come up with a "home-experiment-gone-wrong" outbreak. Remember, it only takes one person to erroneously develop the next biological weapon. All of this mayhem began from one person, then it affected hundreds, who flew to other countries and affected millions. We need to invest in pandemic containment and expand on the right strategy. COVID-19 isn't the first pandemic, and it sure won't be the last, and off-target mutations might not be the only possible explanation. Are we learning any lesson from this at all? Are we prepared for the next outbreak?

Conclusion.

SPACEX FALCON HEAVY ROCKET BOOSTERS LANDING SIMULTANEOUSLY.

Image 11.1 via SpaceX. Scan the QR code to watch the historic moment.

We reside in a world where algorithm decides your fate. Have you used Tinder before? If anyone met your life-partner using a match-making app, then your fate was determined by an algorithm. And this is just the beginning. We are already living in a world dominated by the power of algorithms, and as these artificial "beings" make jobs redundant, distribution of wealth and power will still be imbalanced, and continue to shift to whoever holds the legal ownership of these algorithms. The description of artificial intelligence and artificial consciousness will, in the fullness of time, become indistinct.

Science isn't good or evil – it's the way we humans exploit and make use of it. If we can already portray a picture of an actual simulation of artificial brain before 2025, then robot receptionists, driverless cars and fully-automated smart cities are just a decade away. The way technologies are speeding up, people born in the next decade would never be able to envision a world without it. It's time we contemplate forming applicable framework to dissuade developers, investors, and researchers from performing moral gymnastics with emerging ideas.

On a positive note, just look around you – did you ever imagine all of these technologies at hand 10 years ago? The internet, social media and mobile phones have completely changed our lives, which was science fiction in the 50s. If you would like to get an idea of how much the telecom sector alone has progressed since then, take some time off this weekend and watch the season 1, episode 6 of The Crown.

In fact, some of the existing technologies were theories in the early 2000. Sending a rocket to space and bringing the same rocket back was a completely hypothetical concept.

Now, SpaceX has performed the full-cycle using AI – sending a rocket to the outer space, and bringing the vessel back to earth to a precise location, and re-used that same booster.[1] In recent years, we have witnessed breakthroughs that were unfathomable – simultaneously bringing back two used *falcon rocket boosters*.[2] The technology is expanding so rapidly that humans are anticipated to colonise other planets of the solar system by 2030. Exponential progress is not just fantasy; it is a part of our destiny.

Every day new ideas are coming up that might become the next great revolution. These impressive concepts are not only shifting perspective towards a disruptive business idea, but also our potential future lives. However, there is a limit to everything, therefore, to survive as human species and to protect the future of the next generation, moral codes and ethical framework is an obligation for us. Over the next decade, as more researchers corroborate ongoing developments, humans will have a better understanding with regards to the impact of the technologies that are discussed in this book. These technologies are potentially explosive bets to make for investors. Over the next decade, entrepreneurship will be influenced by the birth of even more appealing ideas. Emerging technologies are destined to change the world of business.

We are reaching the limits to how much power can be packed into a mobile phone using traditional computing systems. Therefore, the neuromorphic architecture and memristors are going to replace microprocessors that will be embedded in mobile phones. Carbon nanotubes will replace silicon. Our phones will not need any algorithm to be intelligent, because the hardware itself will be capable of learning everything about us. We are also reaching a threshold to how much data can be packed in a storage device. Hence, synthetic biology will be the next scientific pursuit for us to start storing long-term data. The cost of DNA analysis has been steadily going down for the past 20 years. Genetic profile decoding or "reading" costs a fraction of what it used to 19 years ago. The cost of writing onto synthetic DNA will go down significantly over the next decade.

From 5-inch floppy disks for 1MB data, we will witness startups bringing hardware and software that can pack tens of thousands of terabytes of data with the digital memory using synthetic DNA. By the end of this decade, we may start to use synthetic DNA as a part of our personal computers. It could also assist us in interplanetary travel. Astronauts will need to carry a significant amount of data to and from the earth once we start colonising Mars and other planets in the solar system. We will use DNA for data storage and archiving, and eventually transport them to outer-terrestrial colonies.

Creating designer babies is a matter of ethical issue; although, advances in altering genome using CRISPR could completely knockout inherited diseases from the children that are yet to be born. More scientific research is required to reduce off-target mutations and side effects that could cause more trouble than expected. One thing is guaranteed, that this next decade, will undoubtedly be the era for building the foundation for the next century – whether it's a revolution in personal computing or climate change. We need ideas that would benefit humanity, visions that can benefit the future, such as discovering a way to store all the valuable intelligence in DNA, and we're talking about almost everything we know. This could include copies of the knowledge that humanity has gathered over thousands of years so that it can be passed on from generation to generation.

Furthermore, the real-world application of disruptive technologies such as artificial intelligence to process data is also vital. Before we colonise other planets, we must learn to deal with pandemics. Gates recently posted a new blog explaining why COVID-19 a significant threat and a "once-in-a-century pathogen".[3] He explains the importance of making further considerable systematic changes, including disease surveillance, application of machine learning in the detection of diseases and international collaboration in data sharing. Scientists and researchers also believe that sharing experiences is critical for learning about such novel pathogens and that more investment is required for such purposes.[4] The governments, NGOs and the private sector need to work together in synchronisation to help prevent future pandemics. Blockchain technology will be instrumental in creating a global platform where the researchers could share genetic material and clinical data. Organisations such as GLOPID-R is allowing such collaboration. Elsevier has opened a dedicated, free global *coronavirus information centre* for efficient sharing of clinical research among scientists and those who are interested in reading the recent findings.[5]

New technologies can aid in developing such platforms for secure and private data sharing. Having a blockchain-based global platform for research collaboration would allow scientists, researchers, governments and corporations around the world to collaborate and share data effectively. Blockchain technology allows the data to be shared globally in a matter of seconds and also provides the security required for sharing genetic data. Using an access key, various types of users could share their genetic data for them to be used by scientists and researchers to understand more about these pathogens.

If such a platform is made open to patients around the world, they can confidentially share their data with the research organisations and have the stamp of safety from blockchain that will allow untampered genetic data storage. Controlling uncertainty during a pandemic will be much easier by the widespread application of technologies available to us. Our research work at Imperial in 2020 will focus on comprehending and designing a procedure that allow clinicians, researchers, and general users to collaboratively share their data for accelerated diagnosis and prevention of infectious disease. The outcome of the research will be published in a few months.

This book does not discuss other technologies that are at the cusp of a revolution – quantum computing, quantum entanglement, cryogenics, interplanetary travel, nanotechnology, colonisation of the solar system and so on. This is a non-exhaustive list of some astounding technologies that are on the verge of discoveries. These ideas won't affect consumer lives over the next decade; however, we will witness some breakthrough use cases. By 2040, more science fictions are going to become a reality and eventually be a part of our lives. The path to a scientific invention is incredibly messy and experimental. If a positive outcome is achieved and millions of lives are made better by the outcome of a product, it's guaranteed to have a long-lasting positive impact. By then, we will be better prepared for a pandemic, because the technology will allow us to speed up many intricate procedures.

We can't label these technologies and concepts as gimmicks. In perpetual reality, these are well-thought-out ideas that are going to alter the appearance of our society. Existing businesses will continue to undertake model transformation, by speedily progressing in the understanding of how new technologies can enhance an idea. Therefore, decisions made by all of us – collectively the society is going to have a contribution towards the lives of the next generation. Any dystopian outcome depends on how the technologies are applied and who are funding these companies. Whether as a potential entrepreneur or investor, it is ultimately up to us to determine what steps to take. Before exploiting the power of these emerging technologies, humans must consider moral standards and decide on what to pursue. Unless ethical boundaries are painstakingly redefined, it's hard to predict what catastrophic event is waiting for us in the imminent future. Ultimately, the post-singularity phase will result in many innovators to take a step back and re-think their strategies, with regards to their aim, and collateral damages from their innovation. Achieving singularity and its remanence of cataclysmic events might assist in advancing towards a deliverance. Nonetheless, one idea is guaranteed, that over the next century, humans are foreordained to share automated computational intelligence.

Abbreviations.

ALU – Arithmetic Logic Unit

AMF – Arch Mission Foundation

ATGC – Adenine, Thymine, Cytosine, Guanine

AV – Autonomous Vehicle

AVR – Active Virtual Reality

B2C – Business to Consumer

BCI – Brain Computing Interface

BMI – Brain Machine Interface

CAPTCHA – Completely Automated Public Turing test to tell Computers and Humans Apart

CFR – Case Fatality Rate

CNN – Convolutional Neural Network

CPU – Central Processing Unit

CRI – Clinical Research and Innovation

CRISPR – Clustered Regularly Interspaced Short Palindromic Repeats

CAS9 or CAS13 – Cascade 9 or Cascade 13

DARPA – Defense Advanced Research Project Agency

DLR – Docklands Light Railway

DMF – Digital Microfluidics

DNA – Deoxyribonucleic acid

DVS – Dynamic Vision Sensor

Eden – Energy Efficient Deep Neuromorphic Network

EEG – Electroencephalography

EV – Electric Vehicle

FANG – Facebook, Amazon, Netflix, Google

FDA – Federal Drug Administration

FLOPS – Floating Point Operations Per Second

FOV – Field of View

FPS – Framerate Per Second

FSD – Full Self Driving

GAN – General Adversarial Network

GHz – Gigahertz

GPU – Graphics Processing Unit

HIV – Human Immunodeficiency Virus

HMD – Head Mounted Display

IoT – Internet of Things

IPO – Initial Public Offering

JAXA – Japan Aerospace Exploration Agency

KWH – Kilo Watt Hour

LIDAR – Light Detection and Ranging

MEA – Microelectrode Array

MERS – Middle Eastern Respiratory Syndrome

MHz – Megahertz

GHz – Gigahertz

GLOPID-R – Global Research Collaboration For Infectious
Disease Preparedness

MLA – Machine Learning Algorithm

NASA – National Aeronautics and Space Administration

NFC – Near Field Communication

NHS – National Health Service

NGO – Non-Government Organisation

NLP – Natural language Processing

NYSE – New York Stock Exchange

OPEC – Organization of the Petroleum Exporting
Countries

PB – Petabyte

PHEV – Plugin Hybrid Electric Vehicle

PVR – Passive Virtual Reality

RAM – Random Access Memory

RNN – Recurrent Neural Network

SARS – Server Acute Respiratory Syndrome

SHERLOCK - Specific High Sensitivity Enzymatic Reporter unlocking

SUV – Sports Utility Vehicle

SyNAPSE – Systems of Neuromorphic Adaptive Plastic Scalable Electronics

TB – Terabyte

TOPS – Trillion Operations Per Second

TTS – Text to Speech

VC – Venture Capital

YOLO – You Only Look Once

Index.

Table of Figures.

5.3 Wikimedia. (2017) 京コンピュータ (32588659510).jpg. Available: https://commons.wikimedia.org/wiki/File:%E4%BA%AC%E3%82%B3% E3%83%B3%E3%83%94%E3%83%A5%E3%83%BC%E3%82%BF_(325 88659510)jpg. Last accessed 4 February 2019. licensed under the Creative Commons Attribution 2.0 Generic (CC BY 2.0).

6.1 IBM Research. (2016) *IBM Neurosynaptic System (1)*. Available: https://www.flickr.com/photos/ibm_research_zurich/26101819075/in/ph otolist-Vets97-xc7yzG-wwCtkd-FLwDrn-ERh5j4. Last accessed 2 June 2019. Licensed under Creative Commons Attribution-NoDerivs 2.0 Generic (CC BY-ND 2.0).

7.1 Quartz. (2019) *The world, s famous supercomputer by year.* Available: https://s3.us-east-1.amazonaws.com/qz-production-atlas-assets/charts/atlas_SJw9IPFe7@2x.png. Last accessed 3 September 2019.

8.1 Musk, E. and Neuralink (2019) An integrated brain-machine interface platform with thousands of channels. *bioRxiv.* 703801; doi: https://doi.org/10.1101/703801. Licensed under Creative Commons Attribution-NoDerivs International (CC BY-ND 4.0).

8.2 Musk, E. and Neuralink (2019) An integrated brain-machine interface platform with thousands of channels. *bioRxiv.* 703801; doi: https://doi.org/10.1101/703801. Licensed under Creative Commons Attribution-NoDerivs International (CC BY-ND 4.0).

9.2 Jussi Puikkonen/KNAW. (2016) *Jennifer Doudna.* Available: https://www.flickr.com/photos/79173061@N08/26658739920. Last accessed 2 September 2019. Licensed under the Creative Commons Attribution 2.0 Generic (CC BY 2.0).

9.5 Ping, Z., Ma, D., Huang, X., Chen, S., Liu, L., Guo, F., Zhu, S., Shen, Y. (2019) Carbon-based archiving: current progress and future prospects of DNA-based data storage. *Gigascience.* 8 (6), giz075. DOI: 10.1093/gigascience/giz075. Licensed under Creative Commons Attribution 4.0 International (CC BY 4.0).

9.6 Newman, S., Stephenson, A. P., Willsey, M., Nguyen, B. H., Takahashi, C. N., Strauss, K. & Ceze, L. (2019) High density DNA data storage library via dehydration with digital microfluidic retrieval. *Nature Communications.* 10 (1076). Doi: https://doi.org/10.1038/s41467-019-09517-y. Licensed under Creative Commons Attribution 4.0 International (CC BY 4.0).

9.8 Freeberg, A. and NASA/GSFC (2009) *The Moon - Resources for Finding High-Res Stills.* Available: http://svs.gsfc.nasa.gov/10405. Last accessed 2 September 2019.

Bibliography.

CHAPTER 1

[1] Brown, M. (2019) *Elon Musk Smokes Weed and Talks Cybernetic AI. Collectives on Joe Rogan.* Available: https://www.inverse.com/article/48756-elon-musk-smokes-weed-and-talks-cybernetic-a-i-collectives-on-joe-rogan. Last accessed 4 July 2019.

[2] Revell, T. (2017) *Amputees control virtual prosthetic arm using nerve signals Read more: https://www.newscientist.com/article/2120461-amputees-control-virtual-prosthetic-arm-using-nerve-signals/#ixzz5yrLqx325.* Available: https://www.newscientist.com/article/2120461-amputees-control-virtual-prosthetic-arm-using-nerve-signals/. Last accessed 12 July 2019.

[3] Edwards, J. (2003). Building the Great Pyramid: Probable Construction Methods Employed at Giza. *Technology and Culture.* 44(2). 340-354.

[4] Brown, M. (2019) *SpaceX Has a Bold Timeline for Getting to Mars and Starting a Colony.* Available: Revell, T. (2017) Amputees control virtual prosthetic arm using nerve signals Read more: https://www.newscientist.com/article/2120461-amputees-control-virtual-prosthetic-arm-using-nerve-signals/#ixzz. Last accessed 4 August 2019.

[5] Airbus SAS (2018) *Ultra Long Range A350 XWB goes the distance.* Available: https://www.airbus.com/newsroom/news/en/2018/09/ultra-long-range-a350-xwb-goes-the-distance.html. Last accessed 4 August 2019.

[6] BBC. (2019) *Boeing 737 Max: What went wrong?* Available: https://www.bbc.com/news/world-africa-47553174. Last accessed 3 August 2019.

[7] Deloitte (2017) *Using Blockchain & Internet-of-Things in supply chain traceability.* USA: Deloitte US.

[8] Galambos, P., Imre, P., J. Rudas, I. (2014) Merged Physical and Virtual Reality in Collaborative Virtual Workspaces: the VirCA Approach. *Institute for Computer Science and Control, Hungarian Academy of Sciences Kende.* 13-17.

[9] Simon, M. (2018) *Lab-Grown Meat Is Coming, Whether You Like It or Not.* Available: https://www.wired.com/story/lab-grown-meat/. Last accessed 3 August 2019.

[10] Li Da Xu, Eric L. Xu and Ling Li. (2018) Industry 4.0: state of the art and future trends. *International Journal of Production Research*. 56, 2941-2962.

[11] Parmar, A. (2017). *Tanmay Bakshi | Interview at GOOGLE | 13 year old boy*. Available: https://www.youtube.com/watch?v=ZoNNjwkLTP4. Last accessed 1 November 2019.

[12] Drake, D. (2015) *6 Start-up Exit Strategies for Investors*. Available: https://www.huffpost.com/entry/six-startup-exit-strategies_b_8254780?guce_referrer=aHR0cHM6Ly93d3cuZ29vZ2xlLm NvLnVrLw&guce_referrer_sig=AQAAAKM7ksIdlaCfYrdeuA4AGR7jNusH J_9HhP79eF2-Ajp-DCjMseGx5ZwFhCMn. Last accessed 4 August 2019.

[13] Streitfeld, D. (2018) *Amazon Hits $1,000,000,000,000 in Value, Following Apple*. Available: https://www.nytimes.com/2018/09/04/technology/amazon-stock-price-1-trillion-value.html. Last accessed 15 August 2019.

[14] Salinas, S. (2018) *A year ago the FAANG stocks were a hot buy — here's where they stand heading into 2019*. Available: https://www.cnbc.com/2018/12/31/faang-stocks-2018-performance.html. Last accessed 21 August 2019.

[15] Wharton School of the University of Pennsylvania. (2012) *Investor Sentiment and Stock Prices: Explaining the Ups and Downs*. Available: https://knowledge.wharton.upenn.edu/article/investor-sentiment-and-stock-prices-explaining-the-ups-and-downs/. Last accessed 29 August 2019.

[16] Lee, X. E. (2018) *No profit? No problem. Investors keep snapping up loss-making companies*. Available: https://www.cnbc.com/2018/08/29/no-profits-no-problem-the-economy-has-a-growing-appetite-for-unprofitable-companies.html. Last accessed 4 August 2019.

CHAPTER 2

[1] Mobile Year Zero. (2019) *Ivan Sutherland Virtual Reality in the 1960s*. [Online Video]. 28 September 2015. Available: https://www.youtube.com/watch?v=Hp7YgZAHLos. [Accessed: 4 June 2019].

[2] VRHappening. (2015) Available: http://www.vrhappening.com/wp-content/uploads/2015/11/US3050870-2.png. Last accessed 4 April 2019.

[3] Beavis, G. (2018) *I just watched Avengers: Infinity War in 4DX and I got punched in the head...twice*. Available: https://www.techradar.com/news/i-just-watched-avengers-infinity-war-in-4dx-and-i-have-the-bruises-to-prove-it. Last accessed 8 April 2019.

[4] Brockwell, H. (2016) *Forgotten genius: the man who made a working VR machine in 1957*. Available: https://www.techradar.com/news/wearables/forgotten-genius-the-

man-who-made-a-working-vr-machine-in-1957-1318253/2. Last accessed 4 April 2019.

[5] BBC. (2018) *The visionary behind Virtual Reality: Jaron Lanier - BBC Ideas- BBC Ideas.* Available: https://www.youtube.com/watch?v=2oNQK52Va3c. Last accessed 5 April 2019.

[6] Rothman, M. (1993) *Disney's Virtual World puts a new spin on VR.* Available: https://variety.com/1993/biz/news/disney-s-virtual-world-puts-new-spin-on-vr-108733/. Last accessed 1 August 2019.

[7] Virtual Reality Society. (2017) *The Unreleased Sega VR Headset – So Much Effort Squandered.* Available: https://www.vrs.org.uk/unreleased-sega-vr-headset-much-effort-squandered/. Last accessed 6 April 2019.

[8] Gibbs, S. (2015) *Google Maps: a decade of transforming the mapping landscape.* Available: https://www.theguardian.com/technology/2015/feb/08/google-maps-10-anniversary-iphone-android-street-view. Last accessed 5 March 2019.

[9] O'Kane, S. and Statt, N. (2017) *This is Google Jump's next-generation VR camera rig.* Available: https://www.theverge.com/circuitbreaker/2017/4/24/15405540/yi-technology-halo-360-vr-google-jump-start-camera. Last accessed 5 March 2019.

[10] Chang, L. (2017) *Google has shipped 10 million Cardboard VR headsets since launch in 2014.* Available: https://www.digitaltrends.com/virtual-reality/google-cardboard-10-million/. Last accessed 5 March 2019.

[11] Heath, A and Shead, S. (2017) *Has Mark Zuckerberg's $2 Billion Bet on Oculus Paid Off?* Available: https://www.inc.com/business-insider/mark-zuckerberg-facebook-2-billion-deal-oculus-controversy-palmer-luckey.html. Last accessed 5 March 2019.

[12] Nafarrete, J. (2017) *Google Buying HTC's Pixel Team for $1.1 Billion.* Available: https://vrscout.com/news/google-acquires-htc-smartphone-1-billion/. Last accessed 6 March 2019.

[13] Meyer. D. (2017) *This Secretive Augmented Reality Firm Just Raised Another $502 Million.* Available: https://fortune.com/2017/10/18/magic-leap-502-million-google-alibaba/. Last accessed 6 March 2019.

[14] IamVR Official. (2019) Whale Surprise Jumps into a Gym in Mixed Reality (Exciting) by Magic Leap. [Online Video]. 4 May 2019. Available: https://www.youtube.com/watch?v=LM0T6hLH15k. [Accessed: 16 June 2019].

[15] Yang, P. (2016) *The Untold Story of Magic Leap, the World's Most Secretive Startup.* Available: https://www.wired.com/2016/04/magic-leap-vr/. Last accessed 2 March 2019.

[16] PlayStation. (2017) *PlayStation VR: The Ultimate FAQ.* Available: https://blog.us.playstation.com/2017/10/02/playstation-vr-the-ultimate-faq/. Last accessed 15 March 2019.

[17] Z CAM. (n.d.) *Z CAM launches new professional stereoscopic VR camera – Z CAM V1.* Available: http://www.z-cam.com/z-cam-launches-new-professional-stereoscopic-vr-camera-z-cam-v1/. Last accessed 23 June 2019.

[18] The Drum. (2017) *Netflix, Ikea, Coca-Cola, Burger King and more: 2017's top creative PR stunts.* Available: https://www.thedrum.com/news/2017/09/08/netflix-ikea-coca-cola-burger-king-and-more-2017s-top-creative-pr-stunts. Last accessed 6 March 2019.

[19] Tan, E. & Page, J. (2017) *Audi rolls out global VR experience to get people back into the showroom.* Available: https://www.campaignlive.co.uk/article/audi-rolls-global-vr-experience-people-back-showroom/1441935. Last accessed 6 March 2019.

[20] S. Elbamby, M., Perfecto, C., Bennis, M., Doppler, K. (2018) Towards Low-Latency and Ultra-Reliable Virtual Reality. *Centre for Wireless Communications.*

[21] Reed, C. (2018) *7 Things You Can Do to Overcome VR Motion Sickness.* Available: https://uploadvr.com/7-ways-overcome-vr-motion-sickness/. Last accessed 2 March 2019.

[22] Scott. H. (2019) *The Best PS4 Deals on September 2019.* Available: https://www.tomsguide.com/us/best-ps4-deals,news-28637.html. Last accessed 6 September 2019.

[23] Greenwald, W. (2019) *The Best VR (Virtual Reality) Headsets for 2019.* Available: https://uk.pcmag.com/virtual-reality/75926/the-best-vr-virtual-reality-headsets. Last accessed 25 September 2019.

[24] Vive. (n.d.) *VIVE Pro Full Kit | The professional-grade VR headset.* Available: https://www.vive.com/uk/product/vive-pro-full-kit/?gclid=EAIaIQobChMIl9a3iJDd4wIVSLTtCh1-zAMgEAQYASABEgLeEvD_BwE. Last accessed 6 September 2019.

[25] Jay. (2016) *Field of View for Virtual Reality Headsets Explained.* Available: https://vr-lens-lab.com/field-of-view-for-virtual-reality-headsets/. Last accessed 5 September 2019.

[26] Martindale, J. (2018) *Oculus Rift vs. HTC Vive.* Available: https://www.digitaltrends.com/virtual-reality/oculus-rift-vs-htc-vive/. Last accessed 7 September 2019.

[27] Carbotte, K. (2019) *Pimax 5K Plus Review: A Fresh Look at Ultrawide VR.* Available: https://www.tomshardware.com/reviews/pimax-5k-plus-vr-headset,5990.html. Last accessed 2 September 2019.

[28] Beavis, G. (2019) *OnePlus 7 Pro 5G beats Samsung, Oppo and LG in speed tests.* Available: https://www.techradar.com/news/oneplus-7-pro-5g-beats-samsung-oppo-and-lg-in-speed-tests. Last accessed 6 September 2019.

[29] Moore, B. (2019) *HTC's new Vive Cosmos VR headset has inside-out tracking and a high-res display.* Available: https://www.pcgamer.com/htcs-new-vive-cosmos-vr-headset-has-

inside-out-tracking-and-a-high-res-display/. Last accessed 7 September 2019.

[30] Road to VR. (2018) CLIP: HaptX Haptic Force Feedback Gloves. [Online Video]. 26 October 2018. Available: https://www.youtube.com/watch?v=LM0T6hLH15k. [Accessed: 2 September 2019].

[31] McDuffus, E. Nishijo, M. Patel, R. (2018) *Does Passive Virtual Reality Create A Greater Sense of Presence Than 2D Video?* London: Imperial College School of Medicine.

[32] U.Kühnapfel, H.K.Çakmak and H.Maaß. (2000) Endoscopic surgery training using virtual reality and deformable tissue simulation. *Computers & Graphics.* 24 (1), 671-682. DOI: 10.1016/S0097-8493(00)00070-4.

[33] Mimic Technologies. (n.d.) *Simulator for Intuitive Surgical®.* Available: https://mimicsimulation.com/inside-dv-trainerpartnership/. Last accessed 6 September 2019.

[34] The University of Louisville. (2018) Virtual reality surgery training. [Online Video]. 7 September 2017. Available: https://www.youtube.com/watch?v=sOOwaCvJjzc. Last accessed: 6 September 2019.

[35] Narendranathan, D. Kalair, S. Mehta, S. (2019) *Comparing the Effectiveness of Meditation through Virtual Reality A4 to Commercial Applications in Reducing Symptoms of Anxiety.* London: Imperial College School of Medicine.

[36] Facebook Technologies. (n.d.) *How do I use the Oculus Rooms.* Available: https://support.oculus.com/1611453315823320/. Last accessed 2 September 2019.

[37] UploadVR. (2018) Facebook VR Research: Photorealistic Face Tracked Avatars. [Online Video]. 4 March 2019. Available: https://www.youtube.com/watch?v=86-tHA8F-zU. Last accessed: 15 September 2019.

[38] Vice. (2018) *VR Treadmill Overview – March 2018.* Available: https://packet39.com/blog/2018/03/25/vr-treadmill-overview-march-2018/. Last accessed 18 September 2019.

[39] Fink, C. (2019) *Virtuix Omni Rides VR Esports Explosion To One Million Plays.* Available: https://www.forbes.com/sites/charliefink/2019/03/04/virtuix-omni-rides-vr-esports-explosion-to-one-million-plays/#61505a7a5c53. Last accessed 11 September 2019.

[40] Perez, S. (2019) *Google's 'Digital Wellbeing' features hit more devices, including Samsung Galaxy S10.* Available: https://techcrunch.com/2019/02/21/googles-digital-wellbeing-features-hit-more-devices-including-samsung-galaxy-s10/. Last accessed 12 September 2019.

[41] Quan-Haase, Anabel & Young, Alyson. (2010) Uses and Gratifications of Social Media: A Comparison of Facebook and Instant Messaging.

Bulletin of Science, Technology & Society. 30. 350-361. Doi: 10.1177/0270467610380009.

[42] Griffiths, M. D. (2018) *Addicted to Social Media?* Available: https://www.psychologytoday.com/gb/blog/in-excess/201805/addicted-social-media. Last accessed 7 September 2019.

CHAPTER 3

[1] Randewich, N. (2020) *Tesla's market value zooms past that of GM and Ford - combined.* Available: https://www.reuters.com/article/us-usa-stocks-tesla/teslas-market-value-zooms-past-that-of-gm-and-ford-combined-idUSKBN1Z72MU. Last accessed 2 February 2020.

[2] NASA's Goddard Space Flight Center. (2015) *The Antarctic Ozone Hole Will Recover.* Available: https://svs.gsfc.nasa.gov/30602. Last accessed 1 September 2019.

[3] Smart Energy GB. (n.d.) *WE'RE WORKING TOWARDS A SMARTER AND GREENER BRITAIN.* Available: https://www.smartenergygb.org/en. Last accessed 16 September 2019.

[4] Blackall, M. (2019) *Extinction Rebellion protests block traffic in five UK cities.* Available: https://www.theguardian.com/environment/2019/jul/15/extinction-rebellion-protests-block-traffic-in-five-uk-cities. Last accessed 12 September 2019.

[5] BBC. (2019) *UK Parliament declares climate change emergency.* Available: https://www.bbc.co.uk/news/uk-politics-48126677. Last accessed 1 September 2019.

[6] Shell. (2018) *Disclaimer.* Available: https://reports.shell.com/annual-report/2018/servicepages/disclaimer.php. Last accessed 12 September 2019.

[7] Sawe, Benjamin Elisha. "Biggest Oil Companies In The World." WorldAtlas, Dec. 5, 2018, worldatlas.com/articles/biggest-oil-companies-in-the-world.html.

[8] Deloitte. (n.d.) *Battery Electric Vehicles.* Available: https://www2.deloitte.com/content/dam/Deloitte/uk/Documents/manufacturing/deloitte-uk-battery-electric-vehicles.pdf. Last accessed 8 February 2019.

[9] Key, J. (2018). *Online Car Sales: Myth or Reality?.* Available: https://www.keyprinciples.co.uk/online-car-sales-myth-or-reality/. Last accessed 2 February 2019.

[10] Carleton, P. (2019) *How car depreciation affects your car's value.* Available: https://www.finder.com/what-is-car-depreciation. Last accessed 4 September 2019.

[11] Pinola, M. (2019) *When Is Leasing a Car Better Than Buying?*. Available: https://lifehacker.com/when-is-leasing-a-car-better-than-buying-5858640. Last accessed 3 September 2019.

[12] Elliott, A. F. (2018) *Compared: The new companies shaking up the car hire industry*. Available: https://www.telegraph.co.uk/travel/advice/carpooling-sharing-companies-rated/. Last accessed 9 May 2019.

[13] Lambert, F. (2019) *BMW and Mercedes-Benz partner on next-gen autonomous vehicles*. Available: https://electrek.co/2019/02/28/bmw-mercedes-benz-partner-autonomous-vehicles/. Last accessed 6 September 2019.

[14] Tobin, D. (2019) *2019 Diesel tax: new charges and surcharges for UK drivers*. Available: https://www.buyacar.co.uk/cars/diesel-cars/460/2019-diesel-tax-new-charges-and-surcharges-for-uk-drivers. Last accessed 6 September 2019.

[15] Burgess, R. (2017) *Islington to introduce £2 diesel surcharge for parking*. Available: https://www.autocar.co.uk/car-news/industry/islington-introduce-%C2%A32-diesel-surcharge-parking. Last accessed 7 May 2019.

[16] Haining, C. (2018) *Audi e-tron vs Mercedes EQC vs Tesla Model X vs Jaguar I-Pace: Premium electric SUVs compared*. Available: https://www.carbuyer.co.uk/tips-and-advice/165325/audi-e-tron-vs-mercedes-eqc-vs-tesla-model-x-vs-jaguar-i-pace-premium. Last accessed 17 May 2019.

[17] Autoexpress. (2012) *Tesla Roadster (2008-2013) review*. Available: https://www.autoexpress.co.uk/tesla/roadster. Last accessed 22 May 2019.

[18] Hotten, R. (2015) *Volkswagen: The scandal explained*. Available: https://www.bbc.co.uk/news/business-34324772. Last accessed 7 May 2019.

[19] Roberson, B. (2018) *$225 Million In New Funding Gives Comatose EV Startup Faraday Future A Shot At An Actual Future*. Available: https://www.forbes.com/sites/billroberson/2019/05/01/225-million-in-new-funding-gives-comatose-ev-startup-faraday-future-a-shot-at-an-actual-future/#603087e8660b. Last accessed 8 September 2019.

[20] Muoio, D. (2016) *A company you've never heard of is quietly leading the driverless-car revolution*. Available: https://www.businessinsider.com/nvidia-driverless-cars-2016-9?r=US&IR=T. Last accessed 7 August 2019.

[21] Tesla. (2019) *Introducing Dog Mode*. [Online Video]. 13 February 2019. Available from: https://www.youtube.com/watch?v=T2rbdMlmpYY. Last accessed: 6 September 2019.

[22] Keeney, T. (2018) *Opinion: Investors are overlooking this incredibly valuable part of Tesla's business*. Available:

https://www.marketwatch.com/story/investors-are-overlooking-this-part-of-teslas-business-2018-08-09. Last accessed 5 May 2019.

[23] Hollister, S. (2019) *Tesla's new self-driving chip is here, and this is your best look yet.* Available: https://www.theverge.com/2019/4/22/18511594/tesla-new-self-driving-chip-is-here-and-this-is-your-best-look-yet. Last accessed 7 September 2019.

[24] Pell, R. (2019) *Tesla and Nvidia spar over 'best' FSD chip.* Available: https://www.eenewspower.com/news/tesla-and-nvidia-spar-over-best-fsd-chip. Last accessed 7 September 2019.

[25] Barnard, M. (2016) *Tesla & Google Disagree About LIDAR — Which Is Right?* Available: https://cleantechnica.com/2016/07/29/tesla-google-disagree-lidar-right/. Last accessed 11 September 2019.

[26] Tanehaus, A. (2017) *Back to the Feature: The Evolution of Car Design and Functionality.* Available: https://www.zipcar.com/ziptopia/city-living/back-to-the-feature-the-evolution-of-car-design-and-functionality. Last accessed 7 May 2019.

[27] Pollard, T. (2019) What are autonomous car levels? Levels 1 to 5 of driverless vehicle tech explained. Available: https://www.carmagazine.co.uk/car-news/tech/autonomous-car-levels-different-driverless-technology-levels-explained/. Last accessed 7 September 2019.

[28] Cleantechnica. (2018) *Tesla-Autopilot-Radar.* [Image] Available: https://cleantechnica.com/files/2018/08/Tesla-Autopilot-Radar.png. Last accessed 6 September 2019.

[29] Wasik, J. (2017) *4 Reasons Why Tesla Is Worth More Than Ford.* Available: https://www.forbes.com/sites/johnwasik/2017/05/31/4-reasons-why-tesla-is-worth-more-than-ford/#45ea734c2893. Last accessed 7 September 2019.

[30] Volvo. (n.d.) *The Future is Electric.* Available: https://group.volvocars.com/company/innovation/electrification. Last accessed 1 August 2019.

[31] Ambler, P. (2018) *Volvo & Geely: The Unlikely Marriage Of Swedish Tech And Chinese Manufacturing Might That Earned Record Profits.* Available: https://www.forbes.com/sites/pamelaambler/2018/01/23/volvo-geely-the-unlikely-marriage-of-swedish-tech-and-chinese-manufacturing-might-that-earned-record-profits/#794b98314ecc. Last accessed 5 May 2019.

[32] Gilroy, R. (2019) *Volvo Posts Record Quarterly Revenue in 2Q.* Available: https://www.ttnews.com/articles/volvo-cars-boosts-cost-cuts-light-declining-profit. Last accessed 5 September 2019.

[33] carwow. (2019) Volvo's Tesla Model 3 revealed - the stunning Polestar 2 EV. [Online Video]. 28 February 2019. Available from:

https://www.youtube.com/watch?v=-VSDvXoabNo [Accessed: 6 September 2019].

[34] Volvo Cars. (2018) Introducing The New S60. [Online Video]. 20 February 2018. Available from: https://www.youtube.com/watch?v=1aLx5GYVI7U [Accessed: 6 May 2019].

[35] Volvo. (n.d.) *The Future is Electric.* Available: https://group.volvocars.com/company/innovation/electrification. Last accessed 1 August 2019.

[36] Toyota (GB) PLC. (2015) *History of the Toyota Prius.* Available: https://blog.toyota.co.uk/history-toyota-prius. Last accessed 6 May 2019.

[37] Lexus. (n.d.). *Why Hybrid?.* Available: https://www.lexus.co.uk/hybrid/why-hybrid/. Last accessed 2 January 2019.

[38] Haining, C. (2018) *Audi e-tron vs Mercedes EQC vs Tesla Model X vs Jaguar I-Pace: Premium electric SUVs compared.* Available: https://www.carbuyer.co.uk/tips-and-advice/165325/audi-e-tron-vs-mercedes-eqc-vs-tesla-model-x-vs-jaguar-i-pace-premium. Last accessed 2 January 2019.

[39] Brodie, J. (2019) *New Mercedes EQC 2019 review.* Available: https://www.autoexpress.co.uk/mercedes/eqc/106827/new-mercedes-eqc-2019-review. Last accessed 7 January 2019.

[40] Krok, A. (2019) *Avengers: Endgame ad brings out Audi E-Tron to help Captain Marvel.* Available: https://www.cnet.com/roadshow/news/avengers-endgame-captain-marvel-audi-e-tron/. Last accessed 6 September 2019.

[41] Lambert, F. (2018) *Tesla still has a 19-month long backlog of Model 3 reservations at current production rate.* Available: https://electrek.co/2018/07/03/tesla-model-3-long-backlog-reservations-production-rate/. Last accessed 7 January 2019.

[42] Volkswagen. (n.d.) *ID. Volkswagen, just electric.* Available: https://www.volkswagen.co.uk/e-mobility/en.html. Last accessed 6 January 2019.

[43] What Car? (n.d.) *Volkswagen Golf GTE review.* Available: https://www.whatcar.com/volkswagen/golf/hatchback/review/n17166. Last accessed 5 September 2019.

[44] Volkswagen. (2019) *Volkswagen e-Golf Zipcar UK Fleets Travels over 250,000 electric miles.* Available: https://www.volkswagen.co.uk/about-us/news/2019/01/volkswagen-e-golf-zipcar-uk/12. Last accessed 6 September 2019.

[45] Deloitte. (n.d.) *Battery Electric Vehicles.* Available: https://www2.deloitte.com/content/dam/Deloitte/uk/Documents/manufacturing/deloitte-uk-battery-electric-vehicles.pdf. Last accessed 5 January 2019.

[46] Udemans, C. (2019) *Struggling EV firm Faraday Future gets another financial lifeline with new $225M investment.* Available: https://techcrunch.com/2019/04/30/faraday-future-gets-another-financial-lifeline/. Last accessed 7 September 2019.

[47] Steven, C. (2019) *Founder Of Electric Vehicle Startup Faraday Files Bankruptcy.* Available: https://www.bloomberg.com/news/articles/2019-10-14/founder-of-electric-vehicle-startup-faraday-files-for-bankruptcy. Last accessed 5 May 2020.

[48] Glon, R. (2020) *Faraday Future FF91: driving the car that nearly didn't happen.* https://www.autocar.co.uk/car-news/new-cars/faraday-future-ff91-driving-car-nearly-didnt-happen. Last accessed: 5 May 2020.

[49] Kiley, D. (2019) *Ford Invests $500 Million In Hot Electric Truck Startup Rivian.* Available: https://www.forbes.com/sites/davidkiley5/2019/04/24/ford-invests-500-million-in-hot-electric-truck-startup-rivian/#1d58515c1f56. Last accessed 3 September 2019.

[50] Valdes-Dapena, P. (2019) *Ford shows off electric F-150 pickup by towing a freight train.* Available: https://edition.cnn.com/2019/07/23/success/ford-f-150-electric-pickup-tows-train/index.html. Last accessed 6 September 2019.

[51] DeBord, M. (2019) *An all-electric Ford F-150 pickup truck prototype has towed more than a million pounds.* Available: https://www.businessinsider.com/electric-ford-f150-prototype-towed-a-million-pounds-2019-7?r=US&IR=T. Last accessed 7 September 2019.

[52] FORD. (2017) *FORD INVESTS IN ARGO AI, A NEW ARTIFICIAL INTELLIGENCE COMPANY, IN DRIVE FOR AUTONOMOUS VEHICLE LEADERSHIP.* Available: https://media.ford.com/content/fordmedia/fna/us/en/news/2017/02/10/ford-invests-in-argo-ai-new-artificial-intelligence-company.html. Last accessed 2 January 2019.

[53] Rauwald, C and Naughton, K. (2019) *VW, Ford Extend Collaboration to Electric, Self-Driving Cars.* Available: https://www.bloomberg.com/news/articles/2019-07-11/vw-said-to-invest-in-ford-backed-argo-ai-at-7-billion-valuation. Last accessed 3 September 2019.

[54] Pollard. T. (2019) *What are autonomous car levels? Levels 1 to 5 of driverless vehicle tech explain.* Available: https://www.carmagazine.co.uk/car-news/tech/autonomous-car-levels-different-driverless-technology-levels-explained/. Last accessed 5 September 2019.

[55] Baldwin, R. (2019). *Tesla promises 'one million robo-taxis' in 2020.* Available: https://www.engadget.com/2019/04/22/tesla-elon-musk-self-driving-robo-taxi/?guccounter=1&guce_referrer=aHR0cHM6Ly93d3cuZ29vZ2xlLmNv

LnVrLw&guce_referrer_sig=AQAAAKL5yEue1OApwwVHGr0UOvP8bLa
3_6DNVdQkW9fJ. Last accessed 21 September 2019.

[56] Houser, K. (2019) *SEE TESLA'S ENHANCED SUMMON PICK UP A DRIVER IN A PARKING LOT.* Available: https://futurism.com/the-byte/see-teslas-enhanced-summon-parking-lot. Last accessed 4 September 2019.

[57] Korosec, K. (2019) *Waymo's robotaxi pilot surpassed 6,200 riders in its first month in California.* Available: https://techcrunch.com/2019/09/16/waymos-robotaxi-pilot-surpassed-6200-riders-in-its-first-month-in-california/. Last accessed 18 September 2019.

[58] Wang, Y., Chao, W. L., Garg, D., Hariharan, B., Campbell, M., Q. Weinberger, K. (2018) Pseudo-LiDAR from Visual Depth Estimation: Bridging the Gap in 3D Object Detection for Autonomous Driving. *Computer Vision and Pattern Recognition.* 5, https://arxiv.org/abs/1812.07179.

[59] Connor, L. (2016) *10 incredible facts you might not know about the DLR.* Available: https://www.standard.co.uk/lifestyle/london-life/10-incredible-facts-you-might-not-know-about-the-dlr-a3330716.html. Last accessed 7 January 2019.

[60] Ukauthority. (2018) *Public invited to test driverless pods in Greenwich.* Available: https://www.ukauthority.com/articles/public-invited-to-test-driverless-pods-in-greenwich/. Last accessed 4 January 2019.

[61] Heathrow Airport Limited. (2016) *Heathrow press releases.* Available: https://mediacentre.heathrow.com/pressrelease/details/81/Corporate-operational-24/5605. Last accessed 4 January 2019.

[62] Ingram, A. (2019) *Peugeot says level 4 autonomous cars would mean a £13,000 price hike.* Available: https://www.autoexpress.co.uk/peugeot/106233/peugeot-says-level-4-autonomous-cars-would-mean-a-13000-price-hike. Last accessed 5 September 2019.

[63] Brown, T. (2018) *The Impact of Driverless Technology on Independent Driving Jobs.* Available: https://www.itchronicles.com/artificial-intelligence/the-impact-of-driverless-technology-on-independent-driving-jobs/. Last accessed 5 January 2019.

[64] Mills, J. (2018) *SELF-STEERING SYSTEMS TO SHUT DOWN AFTER ONE MINUTE IF DRIVERS TAKE HANDS OFF THE WHEEL.* Available: https://www.driving.co.uk/news/self-steering-systems-shut-one-minute-drivers-take-hands-off-wheel/. Last accessed 5 September 2019.

[65] Pitt, T. (2019) *2025 will be 'tipping point' for electric cars, say experts.* Available: https://www.motoringresearch.com/car-news/2025-tipping-point-for-electric-cars/. Last accessed 4 September 2019.

[66] Staufenberg, J. (2016) *Norway to 'completely ban petrol powered cars by 2025'.* Available:

https://www.independent.co.uk/environment/climate-change/norway-to-ban-the-sale-of-all-fossil-fuel-based-cars-by-2025-and-replace-with-electric-vehicles-a7065616.html. Last accessed 12 September 2019.

[67] Alam, M. R., St-Hilaire, M. and Kunz, T. (2019) Peer-to-peer energy trading among smart homes. *Applied Energy*. 238, 1434-1443. https://doi.org/10.1016/j.apenergy.2019.01.091

[68] Zhang, C, Wu, J., Long, C Chenga. (2016) Review of Existing Peer-to-Peer Energy Trading Projects. *ScienceDirect*, doi: 10.1016/j.egypro.2017.03.737.

[69] Alam, M. R., St-Hilaire, M. and Kunz, T. (2019) Peer-to-peer energy trading among smart homes. *Applied Energy*. 238, 1434-1443. https://doi.org/10.1016/j.apenergy.2019.01.091

[70] GreenMatch. (2019) *Things to Know before Buying a 4kW Solar Panel System*. Available: https://www.greenmatch.co.uk/solar-energy/solar-system/4kw-solar-panel-system. Last accessed 4 September 2019.

[71] GreenMatch. (2019) *What Is the Installation Cost for Solar Panels?*. Available: https://www.greenmatch.co.uk/blog/2014/08/what-is-the-installation-cost-for-solar-panels. Last accessed 5 September 2019.

CHAPTER 4

[1] Simplilearn. (2019) *Machine Learning Basics | What Is Machine Learning? | Introduction To Machine Learning | Simplilearn*. [Online Video]. 1 July 2019. Available from: https://www.youtube.com/watch?v=ukzFl9rgwfU. [Accessed: 2 June 2019].

[2] Ritter, J. (2014) *Google's IPO, 10 Years Later*. Available: https://www.forbes.com/sites/jayritter/2014/08/07/googles-ipo-10-years-later/#248042802e6c. Last accessed 2 July 2019.

[3] von Ahn L., Blum M., Hopper N.J., Langford J. (2003) CAPTCHA: Using Hard AI Problems for Security. In: Biham E. (eds) Advances in Cryptology — EUROCRYPT 2003. EUROCRYPT 2003. *Lecture Notes in Computer Science*, vol 2656. Springer, Berlin, Heidelberg.

[4] Google. (2009) *Teaching computers to read: Google acquires reCAPTCHA*. Available: https://googleblog.blogspot.com/2009/09/teaching-computers-to-read-google.html. Last accessed 3 July 2019.

[5] Von Ahn, L., Blum, M., J. Hopper, N., Langford, J. (2008) reCAPTCHA: Human-Based Character Recognition via Web Security Measures. *Science*. 321, 1465-1468. DOI: 10.1126/science.1160379.

[6] Techcrunch. (2007) *Recaptcha: Using Captcha To Digitize Books.* Available: https://techcrunch.com/2007/09/16/recaptcha-using-captchas-to-digitize-books/. Last accessed 26 May 2019.

[7] Philipp Lenssen. (2012) Google Brain. [Online Video]. 5 April 2012. Available from: https://www.youtube.com/watch?v=RupYlWs4EiM. [Accessed: 1 September 2019].

[8] Briggs, P. (2018) *How Canada's AI Research Hubs Lured Facebook, Google and Samsung North.* Available: https://www.emarketer.com/content/how-canada-s-hubs-for-ai-research-lured-facebook-google-and-samsung-north. Last accessed 3 July 2019.

[9] Perez, S. (2012) *Google Now Using ReCAPTCHA To Decode Street View Addresses.* Available: https://techcrunch.com/2012/03/29/google-now-using-recaptcha-to-decode-street-view-addresses/. Last accessed 10 July 2019.

[10] Shin, L. (2012) *Google brain simulator teaches itself to recognize cats.* Available: https://www.zdnet.com/article/google-brain-simulator-teaches-itself-to-recognize-cats/. Last accessed 7 July 2019.

[11] V. Le, Q., Ranzato, M., Monga, R., Devin, M., Chen, K., Corrado, G,. Dean, J., Y. Nig, A. (2012) Building High-level Features Using Large Scale Unsupervised Learning. *Appearing in Proceedings of the 29th International Conference on Machine Learning, Edinburgh, Scotland, UK, 2012*

[12] Shet, V. (2014) *Are you a robot? Introducing "No CAPTCHA reCAPTCHA".* Available: https://security.googleblog.com/2014/12/are-you-robot-introducing-no-captcha.html. Last accessed 4 July 2019.

[13] Google. (2018) *Introducing reCAPTCHA v3: the new way to stop bots.* Available: https://webmasters.googleblog.com/2018/10/introducing-recaptcha-v3-new-way-to.html. Last accessed 14 July 2019.

[14] Lowensohn, J. (2013) *Google buys Boston Dynamics, maker of spectacular and terrifying robot.* Available: https://www.theverge.com/2013/12/14/5209622/google-has-bought-robotics-company-boston-dynamics. Last accessed 16 July 2019.

[15] Statt, N. (2017) *Alphabet agrees to sell Boston Dynamics to SoftBank.* Available: https://www.theverge.com/2017/6/8/15766434/alphabet-google-boston-dynamics-softbank-sale-acquisition-robotics. Last accessed 28 July 2019.

[16] Medeiros, J. (2019) *How SoftBank ate the world.* Available: https://www.wired.co.uk/article/softbank-vision-fund. Last accessed 4 July 2019.

[17] Pilkington, M. (2014) *The Personal Computers of the 1980s.* Available: https://www.pcgamer.com/uk/personal-computers-1980s/. Last accessed 18 June 2019.

[18] van Gerven, M. and Bohte, S. (2017) Editorial: Artificial Neural Networks as Models of Neural Information Processing. Frontiers in Computational Neuroscience. 11:114. doi: 10.3389/fncom.2017.00114

[19] Schapire R.E. (2003) The Boosting Approach to Machine Learning: An Overview. In: Denison D.D., Hansen M.H., Holmes C.C., Mallick B., Yu B. (eds) *Nonlinear Estimation and Classification. Lecture Notes in Statistics*, vol 171. Springer, New York, NY.

[20] Rouse, M. (n.d.) *machine learning (ML).* Available: https://searchenterpriseai.techtarget.com/definition/machine-learning-ML. Last accessed 2 June 2019.

[21] TensorFlow. (2019) Machine Learning Zero to Hero (Google I/O'19) [Online Video]. 9 May 2018. Available from: https://www.youtube.com/watch?v=VwVg9jCtqaU. [Accessed: 2 June 2019].

[22] Gershenson, C. (2003) Artificial Neural Networks for Beginners. *Neural and Evolutionary Computing (cs.NE).* ArXiv:cs/0308031 [cs:NE].

[23] Edwards, G. (2018) *Machine Learning | An Introduction.* Available: https://towardsdatascience.com/machine-learning-an-introduction-23b84d51e6d0?gi=d36fd5185155. Last accessed 14 July 2019.

[24] Robinson, J. (2019). *How Facebook Scales Machine Learning.* Available: https://medium.com/@jamal.robinson/how-facebook-scales-artificial-intelligence-machine-learning-693706ae296f. Last accessed 14 August 2019.

[25] Yu, A. (2019) *How Netflix Uses AI, Data Science, and Machine Learning—From A Product Perspective.* Available: https://becominghuman.ai/how-netflix-uses-ai-and-machine-learning-a087614630fe. Last accessed 23 June 2019.

[26] Dettmers, T. (2018) *A Full Hardware Guide to Deep Learning.* Available: https://timdettmers.com/2018/12/16/deep-learning-hardware-guide/. Last accessed 4 July 2019.

[27] Lawrence, S., Lee Giles, C., Tsoi, A. C., D. Back, A. (1997) Face Recognition: A Convolutional Neural-Network Approach. *IEEE TRANSACTIONS ON NEURAL NETWORKS.* 8.

[28] Kim, Yoon. (2014). Convolutional Neural Networks for Sentence Classification. *Proceedings of the 2014 Conference on Empirical Methods in Natural Language Processing.* 10.3115/v1/D14-1181.

[29] Krizhevsky, A., Sutskever, I., Hinton, G. E. (2012) ImageNet Classification with Deep Convolutional Neural Networks, DOI: 10.1145/3065386.

[30] Goyal, P. Dollar, P. Grishick, R. Noodrhuis P. Weslowski, L. Kyrola, A. Tulloch, A. Jia, Y. He, K. Accurate, Large Minibatch SGD: Training ImageNet in 1 Hour. *Facebook research*.

[31] Akiba, T., Suzuki, S., Fukuda, K. (2017) Extremely Large Minibatch SGD: Training ResNet-50 on ImageNet in 15 Minutes. arXiv:1711.04325v1 [cs.DC].

[32] He, K., Zhang, X., Ren, S., Sun, J. (2016) Deep Residual Learning for Image Recognition. 770-778. 10.1109/CVPR.2016.90.

[33] Poggio, T and Liao, Q. (2016) Bridging the Gaps Between Residual Learning, Recurrent Neural Networks and Visual Cortex. arXiv:1604.03640.

[34] Mikolov, T. (2010) *Recurrent neural network-based language model.* Available: http://www.fit.vutbr.cz/research/groups/speech/servite/2010/rnnlm_mikolov.pdf. Last accessed 24 July 2019.

[35] Zaremba, W. (2015) RECURRENT NEURAL NETWORK REGULARIZATION. *ICLR 2015*. 1, arXiv:1409.2329v5 [cs.NE].

[36] Sercan O. Arık, Mike Chrzanowski, Adam Coates, Gregory Diamos. (2017) Deep Voice: Real-time Neural Text-to-Speech. *International Conference on Machine Learning (ICML) 2017*. arXiv:1702.07825v2 [cs.CL].

[37] Matsugu, Masakazu & Mori, Katsuhiko & Mitari, Yusuke & Kaneda, Yuji. (2003). Subject Independent Facial Expression Recognition with Robust Face Detection Using a Convolutional Neural Network. *Neural networks : the official journal of the International Neural Network Society*. 16. 555-9. 10.1016/S0893-6080(03)00115-1.

[38] Li, K., Xu, H., Wang, Y., Povey, D., Khudanpur, S. (2018) Recurrent Neural Network Language Model Adaptation for Conversational Speech Recognition.

[39] Li, S., Li, W., Cook, C. (2018) Independently Recurrent Neural Network (IndRNN): Building a Longer and Deeper RNN. *The IEEE Conference on Computer Vision and Pattern Recognition (CVPR), 2018*. 5457-5466.

[40] Google Patents. (2015) *Multiplicative recurrent neural network for fast and robust intracortical brain machine interface decoders*. Available: https://patents.google.com/patent/US10223634B2/en. Last accessed 4 July 2019.

[41] Ciprani, J. (2019) *How to review and turn off Facebook's facial recognition feature*. Available: https://www.cnet.com/how-to/how-to-review-and-turn-off-facebooks-facial-recognition-feature/. Last accessed 11 September 2019.

[42] Mnih, V., Kavukcuoglu, K., Silver, D., A. Rusu, A. (2015) Human-level control through deep reinforcement learning. *Nature*. 518, 529-533. Doi: 10.1038/nature14236.

[43] Marr, B. (2018) *Machine Learning In Practice: How Does Amazon's Alexa Really Work.* Available: https://www.forbes.com/sites/bernardmarr/2018/10/05/how-does-amazons-alexa-really-work/#3abac7e51937. Last accessed 28 July 2019.

[44] Silver, D., Schrittwieser, J., Simonyan, K., Antonoglou, I., Huang, A. (2017) Mastering the game of Go without human knowledge. *Nature.* 550. doi: https://doi.org/10.1038/nature24270.

[45] Knapton, S. (2017) *AlphaGo Zero: Google DeepMind supercomputer learns 3,000 years of human knowledge in 40 days.* Available: https://www.telegraph.co.uk/science/2017/10/18/alphago-zero-google-deepmind-supercomputer-learns-3000-years/. Last accessed 28 July 2019.

[46] Macaulay, T. (2014) *Google DeepMind: the story behind the world's leading AI startup.* Available: https://www.techworld.com/startups/google-deepmind-what-is-it-how-it-works-should-you-be-scared-3615354/. Last accessed 28 July 2019.

[47] Li, Y. (2019) *Using Deep Learning to Improve Usability on Mobile Devices.* Available: https://ai.googleblog.com/2019/04/using-deep-learning-to-improve.html. Last accessed 29 July 2019.

[48] Karras, T., Laine, S., Aila, T. (2019) A Style-Based Generator Architecture for Generative Adversarial Networks. *arXiv.* arXiv:1812.04948 [cs.NE].

[49] Generated.photos. (2019) *100K models.* Available: https://drive.google.com/drive/folders/1wSy4TVjSvtXeRQ6Zr8W98YbSuZXrZrgY. Last accessed 21 September 2019.

[50] Younger, J. (2019) *Google's Artificial Intelligence And Machine Learning Research Priorities: Freelancers, Take Note.* Available: https://www.forbes.com/sites/jonyounger/2019/01/16/googles-ai-and-ml-research-priorities-freelancers-take-note/#7a3c183344c3. Last accessed 29 July 2019.

[51] TensorFlow. (n.d.) *An end-to-end open source machine learning platform.* Available: https://www.tensorflow.org/. Last accessed 29 July 2019.

[52] Google Cloud. (n.d.) *Empowering businesses with Google Cloud AI.* Available: https://cloud.google.com/tpu/. Last accessed 29 July 2019.

[53] Data based on the computation of ResNet 50, a deep neural network with 50 layers that can perform complete ResNet 50 computation under 7.1 minutes. Benchmark data provided MLPerf. Data Source: Google Cloud. (n.d.) *Empowering businesses with Google Cloud AI.* Available: https://cloud.google.com/tpu/. Last accessed 29 July 2019.

[54] IBM. (n.d.) *Watson Machine Learning: Pricing.* Available: https://www.ibm.com/uk-en/cloud/machine-learning/pricing. Last accessed 29 July 2019.

[55] Cody Ogden. (2019). Google Graveyeard. Available: https://killedbygoogle.com. Last accessed 28 October 2019.

[56] Wallace, F. (2019) *The Positive Impact of Artificial Intelligence on the Music Industry.* Available: http://www.prefixmag.com/features/positive-impact-artificial-intelligence-music-industry/205376/. Last accessed 29 July 2019.

[57] Protalinski, E. (2019) *Amazon reports $63.4 billion in Q2 2019 revenue: AWS up 37%, subscriptions up 37%, and 'other' up 37%.* Available: https://venturebeat.com/2019/07/25/amazon-earnings-q2-2019/. Last accessed 29 July 2019.

[58] AWS. (n.d.) *Amazon Managed Blockchain features.* Available: https://aws.amazon.com/managed-blockchain/features/?nc=sn&loc=2. Last accessed 29 July 2019.

[59] Jasper, C. (2019) *Heathrow Airport Wants to Use Artificial Intelligence to Speed Up Landings.* Available: https://skift.com/2019/01/28/heathrow-airport-wants-to-use-artificial-intelligence-to-speed-up-landings/. Last accessed 29 July 2019.

[60]Neiger, C. (2019) *5 Reasons Why Investors Should Believe the Artificial Intelligence Hype.* Available: https://www.fool.com/investing/2019/04/13/reasons-investors-believe-artificial-intelligence.aspx. Last accessed 30 July 2019.

[61] ColdFusion. (2018) Deepfakes - Real Consequences. [Online Video]. 28 April 2018. Available from: https://www.youtube.com/watch?v=dMF2i3A9Lzw. [Accessed: 1 September 2019].

[62] Lyrebird (2017) Lyrebird - Create a digital copy of your voice.[Online Video]. 4 September 2017. Available from: https://www.youtube.com/watch?v=YfU_sWHT8mo [Accessed: 1 September 2019].

[63] Vincent, J. (2019) *ThisPersonDoesNotExist.com uses AI to generate endless fake faces.* Available: https://www.theverge.com/tldr/2019/2/15/18226005/ai-generated-fake-people-portraits-thispersondoesnotexist-stylegan. Last accessed 29 July 2019.

[64] Gault, M. (2019) *This Website Uses AI to Generate the Faces of People Who Don't Exist.* Available: https://www.vice.com/en_us/article/7xn4wy/this-website-uses-ai-to-generate-the-faces-of-people-who-dont-exist. Last accessed 30 July 2019.

[65] Malaria Must Die (2019) David Beckham speaks nine languages to launch Malaria Must Die Voice Petition. [Online Video] 8 April 2017. Available from: https://www.youtube.com/watch?v=QiiSAvKJIHo#action=share [Accessed: 1 September 2019].

[66] Emerging Technology from the arXiv. (2017) *Experts Predict When Artificial Intelligence Will Exceed Human Performance.* Available: https://www.technologyreview.com/s/607970/experts-predict-when-artificial-intelligence-will-exceed-human-performance/. Last accessed 3 July 2019.

[67] Keane, S. (2018) *Congress wrestles with 'deepfake' threat to Facebook.* Available: https://www.cnet.com/news/congress-wrestles-with-deepfake-threat-to-facebook/. Last accessed 30 July 2019.

[68] Oakes, O. (2019) *Deepfake voice tech used good david beckham malaria campaign.* Available: https://www.prweek.com/article/1581457/deepfake-voice-tech-used-good-david-beckham-malaria-campaign. Last accessed 30 July 2019

[69] Kleber, S. (2018) *3 Ways AI Is Getting More Emotional.* Available: https://hbr.org/2018/07/3-ways-ai-is-getting-more-emotional. Last accessed 30 July 2019.

[70] Deepmind. (2017) *Enabling Continual Learning in Neural Networks.* Available: https://deepmind.com/blog/article/enabling-continual-learning-in-neural-networks. Last accessed 31 July 2019.

[71] Goldhill, O. (2018) *The push to create AI-friendly ethics codes is stripping all nuance from morality.* Available: https://qz.com/1412730/the-push-to-create-ai-friendly-ethics-codes-is-stripping-all-nuance-from-morality/. Last accessed 31 July 2019.

CHAPTER 5

[72] Smith, D. (2019) *Artificial Intelligence Can Detect Alzheimer's Disease in Brain Scans Six Years Before a Diagnosis.* Available: https://www.ucsf.edu/news/2019/01/412946/artificial-intelligence-can-detect-alzheimers-disease-brain-scans-six-years. Last accessed 31 July 2019.

[73] Zwanzig, R., Szabo, A. and Bagchi, B. (1992) Levinthal's paradox. *Proc Natl Acad Sci U S A.* 89 (1), doi: 10.1073/pnas.89.1.20.

[74] Deepmind. (2018) *AlphaFold: Using AI for scientific discovery.* Available: https://deepmind.com/blog/article/alphafold. Last accessed 31 July 2019.

[75] Kelly, E. (2019) *DeepMind's AI doctor predicted to transform eye disease diagnosis.* Available:

https://sciencebusiness.net/news/deepminds-ai-doctor-predicted-transform-eye-disease-diagnosis. Last accessed 31 July 2019.

[76] Plummer, L. (2017) *This is how Netflix's top-secret recommendation system works*. Available: https://www.wired.co.uk/article/how-do-netflixs-algorithms-work-machine-learning-helps-to-predict-what-viewers-will-like. Last accessed 3 July 2019.

[77] AP. (2018) *Spotify + The Machine: Using Machine Learning to Create Value and Competitive Advantage*. Available: https://digital.hbs.edu/platform-rctom/submission/spotify-the-machine-using-machine-learning-to-create-value-and-competitive-advantage/. Last accessed 16 July 2019.

[78] Vanian, J. (2017) *Futuristic Robots Are Lending Their Hands in Gap's Warehouse*. Available: https://fortune.com/2017/10/24/gap-robots-kindred-warehouse/. Last accessed 10 August 2019.

[79] Manzotti R and Chella A (2018) Good Old-Fashioned Artificial Consciousness and the Intermediate Level Fallacy. *Frontiers in Robotics and AI*. 5:39. doi: 10.3389/frobt.2018.00039

[80] Scheutz, M. (2014). Artificial emotions and machine consciousness. In K. Frankish & W. Ramsey (Eds.), *The Cambridge Handbook of Artificial Intelligence* (pp. 247-266). Cambridge: Cambridge University Press. doi: 10.1017/ CBO9781139046855.016.

[81] Graziano, M.S.A. (2017) The Attention Schema Theory: A Foundation for Engineering Artificial Consciousness. *Frontiers in Robotics and AI*. 4:60. doi: 10.3389/frobt.2017.00060

[82] van der Velde, F. (2018) In Situ Representations and Access Consciousness in Neural Blackboard or Workspace Architectures. *Frontiers in Robotics and AI*. 5:32. doi: 10.3389/frobt.2018.00032

[83] Kinouchi, Y. and Mackin, J. (2018) A Basic Architecture of an Autonomous Adaptive System With Conscious-Like Function for a Humanoid Robot. *Frontiers in Robotics and AI*. 5:30. doi: 10.3389/frobt.2018.00030

[84] Willingham, A. (2020) *Artificial Intelligence can't technically invent things, says patent office*. Available: https://edition.cnn.com/2020/04/30/us/artificial-intelligence-inventing-patent-office-trnd/index.html. Last accessed: 3 May 2020.

[1] Morris, C. (2019) *Tesla vs. Self-Driving Competition — New MIT Video*. Available: https://cleantechnica.com/2019/02/10/tesla-vs-self-driving-competition-new-mit-video/. Last accessed 2 August 2019.

[2] Lambert, F. (2018) *Tesla owners have driven 1 billion miles with Autopilot activated*. Available: https://electrek.co/2018/11/28/tesla-autopilot-1-billion-miles/. Last accessed 12 August 2019.

[3] JRE Clips. (2019) *Joe Rogan - Elon Musk on Artificial Intelligence*. [Online Video]. 6 September 2018. Available from:

https://www.youtube.com/watch?v=Ra3fv8gl6NE&t=11s. [Accessed: 3 July 2019].

[4] Techopedia. (n.d.) *Definition - What does Supercomputer mean?* Available: https://www.techopedia.com/definition/4599/supercomputer. Last accessed 3 February 2019.

[5] ARM Limited. (2011) *WHAT IS A FLOATING-POINT OPERATION?* Available: http://infocenter.arm.com/help/index.jsp?topic=/com.arm.doc.faqs/ka9805.html. Last accessed 3 January 2019.

[6] Webopedia. (n.d.) *FLOPS.* Available: https://www.webopedia.com/TERM/F/FLOPS.html. Last accessed 3 February 2019.

[7] Hardawar, D. (2016) *NVIDIA's GTX 1070 is a mid-range GPU that feels high-end.* Available: https://www.engadget.com/2016/07/09/nvidia-gtx-1070-review/. Last accessed 3 May 2019.

[8] Stevenson, M. (n.d.) *How many FLOPS is the human brain?* Available: https://www.toytowngermany.com/forum/topic/236060-worlds-fastest-supercomputer-vs-the-human-brain/. Last accessed 31 May 2019.

[9] Saracco, R. (2018) *Simulating the human brain: an exascale effort.* Available: https://cmte.ieee.org/futuredirections/2018/05/10/simulating-the-human-brain-an-exascale-effort/. Last accessed 4 February 2019.

[10] Smolaks, M. (2019) *Commercial spinoffs of Fujitsu's Post-K super 'puter will hit shelves long before exascale daddy switched on.* Available: https://www.theregister.co.uk/2019/04/16/fujitsu_to_start_selling_postk_derivatives_within_12_months/. Last accessed 4 June 2019.

[11] Fujitsu Limited. (2019) *Fujitsu Begins Production of Post-K Also advances productization of commercial units based on the supercomputer technology.* Available: https://www.fujitsu.com/global/about/resources/news/press-releases/2019/0415-01.html. Last accessed 10 September 2019.

[12] Human Brain Project. (2017) *Learning to use neuromorphic computing.* Available: https://www.humanbrainproject.eu/en/follow-hbp/news/learn-to-use-the-neuromorphic-computing/. Last accessed 4 June 2019.

CHAPTER 6

[1] Techopedia. (n.d.) *Von Neumann Architecture.* Available: https://www.techopedia.com/definition/32480/von-neumann-architecture. Last accessed 2 June 2019.

[2] Pktparticle. (n.d.) *Computer Organization | Von Neumann architecture.* Available: https://www.geeksforgeeks.org/computer-organization-von-neumann-architecture/. Last accessed 2 June 2019.

[3] Rouse, M. (n.d.) *RAM (Random Access Memory)*. Available: https://searchstorage.techtarget.com/definition/RAM-random-access-memory. Last accessed 2 June 2019.

[4] González, A., Latorre, F., Magklis, G. (2011) *Processor Microarchitecture: An Implementation Perspective.* San Rafael, California (USA): Morgan & Claypool Publishers.

[5] Computer Hope. (2019) *CPU.* Available: https://www.computerhope.com/jargon/c/cpu.htm. Last accessed 2 June 2019.

[6] Pritchard, P. (n.d.) *How Does RAM Work With the CPU?.* Available: https://www.techwalla.com/articles/how-does-ram-work-with-the-cpu. Last accessed 1 June 2019.

[7] Marchal, P. (1998) John von Neumann: The Founding Father of Artificial Life. *Artificial Life.* 4 (3), 229-235.

[8] The free dictionary. (n.d.) *Heterogeneous system.* Available: https://medical-dictionary.thefreedictionary.com/heterogeneous+system. Last accessed 2 June 2019.

[9] D. Hof, R. (2014) *Neuromorphic Chips.* Available: https://www.technologyreview.com/s/526506/neuromorphic-chips/. Last accessed: 2 August 2019.

[10] Neftci, E. Augustine, C. Paul, S. and Detorakis, G. (2017) Event-Driven Random Back-Propagation: Enabling Neuromorphic Deep Learning Machines. *Frontiers in Neuroscience.* 11:324. doi: 10.3389/fnins.2017.00324.

[11] Techopedia. (n.d.) *Neuromorphic Computing.* Available: https://www.techopedia.com/definition/32953/neuromorphic-computing. Last accessed: 1 June 2019.

[12] Rajendran, B. Sebastian, A. Schmuker, M. Srinivasa, N. & Eleftheriou, E. (2019) Low-Power Neuromorphic Hardware for Signal Processing Applications. *ArXiv, abs/1901.03690.*

[13] Vanarse, A Osseiran, A. and Rassau, A. (2016) A Review of Current Neuromorphic Approaches for Vision, Auditory, and Olfactory Sensors. *Front. Neurosci.* 10:115. doi: 10.3389/fnins.2016.00115.

[14] Martins, N. Angelica, A. Chakravarthy, K. Svidinenko, Y. Boehm, F. Opris, I. Lebedev, M. Swan, M. Garan, S. Rosenfeld, J. Hogg, T. and Freitas, R. (2019) Human Brain/Cloud Interface. *Frontiers in Neuroscience.* 13:112. doi: 10.3389/fnins.2019.00112.

[15] Goldman, B. (2010) *New imaging method developed at Stanford reveals stunning details of brain connections.* Available: https://med.stanford.edu/news/all-news/2010/11/new-imaging-method-developed-at-stanford-reveals-stunning-details-of-brain-connections.html?fbclid=IwAR26teAQf992h_pZ-SQxbdehr9HVUMnNYl9gftTNmwdtfcve7s_k. Last accessed: 2 August 2019.

[16] Swenson, R. (2006) *The Cerebral Cortex.* In: Swenson, R. *REVIEW OF CLINICAL AND FUNCTIONAL NEUROSCIENCE.* Dartmouth Medical School.

[17] Mastin, L. (2019) NEURONS & SYNAPSES. Available: http://www.human-memory.net/brain_neurons.html. Last accessed: 1 June 2019.

[18] Johns Hopkins University. (2018) *Johns Hopkins Scientist Uses EEG Cap to Measure Distraction.* [Online Video]. 4 January 2018. Available: https://www.youtube.com/watch?v=P1rUCce_f4A. [Accessed: 27 August 2019].

[19] Riès, S. Dronkers, N. Knight, R. (2016) Choosing words: left hemisphere, right hemisphere, or both? Perspective on the lateralization of word retrieval. *Annals of the New York Academy of Sciences.* 1369 (1): 111–31. doi:10.1111/nyas.12993.

[20] The Brain Made Simple. (n.d.) *Left and right hemispheres.* Available: http://brainmadesimple.com/left-and-right-hemispheres.html. Last accessed 1 June 2019.

[21] Reber, P. (n.d.) *What is the memory capacity of the human brain?* Available: https://www.scientificamerican.com/article/what-is-the-memory-capacity/?redirect=1. Last accessed 1 June 2019.

[22] Drubach, Daniel. (2000) *Power of A Human Brain.* Available: https://hypertextbook.com/facts/2001/JacquelineLing.shtml. Last accessed: 1 June 2019.

[23] Herculano-Houzel S (2009) The human brain in numbers: a linearly scaled-up primate brain. *Frontiers in Human Neuroscience.* 3:31. doi: 10.3389/neuro.09.031.2009.

[24] IBM. (2008) *IBM Seeks to Build the Computer of the Future Based on Insights from the Brain.* Available: https://www-03.ibm.com/press/us/en/pressrelease/26123.wss. Last accessed: 27 August 2019.

[25] Terdiman, D. (2008) *IBM gets DARPA cognitive computing contract.* Available: https://www.cnet.com/news/ibm-gets-darpa-cognitive-computing-contract/. Last accessed: 29 August 2019.

[26] IBM. (2009) *IBM Moves Closer To Creating Computer Based on Insights From The Brain.* Available: https://www-03.ibm.com/press/us/en/pressrelease/28842.wss. Last accessed: 29 August 2019.

[27] Cascio, J. (2009) *IBM Simulates a Cat-Like Brain: AI or Shadow Minds for Humans?* Available: https://www.fastcompany.com/1462049/ibm-simulates-cat-brain-ai-or-shadow-minds-humans. Last accessed: 29 August 2019

[28] Terdiman, D. (2009) IBM: Computing rivalling human brain may be ready by 2019. Available: https://www.cnet.com/news/ibm-computing-rivaling-human-brain-may-be-ready-by-2019/. Last accessed: 5 August 2019.

[29] IBM. (2011) *IBM Unveils Cognitive Computing Chips.* Available: https://www-03.ibm.com/press/us/en/pressrelease/35251.wss. Last accessed: 5 August 2019.

[30] S. Cassidy, A., Sawada, J., A. Merolla, P., V. Arthur, J., Alvarez-Icaza, R., Akopyan, F., L. Jackson, B. and S. Modha, D. (2016) TrueNorth: a High-Performance, Low-Power Neurosynaptic Processor for Multi-Sensory Perception, Action, and Cognition.

[31] Qiao, N. Mostafa H. Corradi, F. Osswald, M. Stefanini, F. Sumislawska, D. Indiveri, G. (2015) A reconfigurable on-line learning spiking neuromorphic processor comprising 256 neurons and 128K synapses. *Frontiers in Neuroscience.* 9:141. doi: 10.3389/fnins.2015.00141.

[32] IBM. (2011). IBM Unveils Cognitive Computing Chips. Available: https://www-03.ibm.com/press/us/en/pressrelease/35251.wss. Last accessed 3 June 2019.

[33] The Artificial Intelligence Channel. (2017) *IBM Says They Will Be Able to Produce a Brain in a Box By 2020.* [Online Video]. 9 May 2018. Available: https://www.youtube.com/watch?v=yjuE1rFZOHo&t=265s. Last accessed: 12 August 2019.

[34] Dharmendra S. Modha. (n.d.) *Introducing a Brain-inspired Computer.* Available: http://www.research.ibm.com/articles/brain-chip.shtml. Last accessed: 3 June 2019.

[35] S. Cassidy, A., Sawada, J., A. Merolla, P., V. Arthur, J., Alvarez-Icaza, R. , Akopyan, F., L. Jackson, B. and S. Modha, D.. (2014) *TrueNorth: a High-Performance, Low-Power Neurosynaptic Processor for Multi-Sensory Perception, Action, and Cognition.* Available: https://www-03.ibm.com/press/us/en/pressrelease/44529.wss. Last accessed: 1 May 2019.

[36] Smith, L. (2015) Toward a neuromorphic microphone. *Frontiers in Neuroscience.* 9:398. doi: 10.3389/fnins.2015.00398.

[37] Booton, J. (2013) *After Watson, IBM Looks to Build 'Brain in a Box'.* Available: https://www.foxbusiness.com/features/after-watson-ibm-looks-to-build-brain-in-a-box. Last accessed: 1 August 2019.

[38] Wikichip. (n.d.) *Loihi - Intel.* Available: https://en.wikichip.org/wiki/intel/loihi. Last accessed: 1 August 2019.

[39] Feldman, M. (2018) *Intel Ramps Up Neuromorphic Computing Effort with New Research Partners.* Available: https://www.top500.org/news/intel-ramps-up-neuromorphic-computing-effort-with-new-research-partners/. Last accessed: 4 June 2019.

[40] Dr. Mayberry, M. (n.d.) *Intel's New Self-Learning Chip Promises to Accelerate Artificial Intelligence.* Available: https://newsroom.intel.com/editorials/intels-new-self-learning-chip-promises-accelerate-artificial-intelligence/#gs.moesft. Last accessed: 1 August 2019.

[41] Intel Newsroom. (2018) *Intel's 'Loihi' Neuromorphic Chip in the Lab.* [Online Video]. 1 March 2018. Available: https://www.youtube.com/watch?v=cDKnt9ldXv0. [Accessed: 1 August 2019].

[42] APT Advanced Processor Technologies Research Group. (n.d) *SpiNNaker Project.* Available: http://apt.cs.manchester.ac.uk/projects/SpiNNaker/project/. Last accessed: 9 September 2019.

[43] Knight, J. and Furber, S. (2016) Synapse-Centric Mapping of Cortical Models to the SpiNNaker Neuromorphic Architecture. Frontiers in Neuroscience. 10:420. doi: 10.3389/fnins.2016.00420

[44] Weisberger, M. (2018) *New Supercomputer with 1 Million Processors Is World's Fastest Brain-Mimicking Machine.* Available: https://www.livescience.com/64005-worlds-largest-supercomputer-human-brain.html. Last accessed: 18 August 2019.

[45] van Albada, S. Rowley, A. Senk, J. Hopkins, M. Schmidt, M. Stokes, A. Lester, D. Diesmann, M and Furber, S. (2018) Performance Comparison of the Digital Neuromorphic Hardware SpiNNaker and the Neural Network Simulation Software NEST for a Full-Scale Cortical Microcircuit Model. *Frontiers in Neuroscience.* 12:291. doi: 10.3389/fnins.2018.00291

[46] Beal, V. (n.d.) Moore's Law. Available: https://www.webopedia.com/TERM/M/Moores_Law.html. Last accessed: 2 June 2019.

[47] Hazari, A. (2017) *Electronics are about to reach their limit in processing power—but there's a solution.* Available: https://qz.com/852770/theres-a-limit-to-how-small-we-can-make-transistors-but-the-solution-is-photonic-chips/. Last accessed: 18 August 2019.

[48] Rouse, M. (n.d.) memristor. Available: https://whatis.techtarget.com/definition/memristor. Last accessed: 20 August 2019.

[49] IEEE Spectrum. (2008) *6-Minute Memristor Guide.* [Online Video]. 10 December 2008. Available: https://www.youtube.com/watch?v=rvA5r4LtVnc. Last accessed: 20 August 2019.

[50] Esqueda, I. S., Zhao, H. and Wang, H. (2018) Efficient learning and crossbar operations with atomically-thin 2-D material compound synapses. *Journal of Applied Physics*, 124.

[51] Sweatman, W. (2014) THE NEUROGRID – WHAT IT IS AND WHAT IT IS NOT. Available: https://hackaday.com/2014/05/06/the-neurogrid-what-it-is-and-what-it-is-not/. Last accessed: 20 July 2019.

[52] Abate, T. (2014) Stanford bioengineers create circuit board modeled on the human brain. Available: https://news.stanford.edu/pr/2014/pr-neurogrid-boahen-engineering-042814.html. Last accessed: 20 July.

[53] Alom, Md. Zahangir & Josue, Theodore & Rahman, Md & Mitchell, Will & Yakopcic, Chris & Taha, Tarek. (2018). Deep Versus Wide

Convolutional Neural Networks for Object Recognition on Neuromorphic System. 1-8. doi: 10.1109/IJCNN.2018.8489635.

[54] Suleyman, D and King, D. (2019) *Using AI to give doctors a 48-hour head start on life-threatening illness.* Available: https://deepmind.com/blog/article/predicting-patient-deterioration. Last accessed: 22 August 2019.

[55] Université libre de Bruxelles. (2019) *Scientists develop an AI method to improve rare disease diagnosis.* Available: https://medicalxpress.com/news/2019-06-scientists-ai-method-rare-disease.html. Last accessed: 22 August 2019.

[56] Kiral-Kornek, I., Roy, S., Nurse, E., Mashford, B., Karoly, P., Carroll, T., Payne, D., Saha, S., Steven, B., O'Brien, T., Grayden, D., Cook, M., Freestone, D. and Harrer, S. (2017) Epileptic Seizure Prediction Using Big Data and Deep Learning: Toward a Mobile System. *EBioMedicine.* 27, 103-111.

[57] Yellin, T, Aratari, D and Pagliery, J. (2018) *What is bitcoin?* Available: https://money.cnn.com/infographic/technology/what-is-bitcoin/index.html. Last accessed: 4 June 2019.

[58] Owano, N. (2013) Dynamic Vision Sensor tech works like the human retina. Available: https://phys.org/news/2013-08-dynamic-vision-sensor-tech-human.html. Last accessed: 20 July 2019.

[59] Rosenblum, A. (2017) *Air Force Tests IBM's Brain-Inspired Chip as an Aerial Tank Spotter.* Available: https://www.technologyreview.com/s/603335/air-force-tests-ibms-brain-inspired-chip-as-an-aerial-tank-spotter/. Last accessed: 2 August 2019.

[60] Drake, N. (2019) *First-ever picture of a black hole unveiled.* Available: https://www.nationalgeographic.co.uk/space/2019/04/first-ever-picture-black-hole-unveiled. Last accessed: 27 August 2019.

[61] Vu, L. (2017) *Will Brain-Inspired Chips Make a Dent in Science's Big Data Problems?* Available: https://cs.lbl.gov/news-media/news/2017/will-brain-inspired-chips-make-a-dent-in-sciences-big-data-problems/. Last accessed: 27 August 2019.

[62] G. Clark, D., A. Livezey, J., F. Chang, E., E. Bouchard, K. (2018) Spiking Linear Dynamical Systems on Neuromorphic Hardware for Low-Power Brain-Machine Interfaces. *arXiv e-prints.* arXiv:1805.08889 [cs.NE].

[63] Galeon, D. (2018) *Separating Science Fact From Science Hype: How Far off Is the Singularity?* Available: https://futurism.com/separating-science-fact-science-hype-how-far-off-singularity. Last accessed 1 September 2019.

CHAPTER 7

[1] S. Adams, S., Arel, I., Bach, J., Coop, R., Furlan, R., Goertzel, B., Hall, J. S., Samsonovich, A., Scheutz, M., Schlesinger, M., C. Shapiro, S., F. Sowa, J .

(2012) Mapping the Landscape of Human-Level Artificial General Intelligence. *Association for the Advancement of Artificial Intelligence.* ISSN 0738-4602.

[2] Stanford. (n.d.) *History: The 1940's to the 1970s.* Available: https://cs.stanford.edu/people/eroberts/courses/soco/projects/neural-networks/History/history1.html. Last accessed 1 September 2019.

[3] CAUGHILL, P. (2017) *Elon Musk: "The Singularity for This Level of the Simulation Is Coming Soon".* Available: https://futurism.com/elon-musk-the-singularity-for-this-level-of-the-simulation-is-coming-soon. Last accessed 2 August 2019.

[4] Yampolskiy, R. V. (2018) The Singularity May Be Near. 9. DOI: https://doi.org/10.3390/info9080190.

[5] Heylighen, Francis & Campbell, Donald. (1995) Selection of Organization at the Social Level: obstacles and facilitators of metasystem transitions. *World Futures.* doi: 45. 10.1080/02604027.1995.9972560.

[6] Weller, C. (2017) *Meet the first-ever robot citizen — a humanoid named Sophia that once said it would 'destroy humans'.* Available: https://www.businessinsider.com/meet-the-first-robot-citizen-sophia-animatronic-humanoid-2017-10?r=US&IR=T. Last accessed 2 January 2019.

[7] Telegraph Video. (2018) *Sophia the robot takes her first steps.* Available: https://www.telegraph.co.uk/technology/2018/01/08/sophia-robot-takes-first-steps/. Last accessed 7 September 2019.

[8] Griffin, A. (2017) *SAUDI ARABIA GRANTS CITIZENSHIP TO A ROBOT FOR THE FIRST TIME EVER.* Available: https://www.independent.co.uk/life-style/gadgets-and-tech/news/saudi-arabia-robot-sophia-citizenship-android-riyadh-citizen-passport-future-a8021601.html. Last accessed 7 January 2019.

[9] Hart, R. D. (2018) *Saudi Arabia's robot citizen is eroding human rights.* Available: https://qz.com/1205017/saudi-arabias-robot-citizen-is-eroding-human-rights/. Last accessed 2 January 2019.

[10] Hildt, E. (2019) *Artificial Intelligence: Does Consciousness Matter?.* Available: https://www.frontiersin.org/articles/10.3389/fpsyg.2019.01535/full. Last accessed 2 September 2019.

[11] Huszar, F. (2018) *Note on the quadratic penalties in elastic weight consolidation.* Available: https://www.pnas.org/content/pnas/early/2018/02/16/1717042115.full.pdf. Last accessed 2 January 2019.

[12] Moss, S. (2017) *ORNL starts installing Summit, could be the world's most powerful supercomputer.* Available: https://www.datacenterdynamics.com/news/ornl-starts-installing-summit-could-be-worlds-most-powerful-supercomputer/. Last accessed 3 January 2019.

[13] Shostrom, E. L. (1964) Article Metrics Related Articles Cite Share Request Permissions Explore More Download PDF An Inventory for the Measurement of Self-Actualisation. *Educational and Psychological Measurement,* DOI: https://doi.org/10.1177/001316446402400203.

[14] Psy. D, A. O. (2013) *The Theory of Self-Actualisation.* Available: https://www.psychologytoday.com/gb/blog/theory-and-psychopathology/201308/the-theory-self-actualization. Last accessed 2 September 2019.

[15]

[16] Bellis, M. (2019) *Alfred Nobel and the History of Dynamite.* Available: https://www.thoughtco.com/history-of-dynamite-1991564. Last accessed 3 September 2019.

[17] Crowder, J. and Friess, S. (2012) Artificial Psychology: The Psychology of AI.

[18] BostonDynamics. (2018) Testing Robustness. [Online:Video]. 20 February 2018. Available from: https://www.youtube.com/watch?v=aFuA50H9uek. [Accessed: 4 September 2019].

[19] Alexander, D. (2019) *Boston Dynamic Videos Foreshadow Equally Fascinating and Terrifying Future.* Available: https://interestingengineering.com/boston-dynamic-videos-foreshadow-equally-fascinating-and-terrifying-future. Last accessed 6 September 2019.

[20] Baraniuk, C. (2017) *The 'creepy Facebook AI' story that captivated the media.* Available: https://www.bbc.com/news/technology-40790258. Last accessed 6 September 2019.

[21] Griffin, A. (2017) *FACEBOOK'S ARTIFICIAL INTELLIGENCE ROBOTS SHUT DOWN AFTER THEY START TALKING TO EACH OTHER IN THEIR OWN LANGUAGE.* Available: https://www.independent.co.uk/life-style/gadgets-and-tech/news/facebook-artificial-intelligence-ai-chatbot-new-language-research-openai-google-a7869706.html. Last accessed 6 September 2019.

[22] Wehner, M. (2017) *Facebook engineers panic, pull the plug on AI after bots develop their language.* Available: https://bgr.com/2017/07/31/facebook-ai-shutdown-language/. Last accessed 2 September 2019.

[23] McKay, T. (2017) *No, Facebook Did Not Panic and Shut Down an AI Program That Was Getting Dangerously Smart.* Available: https://gizmodo.com/no-facebook-did-not-panic-and-shut-down-an-ai-program-1797414922. Last accessed 7 September 2019.

[24] Novet,J. (2017) *Facebook AI researcher slams' irresponsible' reports about a smart bot experiment.* Available: https://www.cnbc.com/2017/08/01/facebook-ai-experiment-did-not-end-because-bots-invented-own-language.html. Last accessed 6 September 2019.

[25] Boyd, R. (2008) *Do People Only Use 10 Percent of Their Brains?*. Available: https://www.scientificamerican.com/article/do-people-only-use-10-percent-of-their-brains/. Last accessed 7 September 2019.

[26] Sgantzos, K. and Grigg, I . (2019) Artificial Intelligence Implementations on the Blockchain. Use Cases and Future Applications. *Future Internet.* 11 (8), 170 DOI: https://doi.org/10.3390/fi11080170.

[27] Sze, D. (2015) *Maslow: The 12 Characteristics of a Self-Actualised Person.* Available: https://www.huffpost.com/entry/maslow-the-12-characteris_b_7836836?guccounter=2. Last accessed 6 September 2019.

[28] Tarantola, A. (2019) *Tomorrow's 'general' AI revolution would grow from today's technology.* Available: https://www.engadget.com/2019/05/14/artificial-general-intelligence-revolution/?guce_referrer=aHR0cHM6Ly93d3cuZ29vZ2xlLmNvVVRLw&guce_referrer_sig=AQAAAEVQRpBAIPk-cBLmLJtT2vvb1enYfjhmeYDOhaOxbLDkSMicc. Last accessed 2 September 2019.

[29] Shead, S. (2019) *DeepMind's Mysterious Ethics Board Will Reportedly 'Control' AGI If It's Ever Created.* Available: https://www.forbes.com/sites/samshead/2019/03/14/deepminds-mysterious-ethics-board-will-reportedly-control-agi-if-its-ever-created/#5693d60052a9. Last accessed 6 September 2019.

CHAPTER 8

[1] Hayes, T. (2018) *Blade Runner 2049 review: the future's still questionable.* Available: https://www.bfi.org.uk/news-opinion/sight-sound-magazine/reviews-recommendations/blade-runner-2049-denis-villeneuve-future-questionable. Last accessed 8 September 2019.

[2] Vincent, A. (2017) *Black Mirror is coming true in China, where your 'rating' affects your home, transport and social circle.* Available: https://www.telegraph.co.uk/on-demand/2017/12/15/black-mirror-coming-true-china-rating-affects-home-transport/. Last accessed 8 September 2019.

[3] Brooks, J. (2017) *Swedish workers implanted with microchips to replace cash cards and ID passes.* Available: https://www.independent.co.uk/news/world/europe/sweden-workers-microchip-implant-cash-card-id-pass-replace-employee-hand-epicenter-rice-grain-size-a7670551.html. Last accessed 8 September 2019.

[4] The Week. (2018) *Major UK firms to microchip employees.* Available: https://www.theweek.co.uk/97695/major-uk-firms-to-microchip-employees. Last accessed 8 September 2019.

[5] N.Abdulkader, S., Atia, A., M.Mostafa and M. (2015) Brain-computer interfacing: Applications and challenges. *Egyptian Informatics Journal.* 16, 213-230.

[6] Orlowski, A. (2018) *Microsoft wants to patent mind control.* Available: https://www.theregister.co.uk/2018/01/15/microsoft_bci_patent_applica tion/. Last accessed 8 September 2019.

[7] Controlling Drones With Your Mind. (2015) University of Florida. [Online Video]. 7 April 2015. Available from: https://www.youtube.com/watch?v=hLjxMjBlB9k. [Accessed: 7 September 2019].

[8] Joe Rogan - Elon Musk on Artificial Intelligence (2018) University of Florida. [Online Video]. Available from: https://www.youtube.com/watch?v=Ra3fv8gl6NE. [Accessed: 7 September 2019].

[9] Tang, J., Liu, Y., Hu, D., and Zhou, Z. (2018) Towards BCI-actuated smart wheelchair system. *Biomed Eng Online.* 17 (1), 111.

[10] Watson, F., Ruck, R., Naik, S. (2018) *Measuring the effect of interaction on immersion in a virtual environment.* London: Imperial College London.

[11] Waldert, S. (2016) Invasive vs. Non-Invasive Neuronal Signals for Brain-Machine Interfaces: Will One Prevail. *Frontiers in Neuroscience.* 10:295, doi: 10.3389/fnins.2016.00295.

[12] R. B. Martins, N., Angelica, N., Chakravarthy, K., Svidinenko, Y., J. Boehm, F., Opris, I., A. Lebedev, M., Swan, M. A. Garan, S., V. Rosenfeld, J. (2019) Human Brain/Cloud Interface. *Frontiers in Neuroscience.* 13:112, DOI: 10.3389/fnins.2019.00112.

[13] Mitrasinovic, S., Brown, S., T. Schaefer, A., D. Chang, S., Appelboom, G. (2018) Silicon Valley new focus on brain computer interface: hype or hope for new applications? *OPINION ARTICLE.* 1.

[14] Controlling Drones With Your Mind. (2015) University of Florida. [Online Video]. 6 April 2015. Available from: https://www.youtube.com/watch?v=Ra3fv8gl6NE. Last accessed: 7 September 2019.

[15] Advanced Bionics. (n.d.) *Accessories that fit your style – and your life.* Available: https://advancedbionics.com/us/en/home/products/accessories.html. Last accessed 6 September 2019.

[16] Park CH, Chang WH, Lee M, Kwon GH, Kim L, Kim S. T, Kim Y. H. (2015) Which motor cortical region best predicts imagined movement?. *Neuroimage.* 113, pp.101-110. DOI: 10.1016/j.neuroimage.2015.03.033.

[17] Musk, E. and Neuralink (2019) An integrated brain-machine interface platform with thousands of channels. *bioRxiv.* 703801; doi: https://doi.org/10.1101/703801.

[18] Neuralink. (2019) Neuralink Launch Event. [Online Video] Available: https://www.youtube.com/watch?v=r-vbh3t7WVI&feature=youtu.be. Last accessed 23 September 2019.

[19] Haselton, T. (2018) *https://www.cnbc.com/2018/09/07/elon-musk-discusses-neurolink-on-joe-rogan-podcast.html.* Available: https://www.cnbc.com/2018/09/07/elon-musk-discusses-neurolink-on-joe-rogan-podcast.html. Last accessed 7 September 2019.

[20] Al-Khalili, J (2017) *What's Next? : Even Scientists Can't Predict the Future – or Can They?.* London: Profile Books.

CHAPTER 9

[1] U.S. Department of Energy. (2000) *PRESIDENT CLINTON ANNOUNCES THE COMPLETION OF THE FIRST SURVEY OF THE ENTIRE HUMAN GENOME.* Available: https://web.ornl.gov/sci/techresources/Human_Genome/project/clinton1.shtml. Last accessed 29 August 2019.

[2] Venter, J. C., Adams, M., W. Myers, E., W. Li, P., J. Mural, R., Grange. (2001) The Sequence of the Human Genome. *American Association for the Advancement of Science.* 291, 1304-1351, DOI: 10.1126/science.1058040.

[3] Kari M. Severson, Mallozzi, M., Driks, A., and L. Knight, K. (2010) B Cell Development in GALT: Role of Bacterial Superantigen-Like Molecules. *The Journal of Immunology.* 184 (12), 6782-6789; DOI: https://doi.org/10.4049/jimmunol.1000155.

[4] U.S National Library of Medicine. (n.d.) *What are genome editing and CRISPR-Cas9?* Available: https://ghr.nlm.nih.gov/primer/genomicresearch/genomeediting. Last accessed 29 August 2019.

[5] Breakthroughprize. (n.d.) *Jennifer A. Doudna.* Available: https://breakthroughprize.org/Laureates/2/L63. Last accessed 29 August 2019.

[6] Puikkonen, J. (2016) *Jennifer Doudna.* [Image : Online] Available: https://www.flickr.com/photos/79173061@N08/26658739920/. Last accessed 22 September 2019.

[7] CDC. (2020). 1918 Pandemic (H1N1 virus). Available: https://www.cdc.gov/flu/pandemic-resources/1918-pandemic-h1n1.html. Last accessed February 2 2020.

[8] https://www.nejm.org/doi/pdf/10.1056/NEJMra1000449

[9] NHS (2019) *Swine flu (H1N1)* Available: https://www.nhs.uk/conditions/swine-flu/. Last accessed 1 March 2020

[10] Roos R. (2012) *CDC estimate of global H1N1 pandemic deaths: 284,000.* Available: http://www.cidrap.umn.edu/news-perspective/2012/06/cdc-estimate-global-h1n1-pandemic-deaths-284000. Last accessed 1 March 2020.

[11] WHO. (2020) *Ebola virus disease.* Available: https://www.who.int/news-room/fact-sheets/detail/ebola-virus-disease. Last accessed February 4, 2020.

[12] Harrison, C. (2020) *Coronavirus puts drug repurposing on the fast track.* Available: https://www.nature.com/articles/d41587-020-00003-1. Last accessed 1 March 2020.

[13] Paules, C. I., Marston, H. D., Fauci, A. S. (2020) Coronavirus Infections—More Than Just the Common Cold. *JAMA.* 323 (8), 707-708. doi:10.1001/jama.2020.0757.

[14] Josephine, M. (2020). *Coronavirus: China's first confirmed Covid-19 case traced back to November 17.* Available: https://www.scmp.com/news/china/society/article/3074991/coronavirus-chinas-first-confirmed-covid-19-case-traced-back. Last accessed 14 March 2020.

[15] Clinical features of patients infected with 2019 novel coronavirus in Wuhan, China. *The Lancet,* 395 (10223), 495-506.

[16] Schawrtz, D & Graham, A. (2020) Potential Maternal and Infant Outcomes from Coronavirus 2019-nCoV (SARS-CoV-2) Infecting Pregnant Women: Lessons from SARS, MERS, and Other Human Coronavirus Infections. *Viruses 2020,* 12(2), 194; https://doi.org/10.3390/v12020194

[17] Dorigatti, I., Okell, L., Cori, A., Imai, N. (2020) *Report 4: Severity of 2019-novel coronavirus (nCoV).* WHO Collaborating Centre for Infectious Disease Modelling MRC Centre for Global Infectious Disease Analysis. Imperial College London.

[18] Real-Time Estimation of the Risk of Death from Novel Coronavirus (COVID-19) Infection: Inference Using Exported Cases J. Clin. Med. 2020, 9(2), 523; DOI: 10.3390/jcm9020523.

[19] Campbell, D. (2020). *UK coronavirus crisis 'to last until spring 2021 and could see 7.9m hospitalised'.* Available: https://www.theguardian.com/world/2020/mar/15/uk-coronavirus-crisis-to-last-until-spring-2021-and-could-see-79m-hospitalised. Last accessed 16 March 2020.

[20] Gootenberg, J. S., Abudayyeh, O.O. et al. Nucleic acid detection with CRISPR-Cas13a/C2c2. Science. Online first: April 13, 2017. DOI: 10.1126/science.aam9321

[21] McGovern Institute. (2020) *Enabling coronavirus detection using CRISPR-Cas13: An open-access SHERLOCK research protocol.* Available: https://mcgovern.mit.edu/2020/02/14/enabling-coronavirus-detection-using-crispr-cas13-an-open-access-sherlock-research-protocol/. Last accessed 1 March 2020.

[22] McGovern Institute. (2020) *Enabling coronavirus detection using CRISPR-Cas13: An open-access SHERLOCK research protocol.* Available: https://mcgovern.mit.edu/2020/02/14/enabling-coronavirus-

detection-using-crispr-cas13-an-open-access-sherlock-research-
protocol/. Last accessed 1 March 2020.

[23] Cepheid. (2020) *Cepheid and Sherlock Biosciences Establish
Collaboration on New GeneXpert Tests for Infectious Diseases and
Oncology Leveraging CRISPR Technology.* Available:
https://www.prnewswire.com/news-releases/cepheid-and-sherlock-
biosciences-establish-collaboration-on-new-genexpert-tests-for-
infectious-diseases-and-oncology-leveraging-crispr-technology-
301013198.htm. Last accessed 10 March 2020.

[24] Potenza, A. (2019) *This company is making an at-home CRISPR kit to
find out what's making you sick.* Available:
https://www.theverge.com/2018/4/26/17281724/mammoth-biosciences-
crispr-diagnostic-tool-disease-detection. Last accessed 2 March 2020.

[25] Wigton, K. (2020) *Individual response to COVID-19 'as important' as
government action.* Available:
https://www.imperial.ac.uk/news/195976/individual-response-covid-19-
important-government-action/. Last accessed 10 March 2020.

[26] AP. (2020) *Trial of Moderna's coronavirus vaccine starts Monday,
government official says.* Available:
https://fortune.com/2020/03/15/coronavirus-vaccine-moderna-trial-
start/. Last accessed 15 March 2020.

[27] Public Affairs, UC Berkeley. (2019) *Patent office renews dispute over
patent rights to CRISPR-Cas9.* Available:
https://news.berkeley.edu/2019/06/25/patent-office-renews-dispute-
over-patent-rights-to-crispr-cas9/. Last accessed 29 August 2019.

[28] Sanders, R. (2019) *UC receives fourth CRISPR patent; three more on
the way.* Available: https://news.berkeley.edu/2019/04/23/uc-issued-
fourth-crispr-patent-three-more-on-the-way/. Last accessed 29 August
2019.

[29] Yahoo Finance. (n.d.) *Sangamo Therapeutics, Inc. (SGMO).* Available:
https://uk.finance.yahoo.com/quote/sgmo?ltr=1&guccounter=1. Last
accessed 29 August 2019.

[30] Merckgroup. (2018) *Merck and genOway Form CRISPR/Cas9 Strategic
Alliance to Develop Rodent Models.* Available:
https://www.merckgroup.com/en/news/crispr-strategic-alliance-10-12-
2018.html. Last accessed 29 August 2019.

[31] Rosenbaum, L. (2020) *Mammoth Biosciences Raises $45 Million For
Crispr Diagnostics—And Its Tech Is Already Being Used Against
Coronavirus.* Available:
https://www.forbes.com/sites/leahrosenbaum/2020/01/30/mammoth-
biosciences-raises-45-million-to-create-crispr-diagnostic-tests-and-its-
tech-is-already-being-used-against-coronavirus/#4c6ba1aa56c9. Last
accessed 2 March 2020.

[32] Cumbers, J. (2020) *The Synthetic Biology Companies Racing To Fight
Coronavirus.* Available:

https://www.forbes.com/sites/johncumbers/2020/02/05/seven-synthetic-biology-companies-in-the-fight-against-coronavirus/#6dcca04e16ef. Last accessed 2 March 2020.

[33] Nanalyze. (2019) *6 CRISPR Applications from Healthcare Startups.* Available: https://www.nanalyze.com/2018/08/crispr-applications-healthcare-startups/. Last accessed 30 August 2019.

[34] Genetic Engineering & Biotechnology News. (2019) *Base Editing Drug Developer Beam Therapeutics Raises $135M in Series B Financing.* Available: https://www.genengnews.com/news/base-editing-drug-developer-beam-therapeutics-raises-135m-in-series-b-financing/. Last accessed 30 August 2019.

[35] Vinluan, F. (2018) *Refuge Bio Turns to China for $25M Financing of Precision CRISPR R&D.* Available: https://xconomy.com/san-francisco/2018/05/02/refuge-bio-turns-to-china-for-25m-financing-of-precision-crispr-rd/. Last accessed 30 August 2019.

[36] Soriano V. Hot News: Gene Therapy with CRISPR/Cas9 Coming to Age for HIV Cure. *National Center for Biotechnology Information, U.S. National Library of Medicine.*

[37] Gao, D., Smith, S., Spagnuolo, M., Rodriguez, G., Blenner, M. (2018) Dual CRISPR-Cas9 Cleavage Mediated Gene Excision and Targeted Integration in Yarrowia lipolytica. *National Center for Biotechnology Information, U.S. National Library of Medicine.* 13 (9), doi: 10.1002/biot.201700590.

[38] Editas Medicine. (2019) *What if we could repair broken genes?.* Available: https://editasmedicine.com/company-overview/. Last accessed 30 August 2019.

[39] Hagenaars, S. P., Hill, W. D., Harris, S. E., Ritchie, S. J. (2017) Genetic prediction of male pattern baldness. *Journals Plos.* https://doi.org/10.1371/journal.pgen.1006594.

[40] Reuters. (2019) *UK cost watchdog recommends Novartis' blindness therapy Luxturna.* Available: https://uk.reuters.com/article/uk-novartis-britain/uk-cost-watchdog-recommends-novartis-blindness-therapy-luxturna-idUKKCN1VO2UC. Last accessed 15 September 2019.

[41] Rainey, M. (2019) *The Most Expensive Drug in the World — for Now.* Available: https://www.thefiscaltimes.com/2019/05/28/Most-Expensive-Drug-World-Now. Last accessed 2 September 2019.

[42] Miller, J. and Humer, C. (2019) *Novartis $2 million gene therapy for rare disorder is world's most expensive drug.* Available: https://uk.reuters.com/article/uk-novartis-genetherapy/novartis-2-million-gene-therapy-for-rare-disorder-is-worlds-most-expensive-drug-idUKKCN1SU2BB. Last accessed 13 October 2019.

[43] Zayner, J. (2018) *DIY Human CRISPR Myostatin Knock-Out.* Available: https://www.youtube.com/watch?v=o6A9bbDl6fo. Last accessed 2 September 2019.

[44] Chen, A. (2018) *A biohacker injected himself with a DIY herpes treatment in front of a live audience.* Available: https://www.theverge.com/2018/2/5/16973432/biohacking-aaron-traywick-ascendance-biomedical-health-diy-gene-therapy. Last accessed 2 September 2019.

[45] Brown, K. (2018) *CEO Who Tested DIY Herpes Treatment Locks Himself in Lab as Fellow Biohackers Abandon Him.* Available: https://gizmodo.com/ceo-who-tested-diy-herpes-treatment-locks-himself-in-la-1822933670. Last accessed 3 September 2019.

[46] Nisen, M. (2019) *A $2.1 Million Drug Price Record Is Made to Be Broken.* Available: https://www.bloomberg.com/opinion/articles/2019-05-28/novartis-record-2-1-million-drug-price-is-made-to-be-broken. Last accessed 15 September 2019.

[47] Mole, B. (2019) *Genetic self-experimenting "biohacker" under investigation by health officials.* Available: https://arstechnica.com/science/2019/05/biohacker-who-tried-to-alter-his-dna-probed-for-illegally-practicing-medicine/. Last accessed 6 September 2019.

[48] A. Doudna, J. and Charpentier, E. (2014) The new frontier of genome engineering with CRISPR-Cas9. *Science.* 346 (6213), 1258096. DOI: 10.1126/science.1258096

[49] Cohen, J. (2019) *New call to ban gene-edited babies divides biologists.* Available: https://www.sciencemag.org/news/2019/03/new-call-ban-gene-edited-babies-divides-biologists. Last accessed 1 September 2019.

[50] Gallagher, J. (2017) *UK scientists edit DNA of human embryos.* Available: https://www.bbc.com/news/health-41269200. Last accessed 1 September 2019.

[51] Burt, A. (2003) Site-specific selfish genes as tools for the control and genetic engineering of natural populations. *Proc. R. Soc. Lond.* 270, 921–928. doi: 10.1098/rspb.2002.2319

[52] Stein, R. (2019) *Scientists Release Controversial Genetically Modified Mosquitoes In High-Security Lab.* Available: https://www.npr.org/sections/goatsandsoda/2019/02/20/693735499/scientists-release-controversial-genetically-modified-mosquitoes-in-high-securit?t=1567122115414. Last accessed 1 September 2019.

[53] Osbourne, H. (2018). *MALARIA AND CRISPR: GENE EDITING CAUSES COMPLETE COLLAPSE OF MOSQUITO POPULATION IN 'MAJOR BREAKTHROUGH' FOR DISEASE ERADICATION.* Available: https://www.newsweek.com/malaria-gene-editing-crispr-mosquitoes-1135871. Last accessed 12 July 2019.

[54] Robitzski, D. (2019). *A Trial That Gene-Hacked Mosquitoes to Stop Breeding Has Backfired Spectacularly.* Available: https://www.sciencealert.com/a-trial-that-gene-hacked-mosquitoes-to-

stop-breeding-has-backfired-spectacularly. Last accessed 18 September 2019.

[55] Garziera, L., Pedrosa, M. C., de Souza, F. A., Gómez, M., Moreira, M. B., Virginio, J. F., Capurro, M. L. and Carvalho, D. O. (2017) Effect of interruption of over-flooding releases of transgenic mosquitoes over wild population of Aedes aegypti: two case studies in Brazil. *Entomol Exp Appl*, 164, 327-339. doi:10.1111/eea.12618

[56] Evans, B.R., Kotsakiozi, P., Costa-da-Silva, A.L. et al. (2020) Editorial Expression of Concern: Transgenic Aedes aegypti Mosquitoes Transfer Genes into a Natural Population. *Sci Rep* 10, 5524. https://doi.org/10.1038/s41598-020-62398-w

[57] Cyranoski, D. (2019) *China set to introduce gene-editing regulation following CRISPR-baby furore.* Available: https://www.nature.com/articles/d41586-019-01580-1. Last accessed 1 September 2019.

[58] Todd Bergman, M. (2019) *Perspectives on gene editing.* Available: https://news.harvard.edu/gazette/story/2019/01/perspectives-on-gene-editing/. Last accessed 1 September 2019.

[59] Sataline, S. (2018) *Scientist in China defends human embryo gene editing.* Available: https://www.theguardian.com/science/2018/nov/28/scientist-in-china-defends-human-embryo-gene-editing. Last accessed 1 September 2019.

[60] Roy, B., Zhao, J., Yang, C., Luo, W., Xiong, T., Li, Y. et al. (2018) CRISPR/Cascade 9-Mediated Genome Editing-Challenges and Opportunities. *Frontiers in Genetics.* https://doi.org/10.3389/fgene.2018.00240.

[61] Lovell-Badge R. (2019) CRISPR babies: a view from the centre of the storm. *The Company of Biologists Ltd.* 146 (3), doi: 10.1242/dev.175778.

[62] Li J. R. , Walker, S., Nie, J. B., Zhang X. Q. (32-38) Experiments that led to the first gene-edited babies: the ethical failings and the urgent need for better governance. *J Zhejiang Univ Sci B.* 20 (1), DOI: 10.1631/jzus.B1800624.

[63] Ma Y, Zhang L, Qin C1. (2019) The first genetically gene-edited babies: It's "irresponsible and too early". *Animal Model Exp Med.* 2 (1), 1-4.

[64] Wang H. and Yang H. (2019) Gene-edited babies: What went wrong and what could go wrong. *PLoS Bio.* 17,(4).

[65] Chen, A. (2019) *China confirms scientist genetically engineered babies — and more are on the way.* Available: https://www.theverge.com/2019/1/22/18192961/crispr-genetic-engineering-baby-ethics-scientist-china-investigation-he-jiankui. Last accessed 1 September 2019.

[66] National Human Genome Research Institute. (n.d.) *Genetic Disorders.* Available: https://www.genome.gov/For-Patients-and-Families/Genetic-Disorders. Last accessed 2 September 2019.

[67] Ho NC, Park SS, Maragh KD, EM. G. (2003) Famous people and genetic disorders: from monarchs to geniuses--a portrait of their genetic illnesses. *Am J Med Genet A*. 118A (2), 187-96.

[68] Glenza, J. (2019) *This all-male council in Texas just voted to ban abortion*. Available: https://www.theguardian.com/world/2019/jun/14/abortion-texas-waskom-all-white-male-council. Last accessed 2 September 2019.

[69] NEERGAARD, L. (2018) *AP-NORC Poll: Edit baby genes for health, not smarts*. Available: https://www.apnews.com/ef1161deac194f2ca1fd99457dc2cf15. Last accessed 1 September 2019.

[70] Caplan, A. (2019) Getting serious about the challenge of regulating germline gene therapy. *PLoS Bio*. 17 (4). doi: 10.1371/journal.pbio.3000223.

[71] Moschos, S. (2018) *GENE THERAPY IS NOW AVAILABLE, BUT COULD COST MILLIONS OVER A LIFETIME, SAYS SCIENTISTS*. Available: https://www.independent.co.uk/life-style/health-and-families/gene-therapy-cost-rare-genetic-diseases-treatment-expensive-research-a8275391.html. Last accessed 2 September 2019.

[72] Lin, J., Wong, K. C. (2018) Off-target predictions in CRISPR-Cas9 gene editing using deep learning. *Bioinformatics*. 34 (17), i656–i663, https://doi.org/10.1093/bioinformatics/bty554.

[73] Reardon, S. (2019) *CRISPR gene-editing creates wave of exotic model organisms*. Available: https://www.nature.com/articles/d41586-019-01300-9. Last accessed 1 September 2019.

[74] F. Voytas, D. (2015) *ENGINEERING PLANT GENOMES USING CRISPR/CAS SYSTEMIS*. Available: https://patentimages.storage.googleapis.com/74/87/f1/5a836eb98d0f61/US20150167000A1.pdf. Last accessed 1 September 2019.

[75] M.Schaeffer, S., A.Nakata, P.. (2015) CRISPR/Cas9-mediated genome editing and gene replacement in plants: Transitioning from lab to field. *Plant Science*. 240, 130-142, https://doi.org/10.1016/j.plantsci.2015.09.011.

[76] Emily Waltz. (2016) *Gene-edited CRISPR mushroom escapes US regulation*. Available: https://www.nature.com/news/gene-edited-crispr-mushroom-escapes-us-regulation-1.19754. Last accessed 22 September 2019.

[77] Hussain, B. Lucas, SJ. Budak, H. (2018) CRISPR/Cas9 in plants: at play in the genome and at work for crop improvement. *Brief Funct Genomics*. 17 (5), 319-328. doi: 10.1093/bfgp/ely016.

[78] Christian, J. (2019) *BILL GATES BACKED STARTUP IS USING CRISPR TO GROW LAB MEAT*. Available: https://futurism.com/neoscope/bill-gates-startup-crispr-lab-meat. Last accessed 21 September 2019.

[79] Cyranoski, D. (2018) *Japan set to allow gene editing in human embryos.* Available: https://www.nature.com/articles/d41586-018-06847-7. Last accessed 2 September 2019.

[80] Smith, J. (2019) *UK Company to Develop Next Generation CRISPR Gene Editing.* Available: https://labiotech.eu/medical/horizon-discovery-base-editing-crispr/. Last accessed 2 February 2019.

[81] Greene, T. (2019) *New CRISPR tool could eradicate viral diseases with long-range DNA shredding.* Available: https://thenextweb.com/science/2019/04/17/new-crispr-tool-could-eradicate-viral-diseases-with-long-range-dna-shredding/. Last accessed 2 April 2019.

[82] Houser, K. (2019) *THE US HAS OFFICIALLY STARTED USING CRISPR ON HUMANS.* Available: https://futurism.com/the-byte/us-human-crispr-cancer-patients. Last accessed 21 April 2019.

CHAPTER 10

[1] Church, G., Gao, Y., Kosuri, S. (2012) Next-Generation Digital Information Storage in DNA. *Science.* 337 (6102), 1628. DOI: 10.1126/science.1226355.

[2] Kingston. (n.d.) *Storage Chart.* Available: https://www.kingston.com/en/memory-cards/storage-chart. Last accessed 18 April 2019.

[3] Dormehl, L. (2018) *When we run out of room for data, scientists want to store it in DNA.* Available: https://www.digitaltrends.com/cool-tech/dna-data-catalog-startup/. Last accessed 18 April 2019.

[4] Gartenberg, C. (2018) *Huawei's Nano Memory Cards are replacing microSD on its latest phones.* Available: https://www.theverge.com/circuitbreaker/2018/10/16/17985578/huawei-nano-memory-cards-nm-microsd-replacement-mate-20-pro. Last accessed 21 April 2019.

[5] Hirukawa, A. (2018) *Easy as ATCG: Commercialization of DNA as Data Storage.* Available: https://labiotech.eu/features/commercialization-dna-data-storage/. Last accessed 21 April 2019.

[6] Yim, K. Yu, A. Li, J. Wong, A, Loo, J. Chan, K. Kong, S. Yip, K. Chan, T. (2014). The essential component in DNA-based information storage system: robust error-tolerating module. *Front. Bioeng. Biotechnol.* 6(2), 49, doi: https://doi.org/10.3389/fbioe.2014.00049.

[7] Mayer, C., R. McInroy, G., Murat, P., Van Delft, P., Prof. Balasubramanian, S. (2016) An Epigenetics-Inspired DNA-Based Data Storage System. *Angewandte Chemie International Edition.* 55 (37), 11144–11148. doi: https://doi.org/10.1002/anie.201605531.

[8] Newman, S., Stephenson, A. P., Willsey, M., Nguyen, B. H., Takahashi, C. N., Strauss, K. & Ceze, L. (2019) High density DNA data storage library via dehydration with digital microfluidic retrieval. *Nature Communications.* 10 (1076). Doi: https://doi.org/10.1038/s41467-019-09517-y.

[9] Oxford Gene Technology. (2011) *DNA Storage and Quality.* Available: https://www.ogt.com/resources/literature/403_dna_storage_and_qualit y. Last accessed 7 September 2019.

[10] Ping, Z., Ma, D., Huang, X., Chen, S., Liu, L., Guo, F., Zhu, S., Shen, Y. (2019) Carbon-based archiving: current progress and future prospects of DNA-based data storage. *Gigascience.* 8 (6), giz075. DOI: 10.1093/gigascience/giz075.

[11] Arch Mission Foundation. (n.d.) *Our Vision.* Available: https://www.archmission.org/our-vision. Last accessed 8 September 2019.

[12] Arch Mission Foundation. (n.d.) *Digital data in DNA.* Available: https://www.archmission.org/dna. Last accessed 8 September 2019.

[13] Khalil, A., S., and Collins, J. (2010) Synthetic Biology: Applications Come of Age. *Nat Rev Genet.* 11 (5). 367-379. doi: 10.1038/nrg2775.

[14] BIO. (n.d.) *Synthetic Biology Explained.* Available: https://www.bio.org/articles/synthetic-biology-explained. Last accessed 9 September 2019.

[15] Ossola, A. (2017) *Firestorm brewing as scientists work to create synthetic human DNA.* Available: https://www.cnbc.com/2017/05/02/synthetic-dna-scientist-says-it-could-be-inside-humans-within-5-years.html. Last accessed 9 September 2019.

[16] Steenhuysen, J. (2017) *Artificial life breakthrough after scientists create new living organism using synthetic DNA.* Available: https://www.independent.co.uk/news/science/artificial-life-synthetic-dna-scientists-living-organisms-create-scripps-research-institute-floyd-a8083966.html. Last accessed 9 September 2019.

[17] Duncan, E. (2018) *The Next Best Version of Me: How to Live Forever.* Available: https://www.wired.com/story/live-forever-synthetic-human-genome/. Last accessed 9 September 2019.

[18] Terry, M. (2018) *Moderna Therapeutics Sets Record for Biggest Biotech IPO.* Available: https://www.biospace.com/article/moderna-therapeutics-biggest-ipo-in-biotech-history/. Last accessed 9 September 2019.

[19] Terry, M. (2018) *Can Moderna Live up to the Hype? mRNA Company Increases IPO Goal to $600 Million.* Available: https://www.biospace.com/article/moderna-increases-ipo-goal-to-600-million/. Last accessed 9 September 2019.

[20] Toy, S. (2018) *Moderna: 5 things to know about the largest biotech to IPO.* Available: https://www.marketwatch.com/story/moderna-ipo-5-things-to-know-about-what-could-be-the-largest-biotech-ipo-in-history-2018-12-05. Last accessed 9 September 2019.

[21] Genome Compiler. (n.d.). *Genome Compiler.* Available: http://www.genomecompiler.com/. Last accessed 1 August 2019.

[22] Twist Biosciences. (2016). Twist Bioscience Acquires Genome Compiler to Add Gene Design Capabilities. Available: https://twistbioscience.com/company/press/acquires-genome-compiler. Last accessed 10 September 2019.

[23] Crunchbase. (n.d.). *Desktop Genetics.* Available: https://www.crunchbase.com/organization/desktop-genetics. Last accessed 10 September 2019.

[24] Bloomberg. (n.d.). *Synthetic Genomics Inc.* Available: https://www.bloomberg.com/profile/company/1024783Z:US. Last accessed 10 September 2019.

[25] Khan, M. I., Shin, J. H., & Kim, J. D. (2018). The promising future of microalgae: current status, challenges, and optimization of a sustainable and renewable industry for biofuels, feed, and other products. *Microbial cell factories*, 17(1), 36. doi:10.1186/s12934-018-0879-x

[26] ScienceDaily. (n.d.) *High yield, protein with soybean gene.* Available: https://www.sciencedaily.com/releases/2017/11/171122093049.htm. Last accessed 10 September 2019.

[27] Piper, K. (2019) *The rise of meatless meat, explained.* Available: https://www.vox.com/2019/5/28/18626859/meatless-meat-explained-vegan-impossible-burger. Last accessed 10 September 2019.

[28] Buck, G. (2019). *Lab-grown ice cream presents a labelling challenge for Canadian dairy.* Available: https://nationalpost.com/news/lab-grown-ice-cream-presents-a-labelling-challenge-for-canadian-dairy . Last accessed 6 August 2019.

[29] Cumbers, J. (2019) *Animal-Free Beef Was Just A Start. Synthetic Biology Is Set To Bring Us Dairy, Egg Products And More.* Available: https://www.forbes.com/sites/johncumbers/2019/07/22/impossible-ice-cream-anyone/#297ac8847b02. Last accessed 3 February 2020.

[30] University of Oxford. (2018). *New estimates of the environmental cost of food.* Available: http://www.ox.ac.uk/news/2018-06-01-new-estimates-environmental-cost-food. Last accessed 1 August 2019.

[31] Hancox, D. (2018) *The unstoppable rise of veganism: how a fringe movement went mainstream.* Available: https://www.theguardian.com/lifeandstyle/2018/apr/01/vegans-are-coming-millennials-health-climate-change-animal-welfare. Last accessed 11 September 2019.

[32] Kahleova, H., Fleeman, R., Hlozkova, A., Holubkov. R., and Barnard, N.D. (2018) A plant-based diet in overweight individuals in a 16-week randomized clinical trial: metabolic benefits of plant protein. *Nutrition & Diabetes.* 8 (58), pp 1-10. Doi:10.1038/s41387-018-0067-4.

[33] Radnitz, C., Bonnie Beezhold, B., and DiMatteo, J. (2015) Investigation of lifestyle choices of individuals following a vegan diet for health and ethical reasons. *Appetite.* 90, pp.31-36. Doi: 10.1016/j.appet.2015.02.026.

[34] Kahleova, H.; Levin, S.; Barnard, N. (2017) Cardio-Metabolic Benefits of Plant-Based Diets. *Nutrients.* 9, 848. Doi:10.3390/nu9080848.

[35] Woodbury, C. (2019) Benefits of a Plant Based Diet For Prevention of Cholecystitis. *Nursing Capstones*. 162. Available: https://commons.und.edu/nurs-capstones/162.

[36] University of Oxford. (2019) *Is lab-grown meat really better for the environment?* Available: http://www.ox.ac.uk/news/2019-02-19-lab-grown-meat-really-better-environment. Last accessed 11 September 2019.

[37] Gilchrist, K. (2019) *How Impossible Burger's 'simple' vision won hundreds of millions in funding — and backing from Bill Gates*. Available: https://www.cnbc.com/2019/03/08/bill-gates-backed-impossible-burger-ceo-patrick-brown-on-fighting-meat.html. Last accessed 11 September 2019.

[38] Milman, O. (2019) *Burger King's plant-based Whopper gets glowing review – from a meat lobbyist*. Available: https://www.theguardian.com/business/2019/apr/08/burger-king-impossible-whopper-plant-based-review-meat-lobbyist. Last accessed 11 September 2019.

[39] Impossible Foods Inc. (n.d.) *HEME + THE SCIENCE BEHIND IMPOSSIBLE*. Available: https://impossiblefoods.com/heme/. Last accessed 11 September 2019.

[40] Impossible Foods Inc. (2018) *How GMOs can save civilization (and probably already have)* Available: https://medium.com/impossible-foods/how-gmos-can-save-civilization-and-probably-already-have-6e6366cb893. Last accessed 11 September 2019.

[41] Bellon, T., Manjesh, B. (2019) *Beyond Meat's share price more than doubles in vegan burger maker's IPO*. Available: https://www.reuters.com/article/us-beyondmeat-ipo/beyond-meats-share-price-more-than-doubles-in-vegan-burger-makers-ipo-idUSKCN1S81P4. Last accessed 11 September 2019.

[42] Yahoo Finance. (2020) *BYND*. Available: https://finance.yahoo.com/quote/bynd/. Last accessed 7 May 2020.

[43] HONEST BURGERS. (n.d.) *MENU*. Available: https://www.honestburgers.co.uk/food/burgers/plant/. Last accessed 11 September 2019.

[44] Moss, R. (2018) *3.5 Million People In The UK Are Now Vegan'*. Available: https://www.huffingtonpost.co.uk/entry/35-million-people-in-the-uk-are-now-vegan_uk_5ac49b5ee4b093a1eb2087cb?guce_referrer=aHR0cHM6Ly93d3cuZ29vZ2xlLmNvVi5Lw&guce_referrer_sig=AQAAAG2nFCyi2aTDMocX8w6c. Last accessed 11 September 2019.

[45] Beyond Meat. (2019) *OUR IMPACT*. Available: https://www.beyondmeat.com/about/our-impact/. Last accessed 11 September 2019.

[46] Taylor, K. (2019) *It requires 22 ingredients for the Beyond Burger to replicate the taste and texture of a classic hamburger — here's what they*

are. Available: https://www.businessinsider.com/what-is-in-beyond-meat-burger-2019-5?r=US&IR=T. Last accessed 11 September 2019.
[47] Lipschultz, B and Singer, D. (2019) *Beyond Meat Makes History With the Biggest IPO Pop Since 2008 Crisis.* Available: https://www.bloomberg.com/news/articles/2019-05-02/beyond-meat-makes-history-with-biggest-ipo-pop-since-08-crisis. Last accessed 12 September 2019.
[48] Service, R. F. (2017) *DNA could store all of the world's data in one room.* Available: https://www.sciencemag.org/news/2017/03/dna-could-store-all-worlds-data-one-room. Last accessed 12 September 2019.
[49] Ossola, A. (2017) *Firestorm brewing as scientists work to create synthetic human DNA.* Available: https://www.cnbc.com/2017/05/02/synthetic-dna-scientist-says-it-could-be-inside-humans-within-5-years.html. Last accessed 12 September 2019.
[50] Gibbs, S. (2017) *Hacking a computer using DNA is now a reality, researchers claim.* Available: https://www.theguardian.com/technology/2017/aug/11/hacking-computer-dna-university-of-washington-lab. Last accessed 12 September 2019.
[51] ROBITZSKI, D. (2019) *THIS GUY IS TRYING TO GROW ORGANS IN PIG-HUMAN HYBRIDS.* Available: https://futurism.com/neoscope/grow-organs-pig-human-hybrids. Last accessed 12 September 2019.

CHAPTER 11

[1] WHO. (2020) *WHO Director-General's opening remarks at the media briefing on COVID-19 - 5 March 2020.* Available: https://www.who.int/dg/speeches/detail/who-director-general-s-opening-remarks-at-the-media-briefing-on-covid-19---5-march-2020. Last accessed 6 March 2020.
[2] Boseley, S. (2020). *WHO urges countries to 'track and trace' every Covid-19 case.* Available: https://www.theguardian.com/world/2020/mar/13/who-urges-countries-to-track-and-trace-every-covid-19-case. Last accessed 14 March 2020.
[3] Hellewell, J., Abbott, S., Gimma, A., Bosse, N., Jarvis, C., Russell, T., Munday, J., Kucharski, A., and Edmunds, J. (2020) Feasibility of controlling COVID-19 outbreaks by isolation of cases and contacts. *The Lancet Global Heath.* 8 (3), e305-3450.

CHAPTER 12

[1] Sheetz, M. (2017) *Elon Musk's SpaceX becomes the first private company to launch a reused rocket on a NASA mission.* Available: https://www.cnbc.com/2017/12/15/elon-musks-spacex-becomes-first-to-launch-reused-rocket-on-a-nasa-mission.html. Last accessed 12 September 2019.

[2] Thompson, A. (2019) *SpaceX Falcon Heavy Sticks Triple Rocket Landing with 1st Commercial Launch.* Available: https://www.space.com/spacex-falcon-heavy-triple-rocket-landing-success.html. Last accessed 10 September 2019.

[3] Gates, B. (2020) *How to respond to COVID-19.* Available: https://www.gatesnotes.com/Health/How-to-respond-to-COVID-19. Last accessed 20 March 2020.

[4] https://discovery.ucl.ac.uk/id/eprint/10090633/1/1-s2.0-S1201971220300114-main.pdf

[5] Elsevier. (2020) *Novel Coronavirus Information Center.* Available: https://www.elsevier.com/connect/coronavirus-information-center?dgcid=_SD_banner#research. Last accessed 20 March 2020.

ABOUT THE AUTHOR

Farabi Shayor *BSc MSc MIScT*

Farabi's experience lies in business R&D, developing marketing deliverable, brand identities and working in research-based projects involving applied computational intelligence. He has been conducting research on emerging technologies since 2015, including blockchain and virtual reality. Coming from a mix of finance (BSc) and marketing/research (MSc) background, Farabi has developed vital skills to become an entrepreneur and a researcher, and has gained experience of working with over a hundred companies. He has spoken at a number of international conferences and mentioned on Forbes, The Next Web and Inc Magazine. Currently he is the Head of Research at IntelXSys, and working as a Research Lead for "CRI Module" at Imperial College School of Medicine.

@intelxsys

@intelxsys

ep.intelxsys.com

If you have found this book useful,
please kindly leave a review on Amazon.